ANGLO–GERMAN BUSINESS COLLABORATION

Also by Derek Pugh

(*with David Hickson*)
WRITERS ON ORGANIZATIONS: Fifth Edition
GREAT WRITERS ON ORGANIZATIONS
MANAGEMENT WORLDWIDE: The Impact of Societal Culture on
Organizations around the Globe

(*with Estelle Phillips*)
HOW TO GET A PhD: Second Edition

(*edited*)
ORGANIZATION THEORY: Selected Readings, Fourth Edition

Anglo–German Business Collaboration

Pitfalls and Potentials

Dagmar Ebster-Grosz

and

Derek Pugh

Published in collaboration
with the Anglo-German Foundation

First published 1996 by
MACMILLAN PRESS LTD
Houndmills, Basingstoke, Hampshire RG21 6XS
and London
Companies and representatives
throughout the world

ISBN 0–333–65206–1

1000958398 T

A catalogue record for this book is available
from the British Library.

10   9   8   7   6   5   4   3   2   1
05 04 03 02 01 00 99 98 97 96

Printed and bound in Great Britain by
Antony Rowe Ltd
Chippenham, Wiltshire

To
Maria, my mother (Dagmar)
and
Natalie, my wife (Derek)

Contents

List of Figures

List of Tables

Acknowledgements

This study was designed as a co-operative venture between the Open University Business School, UK (Professor Derek Pugh) and the *Lehrstuhl für Betriebswirtschaftslehre der Universität des Saarlandes*, Germany (Professor Dr Christian Scholz). For the first year, the study was supported by the Anglo–German Foundation who contributed the staff costs of the two research officers: Dr Dagmar Ebster-Grosz in Britain and Mr (later Dr) Marco Schroeter in Germany. For the remainder of the project, the research was financially supported by the two universities. We are grateful to the AGF for their initial financial support which enabled the project to get off the ground, and to Dr Ray Cunningham of the Foundation for his helpful approach throughout the whole work. We wish to acknowledge the German–British Chamber of Industry and Commerce for permission to include Tables 2.1, 2.2 and 2.3.

We are extremely grateful to the 99 managers in Britain and Germany who agreed to be interviewed, and who were prepared to talk so freely about the cross-cultural tasks which they face and the problems which arise.

The British and the German teams made their data available to each other, but made their analyses independently (Scholz, 1993; Schröter, 1994). This volume reports the British team's findings and interpretations. We are grateful to Trevor Lambert of Oxford University (formerly of the Open University) for assistance in the computing aspects of the data analysis. Our heartfelt thanks go to Natalie Pugh, who, as always, gave unstinting support and hospitality throughout the writing of the book.

Open University Business School   DAGMAR EBSTER-GROSZ
                                                     DEREK PUGH

1 The Objectives of the Present Research

'The biggest mistake that I made was that I presumed that Germans are British people speaking another language.' — British manager with many years of experience of working for German companies

'We can learn from each other. We could more relax our style, and the British be more consistent.' — German Chief Executive of a large British subsidiary in Germany

Germany has been called the 'economic engine room of Europe'. Historically this is a development that has been going on for well over a century in spite of losing two world wars, the Nazi period and the post-war split of the country in two parts, one under a western capitalist system, and the other under a Soviet communist regime. Indeed just before the 1990 unification, not only was West Germany economically the leading state in Western Europe and the largest exporter in the world, but East Germany (although very far behind West Germany – producing only 40 per cent of the output per worker) was the most efficient of the Soviet satellites and was being held up by hard-line leaders in the Soviet Union as an example of how Communism could work if people were sufficiently disciplined (cf. Hickson and Pugh, 1995).

This German 'economic miracle', with its economic growth prolonged into the late 1980s, is frequently contrasted with the more turbulent development of the UK economy over the same period. Britain has suffered a decline in manufacturing industry, and a continuous fall in standards of living relative to other countries in the European Union. These changes have been linked to the short-termism which characterizes the British industrial scene, stemming from its domination by the financial expediency of stock market capital.

These very different levels of industrial performance have made the two economic systems a popular topic for comparison with British management commentators (Campbell and Warner, 1993; Lawrence, 1980; Lane, 1992; Randlesome, 1993). Others have examined specific elements within the environments (Budde *et al.*, 1982; Maurice *et al.*, 1980; Prais, 1981) and compared their characteristics. In the British press, the German achievement has became a favourite topic of comparison to the disadvantage of British industry. For example, in an item headed 'Secret report reveals shocking state of industry: British management blamed for failure', *The Sunday Times* claimed in March 1993 that a secret DTI report had found that British industry is fundamentally weak, beset by inferior management, suffering from inadequate investment in new technology and achieving productivity levels at least 25 per cent below its international competitors such as France and Germany (Lorenz and Smith, 1993). These views have led to German investment in Britain being welcomed in the press. The benefits to British firms taken over by German corporations of the German practice of longer term investment are frequently underlined.

However, despite this attention, an appropriate understanding of the nature of the differences in institutional and cultural characteristics between the two countries is often not achieved. Direct comparisons of indicators are made, for example, of overall national productivity levels, without making a proper systemic analysis of the whole environment in each country. But as Whitley and others have argued (Whitley (ed.), 1992), an analysis of managerial and organizational behaviour, and its resulting industrial performance, must be based on an understanding of the national institutional context in which it takes place. In addition, the cultural context will have an important impact on business functioning.

A SYSTEMIC APPROACH TO UNDERSTANDING NATIONAL WORK ENVIRONMENTS

A distinctive characteristic of this study is that it looks at aspects of management in Britain and Germany in the context of their environments. There are many comprehensive definitions of the terms 'environment' and 'culture', but for our purposes we shall use the following:

- by *environment* we refer to the framework in which businesses operate. The environment consists of the social, economic, political and legal institutions which define the scope of business activity;
- by *culture* we mean the shared values and patterns of behaviour which individuals learn and accept from the environment.

The first objective of this study is to offer a contribution to the comparative analysis of British and German economic and work environments in order to explain their effects on the activities of firms in the two countries. Thus organizational behaviour in British and German firms is not seen as only the result of interactions between individuals, organization structures and management styles. It is also affected considerably by the nature of the British and German environments and cultures and the opportunities and constraints that they present.

An adequate basis for comparison needs to incorporate these differing environmental factors in order to correctly interpret economic results. Thus elements such as financial ownership and stability, educational systems and product regulatory frameworks are all part of the distinctive national industrial environment which has its effects on the economic activity of each country. In addition, traditional cultural values of the kind analysed by Hofstede (1980) and Trompenaars (1993) also affect managerial processes and organizational behaviour which, in turn, affect economic performance.

This systemic perspective leads to a contingency approach to the differences between Germany and Britain. Neither the German nor the British culture and institutions can be described as 'right' or 'wrong' for industry as a whole. Each has different strengths and weaknesses which both support and constrain economic activity and organizational behaviour. Advantages and disadvantages for particular types of industries are contingent on these institutional and cultural environments. Not all industries flourish in the German environment, and not all firms wither in the British work culture and institutional infrastructure.

In order to identify the impact of those aspects of the cultural and institutional environment which affect the success of British and German firms, we have, first, developed conceptual schemes, based on the previous literature, for the analysis of the business environments, the characteristics of the markets, and the educational systems of the two countries. Secondly, we have focused our empirical study on the activities of companies which operate in both countries, that is, German parent companies with subsidiaries in Britain, and British parent companies with subsidiaries in Germany. Thirdly, since the study is a cross-cultural one, it does not focus on quantitative economic or industrial indicators. Our information has been collected from managers experienced in British and German cross-cultural business collaboration. While our main informants are the Chief Executives of subsidiaries, the data collected refer to the activities of companies as a whole. By comparing the managers' interpretations of the functioning of a parent company with its subsidiary in another country, we are able to examine the effects of the national environment, the industrial environment and the culture on organizational activities. This focus on institutionally-related cross-cultural comparisons aims to contribute to a more comprehensive understanding of the differences between British and German business activity.

PROBLEMS AT THE INTERFACE IN CROSS-CULTURAL COLLABORATION

The second objective of this study is to focus on the problems that arise from British and German collaboration in business. Our informants have long-term experience of working across the cultural divide. We wish to ascertain how the differences in the institutional environments and national work cultures impact on cross-cultural business activity. What are the problems of management, marketing and organizational behaviour that face a British firm operating in Germany and vice versa? And how are they dealt with? What are the operational pitfalls to avoid when attempting to enter the British or German market? And, not least, what are the potential synergies to be gained from effective methods of co-operation between firms in the two countries?

INTERPRETING THE DATA

Our informants are managers with close involvement in Anglo–German business collaboration. As outlined in Chapter 2, they are asked questions on topics which directly concern them, and are encouraged to reflect on their daily work activities. Nevertheless, in discussing culturally sensitive topics such as differences in management styles and work attitudes, the question of how far the managers are drawing on national stereotypes of the British and German cultures has to be considered.

Individuals come to new situations with a framework of attitudes which enables them to make sense of what would otherwise be difficult to interpret and react to. The function of such attitudes is to give stability to perceptions and emotions in a changing world. When the new context is an international cross-cultural situation, it is inevitable that the attitudes used are influenced by some preconceived views of the nature of the other culture and the people in it. These preconceived stereotypes serve the useful function of helping to interpret the new culture; otherwise the strain of functioning in it would be too great. This is the positive aspect of stereotyping.

But, of course, there are also negative aspects. In particular it is quite difficult for aspects of a stereotype, once adopted, to be changed: stereotypes are self-perpetuating. For example, many Britons hold the stereotype that Germans are hard-working and dour. What happens when such Britons meet a lazy, happy German? Perhaps suprisingly, this does not result in the Britons changing their stereotype, but rather in their thinking that the lazy, happy German was an exception – not a *real* German.

The managers in our study must, like everybody, be subject in some degree to this distorting process. However, they have been involved for many years in working with colleagues of the other nationality and their stereotypes are likely to have developed to take account of this more sophisticated view of the differences in the other culture. When interviewed, our respondents had spent on average 13.5 years in their present company (this ranged from 1 to 40 years; see Table 2.16). And since many of them had previously held jobs abroad or worked for foreign corporations (Table 2.17), this figure represents an underestimate of the average amount of their cross-cultural experience. As the result of their long-term exposure to the cross-cultural work environment, they would have become acculturated to a considerable degree in their partner's culture. This bicultural experience enables them to go beyond the stereotypes.

In considering certain data, however, an additional compensating factor will, on occasion, be used. In addition to classifying and comparing according to the country in which the firm is located, the data will be presented according to the nationality of the managers interviewed. This approach will enable an analysis of how far there is agreement on the nature of British and German management processes across managers from both cultures. Since the original stereotypes of British and German managers about each other are likely to have been different, any current agreement among them on aspects of British and German work culture and organizational behaviour is likely to be grounded in their years of learning from experience.

THE PLAN OF THE BOOK

In Chapter 2, the sample and methods of the study are described with the Interview Schedule used given in an Appendix. The remaining chapters report the findings of the research, and compare them, where appropriate, with other work. Chapter 3 analyzes the nature of the differences between the British and German business environments and shows how certain characteristic configurations of parent–subsidiary collaborations develop. In Chapter 4 the differing nature of marketing in the two countries, and the problems of operating in the two markets, are elaborated. A set of short case studies is given in the Appendix to this chapter as illustrations of the issues raised.

A comparison commonly made between Britain and Germany is the difference in the range of qualifications and skills relevant to business activity. Chapter 5 reports the views of the managers on this topic, and discusses some implications to be drawn. Chapter 6 analyzes the distinctive differences in organizational behaviour in British and German firms as demonstrated in management style, work atmosphere and interpersonal relationships. Parent–subsidiary relationships are examined in Chapter 7. In the final chapter, the study is summarized by reviewing the obstacles, which to the unwary may become pitfalls, in operating cross-culturally. This is followed by suggestions for realising the potential of effective Anglo–German business collaboration.

2 The Sample and Methods of the Study

Extracts from an interview with 'Herr Schmidt', Chief Executive of a German engineering subsidiary in Britain:

> 'The average duration of employment is lower in Britain than in Germany. As soon as the sales people are successful, they want to become managers, and go elsewhere. Whilst our average employment is 15 to 20 years in Germany, it is on average four to five years in Britain. Quality of technical sales staff is well below the Continent. We have to spend a lot of money with new staff on training.'

> 'We also have here more lease contract hire than on the Continent. 50 per cent of our business here is contract hire, it is only 10 per cent in Germany.'

> 'People here are very friendly, especially to my wife, but they are too optimistic about the real potential that a company can achieve. Average knowledge in Germany is much higher, and the average ability. Education is a real weakness of this country.'

> 'I trusted my managers in Germany and Austria to make right decisions. I learned that I have to be more critical here.'

> 'The average amount of money spent on research and development is higher in Germany.'

> 'But British are good marketers. Strong in new ideas, creative. There are a lot of good ideas in this country. They are afraid of the differences in the cultures. They are living on an island. British change their minds often and in the last minute.'

Extracts from an interview with 'Mr Smith', Chief Executive of a German engineering subsidiary in Britain:

> 'It is a myth that Germans are hard workers. They are not commited, particularly at management level. Everything dies in July and August.'

'They are ace clock watchers. We work long hours as a small organization, but we cannot contact them outside their working hours. I have the feeling that there has been, in recent years, a change in culture in Germany. The first generation were hard workers; the second generation has become lazy.'

'At the end of the year they need to get rid of their stocks, and they [the parent company] dump them on us. The first three months of a year are locked in, and they are not interested whether it is realistic. Their whole management and accounting system for sales is wrong. When they ship a machine to us, that counts as a sale on their management accounts. But they do not admit the consolidated accounts. Management in XY [company name] is a fiddle, because they [the senior managers in the parent company] have a personal interest in the business. I had enormous rows with them. At the end of the year they used to take all the machines left over and dump them on our order. Our stock in May was worth a sum which was ten times the sum of our annual turnover! Liabilities moved from a country with low interest rates to one with the highest. We then had to raise a loan half the amount of our annual turnover, so that a small company in the UK can be used as a sales dump. Their excuse is that it keeps the factory going. It is a production-led company.'

'Their flexibility is zero; their logic is zero. Our business costs the overall group a lot of money. The only way to influence them is to persuade them that if they want production they have to be flexible. They are very slow, and they react only when we are aggressive. The Germans respond to who shouts loudest. It is too much of an uphill struggle. They would want us to be a subservient and obedient company.'

'There is a fundamental insecurity deep in the culture. They spend a great length of time to prove that they are not wrong. It is like a red rag to a bull if anyone questions their competence. They can be very generous or very petty. But it's not anything personal. They are best together when on the factory floor solving problems on the customer's premises.'

As discussed in Chapter 1 this study was designed, not just to compare the British and German work systems and institutions, but to investigate the problems generated at the cross-cultural interface between them as illustrated by the two managers quoted above. It was therefore decided to study organizations which have built into their functioning the need for such collaboration – between firms in the two countries and between managers of both nationalities. The sample studied consists primarily of subsidiaries of German companies operating in Britain, and subsidiaries of British companies operating in Germany. In addition a small number of the Head Offices of parent companies in both countries were included.

SAMPLE SELECTION

The Anglo–German Chamber of Commerce in Britain publishes a list of subsidiaries of German companies trading in Britain (Feddersen, 1991). The 967 establishments listed form the population for the British sample of this study. It is stratified by size with a variable sampling factor to ensure that more of the larger organizations are included ($n = 46$). This was done in order to obtain maximum problem coverage. Smaller size subsidiaries, although representing more than a half of the population, tended to show more stereotypical patterns. Table 2.1 gives the size bands of the sample and the population from which it was drawn.

Table 2.2 shows that 15 industrial and commercial sectors were represented out of a total of 29 in the population. Interviews in all these 46 firms were carried out by the British team. 92 per cent of the sample agreed to be interviewed when approached. The refusals were substituted with other firms from the same categories.

Table 2.1 *Population and sample of the subsidiaries of German companies in Britain by size*

Number of employees	Population	Sample
2000 and over	10	4
1000–1999	8	6
500–999	11	6
100–499	123	15
75–99	39	2
20–74	209	8
up to 19	389	5
Total		46

Note: Total number of establishments listed: 967 of which 789 gave number of employees. 271 are stated to have production facilities in the UK.
Source: Feddersen, 1991.

Table 2.2   *Population and sample of the subsidiaries of German companies in Britain by industrial sector*

Sector of industry	Population	Sample
1. Machinery, and Mechanical Appliances and parts thereof	313	15
2. Base metals and articles thereof	119	1
3. Electrical Equipment, Appliances and Parts thereof	112	5
4. Instruments, Apparatus, Optical,... Measuring, Medical, Clocks, Watches...	79	2
5. Vehicles, Aircrafts and Parts thereof, Vesels, Transport Equipment	56	3
6. Plastics, Rubber and Articles thereof	62	3
7. Products of the Chemical and Allied Industries	67	5
8. Mineral Products	12	1
9. Articles of stone, Cement, Asbestos, ... Ceramic products, Glass, Glassware	24	2
10. Vegetable products	10	1
11. Prepared foodstuffs, Beverages, Spirits, Tobacco	24	1
12. Miscellaneous manufactured articles	49	1
13. Textiles and Textile Articles	33	2
14. Printers and Publishers	13	2
15. Banking and Insurance	20	2
Total in sample		46

Note: A total of 29 industrial sectors are listed in the population. The table contains only those sectors represented in the sample.
Source: Feddersen, 1991.

Table 2.3 gives the industrial classification used in the present study, alongside that given by Feddersen (1991) on which the sample was drawn. As will be seen, the categories in the study use the more general Feddersen classes, but specify in greater detail the nature of the business activities pursued by the sample firms.

A population description was not available for Germany. The 45 subsidiaries in the German sample include a range of sectors and sizes. The size distribution of the sample of British subsidiaries in Germany is given in Table 2.4. The industrial sector classification used by Scholz (1994) is given in Table 2.5, together with the more detailed classification, comparable to Table 2.3, developed for this study. Data on 39 of these subsidiaries in Germany were made available by the

Table 2.3 *Distribution of German subsidiaries in Britain in the sample by classification used in the present study*

Classification by Feddersen (1991)		Classification used in the study	
Machinery, and Mechanical		Heavy engineering	7
Appliances and Parts thereof	15	Engineering	8
Base metals and Articles thereof	1	Foundry (making car	
		engine parts)	1
Electrical Equipment,		Consumer electronics	1
Appliances and Parts thereof	5	Electrical	4
Instruments, Apparatus,		Specialities	1
Optical,…Measuring,		Electronics (incl.flexible	
Medical, Clocks, Watches…	2	electronic systems)	1
Vehicles, Aircrafts and Parts		Heavy engineering	1
thereof, Vessels, Transport		Engineering	2
Equipment	3		
Plastics, Rubber and Articles		Accessories for the	
thereof	3	automobile industry	3
Products of the Chemical		Pharmaceutical	2
and Allied Industries	5	Chemical	3
Mineral Products	1	Mineral extraction	1
Articles of stone, Cement,		Products for the building	
Asbestos, … Ceramic products,		industry	1
Glass, Glassware	2	Consumer Industry:	
		(Tableware)	1
Vegetable products	1	Commodity trading	1
Prepared foodstuffs, Beverages,		Consumer industry:	
Spirits, Tobacco	1	(Food industry)	1
Miscellaneous manufactured		Consumer industry:	
articles	1	(Kitchen furniture)	1
Textiles and Textile Articles	2	Consumer industry:	
		(Textiles)	1
		(Purpose clothing)	1
Printers and Publishers	2	Publishers	2
Banking and Insurance	2	Finance	2
Total	46		46

German team. The remaining six interviews were carried out by the British team. In addition, interviews by the British team were carried out in seven parent companies in the UK, and in one parent company in Germany. The industrial sectors of these firms are shown in Table 2.6. They are all large organizations, each employing more than 2000

Table 2.4 *Sample of the subsidiaries of British companies in Germany by size*

Number of employees	Sample
2000 and over	4
1000–1999	4
500–999	2
100–499	14
75–99	6
20–74	3
up to 19	1
Missing data	11
Total	45

Note: A population description is not available.

employees in all their operations. Thus data were collected from 99 organizations in total.

THE NATURE OF THE SAMPLE OF SUBSIDIARY ESTABLISHMENTS

The 91 subsidiaries in the sample were spread over two countries, and, as the tables above show, a range of sizes and industrial sectors. Information on a number of other characteristics was also obtained to enable comparisons to be made. The average length of operation of German subsidiaries in Britain was 23 years, and of British subsidiaries in Germany 20 years. Both samples have a similar normal distribution of institutional age, as Figure 2.1 shows. While some subsidiaries were established in both countries in the decade after the Second World War, the boom in start-ups occured in the 1960s. Since then, new establishments have been formed regularly.

Eleven British subsidiaries in Germany operate under a different name from that of the British parent company, since most were established as a result of takeovers. In addition, keeping the original name in the German market is believed to be beneficial. This compares with only four German subsidiaries in Britain which retained their original British names.

The legal status of the subsidiary in the host country is shown in Table 2.7. A very large majority, 81 per cent, are organizations with a legal identity, using 'Ltd' in Britain and 'Gmbh' in Germany. A small number

Table 2.5 *Distribution of British subsidiaries in Germany in the sample by classification used in the present study*

Classification by Scholz (1993)		Classification used in the study	
Engineering	6	Heavy engineering	2
		Engineering	4
Electrotechnical	7	Consumer electronics	4
		Flexible electronic systems	2
		Specialities: Instruments and Apparatus	1
Building materials	4	Products used in the building Industry	3
		Specialities: Fire protection systems	1
Financial services	4	Finance	4
Chemicals and pharmaceuticals	5	Chemicals	3
		Pharmaceuticals	2
Consumer goods	4	Consumer industry: Personal safety equipment	1
		Office accessories	1
		Food and tobacco	2
Other	12	Pharmaceuticals	2
		Specialities: Instruments and Apparatus	2
		Personal safety systems	1
		Laboratory equipment	1
		Transport services	1
		Mineral extraction	2
		Engineering	2
		Foundry	1
Not listed	3	Engineering	2
		Finance	1
Total	45		45

have greater financial autonomy ('plc' or 'AG'). There are no differences between the British and the German samples. Nor is there a significant difference in the number of branches operated in the host country as Table 2.8 shows.

The formal fit of the subsidiaries into the corporate structure of the parent organization is congruent with the legal status. As Table 2.9 shows, just under three-quarters are independent subsidiaries. A small proportion, 13 per cent, have wider responsibilities on behalf of the

Table 2.6 *Industrial sector of eight parent companies interviewed (with sizes of their subsidiaries in the sample)*

British parent companies	
Industrial sector	
Chemicals	1
Metals and articles thereof	1
Pharmaceuticals	1
Building materials	1
Banking and finance	2
Insurance	1
Total	7
Their subsidiaries in Germany	
Number of employees	
2000 and over	3
300–1999	1
20–299	2*
Up to 19	1
Total	7

German parent company	
Branch of industry	
Vehicle parts	1
Size of subsidiary in Britain	
300–1999	1

Note:
*one of these subsidiaries is not in the sample.

parent company for territories other than their host country. Again the two samples appear homogeneous in this respect.

A further aspect of the relationship with parent companies is the corporate board membership links of the Chief Executives of the subsidiaries. As Table 2.10 shows, there is a range in both samples. While over half are not members of a parent company board, some are members of an intermediate divisional board and others are members of the main board of the corporation. This range reflects the range of subsidiary size and market importance present in the samples.

An important aspect of the functioning of a organization is its management structure. Using the usual classification of organization structures deriving originally from Chandler (1962), Table 2.11 shows the range of

Figure 2.1 *Age of subsidaries in sample*

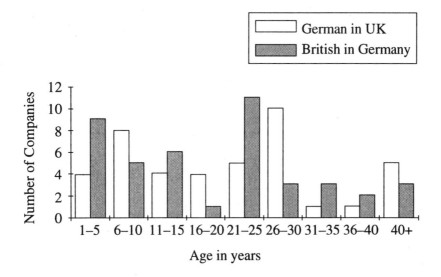

Table 2.7 *Status of subsidiary in the host market*

	Subsidiaries		
	UK in Germany	*German in UK*	*Total*
Registered office	1	3	4
Limited co. (Ltd/Gmbh)	36 (80%)	38 (83%)	74 (81%)
Holding company	0	1	1
Public co. (plc/AG)	6	3	9
Other	2	1	3
Total (= 100%)	45	46	91

structures of the subsidiaries. The basic functional structure is the most usual, with over half the subsidiaries organized in this way. Geographical and product divisional structures and some hybrid types are also found. The British and German samples again appear to be homogeneous with regard to range of structure. The emphasis on functional organization would appear to be related to the fact that most of the companies are of a medium size as shown in Table 2.1 (cf. Pugh and Hickson, 1976).

Table 2.8 *Number of branches in the host country*

| | Subsidiaries | | | | | |
| | UK in Germany | | German in UK | | Total | |
	n	%	n	%	n	%
One branch	17	37	12	26	29	32
HQ and not more than 3 branches	7	16	11	24	18	20
HQ and more than 3 branches	7	16	15	33	22	24
HQ and sub-contractors or independent agents	1	2	4	9	5	5
Missing data	13	29	4	9	17	19
Total	45	100	46	100	91	100

Table 2.9 Nature of the subsidiary's fit into the corporate structure of the parent organization

| | Subsidiaries | | |
	UK in Germany	German in UK	Total
Representative office of the parent company	1	3	4
Independent subsidiary	32 (71%)	34 (74%)	66 (73%)
Responsible for other territories on behalf of the parent company	7 (16%)	5 (11%)	12 (13%)
Other	3	0	3
Missing data	2	4	6
Total (= 100%)	45	46	91

Within the framework of the present interview study, it was not possible to obtain statistical and financial data regarding the comparative business performance of the subsidiaries in the sample. However, all the Chief Executives of subsidiaries were asked to give a qualitative assessment of how their companies had performed during the past year in relation to the targets set by the parent company. Table 2.12 shows that the replies ranged from 'missed the target' to 'exceeded the target', with the commonest response (43 per cent) being 'delivered the target'.

Table 2.10 *Subsidiary CEs' membership of company boards*

| | Subsidiaries | | | | | |
| | UK in Germany | | German in UK | | Total | |
	n	*%*	*n*	*%*	*n*	*%*
Not a member of a board	25	56	24	52	49	54
Member of divisional board	7	16	8	17	15	16
Member of main board	6	13	7	15	13	14
Missing data	7	16	7	15	14	15
Total	45	100	46	100	91	100

Table 2.11 *Organizational structure of the subsidiaries*

| | Subsidiaries | | | | | |
	UK in Germany		German in UK		Total	
Functional	23	(51%)	26	(57%)	49	(54%)
Functional and geographical	3	7	3	7	6	7
Functional and product	7	16	9	20	16	18
Product divisions	5	11	2	4	7	8
Geographical divisions	1	2	0	0	1	1
Missing data	6	13	6	13	12	13
Total (= 100%)	45		46		91	

The table shows little difference in the range of performance achieved in the two samples. All the subsidiaries who missed their targets in both countries claimed their underperformance to be only short term and gave general economic conditions as the cause. Such an outcome is to be expected, since only satisfactorily performing subsidiary ventures are likely to be allowed to continue in operation. Any significant trends towards a permanently lower performance would inevitably lead to closure. But even though all the subsidiaries studied are at least economically viable, there is still a range of performance levels achieved. And, as discussed in Chapter 3 below, there is also a considerable range of potential for successful operation which varies by firm and industry.

Table 2.12   *Achievement of business targets by subsidiaries*

| | Subsidiaries | | | | | |
| | UK in Germany | | German in UK | | Total | |
Achievement	n	%	n	%	n	%
Missed	7	16	7	15	14	15
Missed slightly	5	11	5	11	10	11
Ongoing	3	7	2	4	5	5
Delivered	20	44	19	41	39	43
Exceeded	8	18	9	20	17	19
Missing data	2	4	4	9	6	7
Total	45	100	46	100	91	100

THE RESPONDENTS IN THE INTERVIEWS

One interview was carried out in each of the 99 participating companies. It was conducted with the most senior manager whose role it is to consolidate the flow of information between the two countries, and who would therefore interact on a daily operational basis between both cultures. In the case of most subsidiaries, this task was undertaken by the chief executive, as Table 2.13 shows. In the British subsidiaries in Germany 73 per cent of those interviewed were chief executives. For German subsidiaries in Britain, the figure was 83 per cent. In all but four of the remaining cases the interview was conducted with a senior board member whose task it was to co-ordinate the subsidiary–parent company co-operation. In the parent companies, a senior member of the board of directors would typically have held a position of this nature, and seven of the eight respondents were corporate directors responsible for the subsidiaries' operations. All the managers holding these positions were male.

The topics discussed in this study included important issues of cultural differences in parent–subsidiary relationships, marketing strategy, organizational behaviour and interpersonal relations. It may well have been that the responses obtained would be influenced by the nationalities of managers interviewed. These were therefore noted, and are referred to when quotations are given in the discussion in the following chapters. Table 2.14 gives the nationalities of the managers and their present coun-

Table 2.13 *Respondents' positions in subsidiaries*

	Subsidiaries		
	UK in Germany	German in UK	Total
Chief Executive	33 (73%)	38 (83%)	71 (78%)
Corporate Director	1	6	7
Marketing Director	2	2	4
Financial Director	4	0	4
Personnel Director	1	0	1
Other	4	0	4
Total	45	46	91

Table 2.14 *Nationality of respondents*

	Subsidiaries		Parent companies		
Nationality	UK in Germany	German in UK	UK	German	Total
British	6	34	6	0	46
German	34	12	1	1	48
Other	5	0	0	0	5
Total	45	46	7	1	99

tries of operation. This shows that, in the sample as a whole, there is a general balance of the two nationalities: a total of 46 British nationals and 48 German nationals were interviewed, along with 5 managers of other nationalities (e.g. Belgian, Italian).

The respondents, as shown in Table 2.15, had a range of educational qualifications, from those without qualifications to those with higher degrees. The largest group where those with a relevant university education, although a substantial smaller group had non-university qualifications. They also came from a range of management specialisms as shown in Table 2.16. A characteristic difference here is the preponderance of managers from the technical specialism in the German subsidiaries in the UK, while those in British subsidiaries in Germany came in considerable numbers from a sales or finance background.

The length of employment of the respondents in their current company, shown in Table 2.17, underlines that, as discussed in

Table 2.15   *Education of respondents*

	British subsidiaries in Germany	German subsidiaries in UK	UK parent companies
Without formal qualifications	0	2	0
Relevant formal education	14	8	1
University education non-related	5	3	1
Relevant university education	25	14	2
Higher degrees	1	6	1
Missing data	0	13	2
Total	45	46	7

Note: Data not available for the one German parent company.

Table 2.16   *Management specialism of respondents*

	British subsidiaries in Germany	German subsidiaries in UK	UK parent companies
Technical	5	14	0
Sales and commercial	17	7	2
Marketing	3	7	0
Science	2	3	1
Law	1	0	1
Finance	12	7	2
Administration	0	1	0
Other	3	4	1
Missing data	2	3	0
Total	45	46	7

Note: Data not available for the one German parent company.

Chapter 1, a considerable amount of experience of cross-cultural business collaboration is typical of this group. This is underpinned by the respondents' experience of work in other cross-cultural settings. As shown in Table 2.18, well over half of them has had previous experience of working in foreign firms and/or in foreign locations.

In general, the respondents can be regarded as a typical group of qualified senior managers with considerable involvement in the issues

Table 2.17 *Length of employment of respondent in current company*

Years	British subsidiaries in Germany	German subsidiaries in UK	UK parent companies
0–2	7	7	0
3–5	8	4	0
6–10	4	7	3
11–15	7	6	0
16–20	11	7	0
21–25	3	4	0
26–30	3	4	0
31–35	1	1	1
36–40	0	1	2
Missing data	1	5	1
Total	45	46	7

Note: Data not available for the one German parent company.

Table 2.18 *Respondents' work experience in cross-cultural settings*

	British subsidiaries in Germany	German subsidiaries in UK	UK parent companies
First foreign company worked for in own country	19	15	1
Previously worked for other foreign companies in own country	5	9	0
Long-term work experience abroad only with existing company	5	9	2
Long-term work experience abroad with more than one company	7	7	1
Long-term non-work experience abroad	0	1	0
Other	0	0	2
Missing data	9	5	1
Total	45	46	7

Note: Data not available for the one German parent company.

and problems of Anglo–German business collaboration. In view of their length of experience, they can be expected to respond knowledgeably to the questions asked in the interview.

THE METHODS OF THE RESEARCH

The basic methodology used to collect data in this study is the semi-structured interview. The managers interviewed were found to be very ready to be interviewed and to discuss problems of Anglo–German business collaboration, which they felt as highly relevant to their concerns. As part of the study, three questionnaires were designed and managers were asked to arrange for them to be completed later (by themselves and by colleagues) and returned to the research team by post. However, the overall response rate in Britain and Germany of 40 per cent was not sufficiently high to allow for a convincing analysis. The discussion in this volume is therefore based on the results of the content analysis of the interviews.

THE STRUCTURE OF THE INTERVIEW

After a series of pilot interviews by both teams, some of them in collaboration, an interview schedule was developed.

An innovative aspect of the interviews in this study stems from the fact that respondents were asked to talk, not about themselves, but primarily about their relationship with their parent companies either in Britain or Germany, and about their parent's strengths and weaknesses. So the statements which the interviewees gave about themselves were given indirectly, and usually in support of statements about parent company differences. This lessened the pressure on the interviewees to give 'organizationally appropriate' statements which would highlight the positive aspects of their work environment, and downplay the negative ones. As Stewart *et al.* (1994) put it: 'Britons are readier to break off and philosophise, there is more interaction with the researcher, and the whole exercise is more negotiable. In Germany, it is less of a game, there is less interaction with the researcher, less scope for persuasion or insight into "what is really going on", and less comfort with the uncertainty of the observation exercise' (p. 212). The present approach was designed to reduce these influences on the interviewees in discussing their personal perceptions on topics of work interest. In the British team's experience this approach appears to work with both British and German managers (Table 2.19).

The questions in the interview are given in the Appendix to this chapter. The interview began with a series of standard questions (questions 1–19) to obtain information describing the company, its history, and its product portfolio. Questions were also asked about the company's long- and short-term targets and goals, and the external and internal limitations on the company's performance. Questions on the communication mechanisms between the subsidiary and the parent company were also asked.

The semi-structured part of the interview then followed (questions 20–7). In this section, only very general questions were asked to enable the respondent to elaborate on the issues which were important to him. For example, the opening question was:

What issues tend to arise in co-operating with your German/British partner?

In responding to these open-ended questions, the interviewees developed their answers into a converation with the interviewer, who asked follow-up questions as appropriate. It should be emphasized that the issues raised in reply to these questions concerning, for example, parent–subsidiary relationships, marketing approach and organizational behaviour, derive extra importance from the fact that they were *volunteered* by the respondents.

Finally, a number of other specific questions were asked (questions 28–31) dealing with personnel issues, company image, and the Single European Market.

The interviews were conducted in English or German as appropriate, and, on occasion, in a mixture of the two! Full notes were taken at the British team's interviews by the interviewer and then written up. The German team's interviews were taped and then fully or partially transcribed. The answers to the structured questions were classified and are presented in tables throughout this volume where the data allow. The replies to the unstructured questions were content analysed according to a coding structure devised by the British team, which was subsequently applied by the German team to their own data.

The collaboration of the managers in the interviews and the number of issues raised by them varies considerably between the two teams. Table 2.19 shows a total of 1635 issues collected by both teams. On average, between 22 and 25 issues per company were collected by the British team (in the case of the one German parent company it was 46 issues), whilst on average under six (5.7) issues per company were collected by the German team. For the study as a whole the average was

Table 2.19   *Number of issues raised in each interview*

Interviewed by	Subsidiaries in Britain	Subsidiaries in Germany		Parent companies British	Parent companies German	Total
	UK	UK	Ger.	UK	UK	Both
Number of companies	46	6	39	7	1	99
Number of issues	1062	131	221	175	46	1635
Average per company	23	22	6	25	46	17

Table 2.20   *Issues raised by the managers according to company and country where company is located*

	Subsidiaries British in Germany	Subsidiaries German in Britain	Parent companies British	Parent companies German	Total
Number of companies	45	46	7	1	99
The business environment of Britain and Germany (ch. 3)	26 (7%)	70 (7%)	11 (6%)	6 (13%)	113 (7%)
Market related issues (ch. 4)	18 (5%)	91 (9%)	10 (6%)	3 (7%)	122 7%)
Qualifications and skills of British and German managers (ch. 5)	39 (11%)	191 (18%)	32 (18%)	4 (9%)	266 (17%)
Organizational behaviour (ch. 6)	122 (35%)	363 (34%)	75 (43%)	18 (39%)	578 (35%)
Parent company–subsidiary relationships (ch. 7)	147 (42%)	347 (33%)	47 (27%)	15 (33%)	556 (34%)
Total (=100%)	352	1062	175	46	1635

17 issues per company. This imbalance in the interview content collected by the British and German teams represents a limitation of the study.

The interview process allowed a wide range of topics to be covered. In Table 2.20 they are classifed by main issue, each of which, as indicated, forms the contents of one of the following chapters. The major concerns of the respondents are shown in the table to be those of organizational behaviour in British and German firms (35 per cent), and parent company–subsidiary relationships (34 per cent). These are the most frequent issues raised by both British and German subsidiaries and British and German parent companies. The third most common issue is the differences in qualifications and skill between British and German managers (17 per cent). The remaining two issues are raised consistently but less frequently: differences in the business environment and market related issues have 7 per cent each. In general there are no striking variations in the frequencies of the issues raised by the different subgroups of the sample. Nor are the differences in the frequency of issues raised by British and German managers very great, as Table 2.21 shows. There is some tendency for managers of British nationality to raise market related topics more frequently (9 per cent as against 4 per cent for German managers). In turn, they are slightly more likely to raise topics concerning the business environment (9 per cent compared to 6 per cent).

Table 2.21 *Issues raised by the managers according to their nationality*

	Nationality of respondent			
	British	*German*	*Other*	*Total*
Number of respondents	46	48	5	99
The business environment of Britain and Germany	61 (6%)	52 (9%)	0	113 (7%)
Market related issues	95 (9%)	24 (4%)	3 (12%)	122 (7%)
Qualifications and skills of British and German managers	155 (15%)	110 (18%)	1 (4%)	266 (16%)
Organizational behaviour	355 (35%)	213 (35%)	10 (38%)	578 (35%)
Parent company–subsidiary relationships	340 (34%)	204 (34%)	12 (46%)	556 (34%)
Total (=100%)	1006	603	26	1635

There is, on the whole, therefore, considerable homogeneity in the range and frequency of the issues raised, underlining their importance in the cross-cultural collaborative situation. But, as will be seen in the following chapters, the contents of the statements made varies considerably according to the British or German situation.

COMPARISON OF SAMPLE CHARACTERISTICS

It will be apparent that, in terms of the characteristics considered, the two samples of subsidiaries in Britain and Germany are quite alike. There are some variations, but their distributions for range of size, industry, age since establishment, and legal status are quite comparable. And the same is true in regard to the formal relationship to the parent company, the formal organization structure and the subsidiaries' assessment of their achievement of business targets.

The managers interviewed formed two samples with distributions parallel on several characteristics (respondents' position, length of employment, educational qualifications and experience of cross-cultural business activity) although there was a degree of divergence in the nature of their previous management specialism. And, although a majority of the managers of British subsidiaries of German parent companies were British, and the managers of German subsidiaries of British parent companies were German, there was a balance of nationalities across the two samples. This is important on the occasions when the analysis is carried out by nationality for reasons explained in Chapter 1.

The frequencies of the main issues raised in the interviews also shows, on the whole, considerable similarity, underlining their importance for the managers in the cross-cultural collaborative situation. This degree of homogeneity between the samples on a number of environmental characteristics, structural features, and frequency of issues raised, forms a good basis for allowing comparisons between them concerning management, marketing and organizational behaviour. On these issues, as will be seen in the following chapters, there are important differences to be identified and discussed.

APPENDIX: INTERVIEW SCHEDULE

Interviewer:
  1. Company name:
  2. Interviewee:

-   Position in company:
-   Length of employment with company:
-   Education/Profession:
-   Brief career history:
-   Nationality:
3. Type of ownership of company:
4. Who are the main shareholders or owners?
5. Brief description of the market:
    -   How competitive is your field?
    -   Who are your main competitors?
    -   What proportion of your output do your three largest customers take? Please specify:
    -   What would you say is your competitive advantage?
    -   Which factors are currently limiting your performance:
        -   externally?
        -   internally?
6. Type of business: Manufacturing
    Assembly
    R&D
    Project/Design
    Selling
    Service
    Other
7. Can you give me a brief description of your products, how many major lines there are, and what is their proportion of your turnover.
8. Who is (are) your German/British partner(s)?
    -   Name:
    -   Size:
    -   Type of relationship:
    -   Type of industry:
    -   Partnership established since:
9. Brief Company history:
    -   Established in:
    -   Founder:
    -   Form of establishment:
    -   Organizational, product, and functional changes:
        (If written down, could I have a copy?)
10. How does your company fit into the corporate structure of your organization?
    -   Does your company have an exclusive function for the whole group?
    -   Your rights/responsibilities

- How is your organization structured on the three top levels?
- Do you have an organizational chart, could I have a copy?
- Do you have a separate unit (department, team) for co-operation (or to co-ordinate co-operation) with your British/German partner?
- If yes please specify:

11. How many branches/sites do you have in the UK/Germany?
    - what is their relationship to each other?
12. Main purpose of establishment in the UK/Germany.
13. What targets were you following this year? (Please rank them.)
    - If written down, could I have a copy?
    - Who participated in formulating these targets?
    - How far have you achieved these targets?
    - How would you compare your performance to competition?
    - Any changes for next year?
    - Please specify:
    - Were any of these targets specifically formulated for you by the parent organization?
    - How are these communicated to you?
    - How far can you influence these targets?
14. Are there existing control mechanisms relating to your co-operation with your German/British partner?
    - Please describe:
15. Are there any decisions for which you need the explicit permission of your parent company?
16. How many employees in the UK/Germany directly communicate with the German/British partner:
17. Is there any form of training or induction for the employees involved in the collaboration?
18. What issues tend to arise in the co-operation with your German/British partner?:
19. Do you see any differences in the education of the British and German managers?
20. What was the first thing you (or your colleagues) had to learn (in your current position or when you first became involved in Anglo–German co-operation)?
21. What took you longest to get used to?
22. In what areas do the Germans and the British work best together?
23. In what areas do they have most difficulty in working together?
24. What was your last major strategic decision, and how did it come about?
    - How exceptional was it?

- What consequences?
- How much of a precedent?
- Who participated?
- Were there any delays? If yes where and why?
- Looking now back, do you believe that the decision was a correct one? If yes what are the main benefits?
  If no, what is the loss, and what went wrong?

25. Has the re-opening of the German borders (German re-unification) influenced in any way your co-operation with the German/British partner?

26. What (if anything) would you like to change in your relationship with your parent company?

27. What (if anything) do you believe that your British/German partner would like to change in their relationship with you?

28. Do you have a defined career structure?
    - Appraisal system?

29. Is it expected that some personnel spend a certain period working in Germany/Britain:
    - If yes, who, and for how long?

30. How far do you perceive your company as being British or German? Please express in percentage:
    British ......%   German ......%   Other ......%

31. And finally, what do you hope or fear that the Single European Market will bring for you?

3 Cross-Cultural Collaborative Configurations in Anglo–German Business

'We have a vast feeling of superiority. But it is not the knowledge and the skill which are superior. We only have a very good system. The social and economic infrastructure are the real German trade mark.' — German Managing Director of a British financial subsidiary in Germany

'The Germans are proud of being German. They are loyal shareholders and they support their companies by buying German products. The British too are proud of being British. A Brit will wave the Union Jack as he drives down the M5 motorway in his Toyota.' — British Managing Director of a German engineering subsidiary in Britain

All firms function under business conditions which are set by a combination of their national and industrial environments. For subsidiaries in cross-cultural settings the national environment of the parent company provides a third element of its environment. In order to understand the effects of these influences on the firms in our study, a model of cross-cultural organizations in their environments has been constructed. The three key dimensions of such a model are therefore: (i) the national environment of the parent company; (ii) the national environment of the subsidiary; and (iii) the industry environment. In this chapter, particular configurations of these interacting environments are analyzed.

RELEVANT CHARACTERISTICS OF NATIONAL ENVIRONMENTS

All national environments exhibit a number of important industrially relevant characteristics which affect the workings of the industries within them. The presence of natural resources, the geographical position of the country, its historical heritage and relevant international political actions, all play a role in shaping a national cultural environment. The environmental variables can be grouped under the following four dimensions:

1. The degree of the *stability* of the financial environment and indus-
    trial ownership. This depends on the source and type of finance
    and ownership, and on relevant legislation.
2. The facilitated *speed of response* to suitable strategic managerial
    opportunities. The decision-making and approval procedures
    required by a culture affect the speed of response.
3. The degree of cohesion of the relevant *industrial infrastructure*
    which acts as a catalyst for managerial change. Low cohesion
    allows scope for radical change. Higher cohesion encourages
    resistance to major change whilst supporting incremental
    adjustment. Industrial associations, Chambers of Commerce,
    industrial approval procedures, and relevant industrial, employ-
    ment and environmental law, are key components of such an
    infrastructure.
4. The impact of the *broader cultural environment* in facilitating or
    restricting the supply and demand of industrially relevant inputs
    and outputs. Important factors here are the quality of qualified per-
    sonnel, the availability of a relevant net of suppliers and subcon-
    tractors, the existence of a suitable consumer infrastructure (other
    industries, private consumer groups), and so on.

CHARACTERIZATION OF THE UK AND GERMAN NATIONAL ENVIRONMENTS

Using the above dimensions, Table 3.1 classifies the characteristics of
the British and German environments as recognized in the literature
(Hickson and Pugh, 1995; Lane, 1989; Lane, 1992; Lawrence, 1980;
Randlesome, 1993).

As Table 3.1 shows, most of the UK and German environmental features are polarized towards contrasting values, and have been recognized
as such by previous authors. Thus in regard to the environment of industrial activity, British short-termism in investment linked to the volatility
of stock market equity finance reduces the stability of the financial environment. This is in clear contrast to the German preference for long-
termism in investment on the basis of bank equity and credit finance. The
environment encourages financially-based takeovers in Britain, but
favours organic growth in Germany.

In the British environment, lower capital investment and higher distributed profits which is linked to lower corporate taxation, lead to a less
well-defined industrial infrastructure with a lower emphasis on control.
This may be contrasted with the largely normative industrial infrastruc-

Table 3.1   *Contrasting British and German environmental characteristics*

Liberal (UK)	*Structured (Germany)*
Stability in relation to industrial activity	
Low	*High*
Short-term management	Long-term management
Stock market equity	Bank equity and credit finance
More after-tax profits distributed as dividends	Less after-tax profits distributed as dividends
Impersonal ownership through finance prevails	Large presence of medium-size owner-managed firms
Legitimacy of takeovers	Organic growth
Tendency to lower vertical integration	Tendency to higher vertical integration
Industrial infrastructure	
Less well-defined, largely optional	*Well-defined, largely normative*
Low corprate taxation	High corporate taxation
Less capital investment	More capital investment
Trade associations and Chambers of Commerce are voluntary with low status and low involvement	Trade associations and Chambers of Commerce are statutory and have high status and high involvement
Technical research of lower status and less linked to industry	Technical research of high status and more linked to industry
Speed of managerial response	
High	*Low*
Union traditions versus exclusion of unions (1980s)	Industrial democracy – *Mitbestimmung*
Adversarial bargaining closer to shop floor	Collective bargaining
In management more concern with strategy	In management more concern with operations
Emphasis on profit and marketing	Emphasis on sales and sales volume

ture of Germany, with its higher taxation, lower distributed profits and emphasis on capital investment.

With the German system goes a lower speed of managerial response through a greater concern with operations and a more formal system of

Table 3.1 *Continued*

Liberal (UK)	Structured (Germany)
Broader cultural environment	
Less predictable and volatile	*More predictable and organized*
Political polarization	Industrial self-regulation
State centralised (less able to accommodate individual needs and less stable in policies)	State decentralised (more able to accommodate individual needs and more stable in policies)
Free enterprise	Social market economy
Education for education's sake (less industry linked)	Education is vocational in overall character (more linked to industry)
Decline of apprenticeships	Emphasis on apprenticeships
Lower proportion of graduates	Higher proportion of graduates
Career progress more likely through change of employer	Continuity of employment

collective bargaining and industrial democracy. In Britain, the higher speed of managerial response is based on a greater concern with strategy rather than operations, and the almost complete exclusion of trade unions from decision-making.

In the broader cultural environment, the German adherence to the social market economy values continuity of employment and the vocational character of general education, and utilizes apprenticeships in all industrial fields. This leads to a more predictable industrial environment. In contrast, the greater British emphasis on free enterprise has encouraged education for its own sake with the consequent difficulties of obtaining appropriately skilled personnel in some technical specialisms. Career progress is more likely through a change of employer. This entails a less predictable business environment.

These four areas of difference are themselves interrelated in each country. The less stable financial environment and the less well-defined industrial infrastructure of Britain are congruent with a more volatile business environment. This facilitates a higher speed of managerial response. In Germany, by contrast, the more stable financial environment and the well-defined industrial infrastructure is coupled with a more predictable broader cultural environment. This results in a lower speed of managerial response in the market.

These national patterns as displayed in Table 3.1 allow us to characterize the British environment as *liberal* and the German as *structured*. This

Table 3.2 *Environmental potentials*

Environment	Liberal (UK)	Structured (German)
Maximum scope for:	Financial entrepreneurship	Industrial development
	New opportunities from outside the system	Existing opportunities within the system
Less support for:	Existing developments within the system	New opportunities from outside the system

underlying contrast entails a corresponding difference in the economic potentials of each environment as Table 3.2 suggests. A liberal environment offers maximum scope for financial entrepreneurship with the finance industry developing in its own right with less regard to the effects on other industries. A structured environment encourages industrial development, with the finance industry playing a more supportive role. The liberal environment provides good opportunities for investments from outside the system, while providing relatively less support for developments from within the system. The structured environment has a contrasting effect: giving maximum scope to existing opportunities within the system and providing less support for new opportunities from outside.

CHARACTERISTIC INDUSTRY ENVIRONMENTS

Using the dimensions of Table 3.1, an ideal environmental situation for each industry can be defined based on its current specific requirements for success. The nature of industries differs widely in relation to their needs along these dimensions. A well-established manufacturing industry (such as heavy engineering) will prosper in an environment which is stable and has a well-established supportive infrastructure. But this same environment may well be too cumbersome for a business in which speed and flexibility are key attributes for success (such as consumer electronics).

Industries go through a number of stages – from initial development through rapid growth to maturity – and at different speeds. Industries in the initial stages tend to benefit from a liberal environment, but as they develop into well-established operations, they increasingly depend on the greater support provided by structured environments. In the initial development and rapid growth stages of an industry, the British liberal environment would be more appropriate. For industries in a well-established mature phase their needs would be better supported by a structured environment which provides more stability and longer-term capital support, such as in Germany. After the Industrial Revolution, what is now considered 'traditional' engineering flourished in Britain. But that type of industry later developed more effectively in Germany when its needs for structured support overtook its needs for liberal opportunities.

Through comparing ideal models for individual industries with existing environments, industries can be ranked in terms of their appropriateness to different environments. If an existing environment is congruent with the ideal requirements of an industry, it may be said that the companies of the industry operate in an overall *harmonious* environment. If the existing environment is far from the ideal requirements of the industry, relevant companies operate in a overall *dichotomous* environment.

Applying the model to British and German environments creates a characterization of an appropriate environment for each industry. The environments in both countries differ in some degree from what would be the ideal. But in relation to certain industries the British environment comes closer to the ideal, while for other industries the German environment is closer. Thus, certain types of industry, regardless of nationality of ownership, will have a better potential for development in one of the environments rather than in the other. But not all industries are affected to the same degree by the nature of their environment; some are less affected than others. So a further dimension in the the model must be concerned with the degree of environmental specificity or indifference of each particular industry. All the elements of the model are brought together in Figure 3.1.

AN ENVIRONMENTAL MODEL OF BUSINESS FUNCTIONING IN BRITAIN AND GERMANY

The model of the environmental dependence of industries on their environments is depicted in Figure 3.1. In it the horizontal axis represents the environment as ideally required by the industry, whilst the vertical axis represents the actual national environment. The optimal combination of the industrial and the national environment for individual industries is represented by the diagonal. It shows that consumer electronics, for instance, is currently appropriate for the liberal environment, whilst mechanical engineering is currently appropriate for the structured environment. The figure also shows that mechanical engineering in Britain is not at its optimal point in relation to the combina-

Figure 3.1   *National environment – industrial environment relationship*

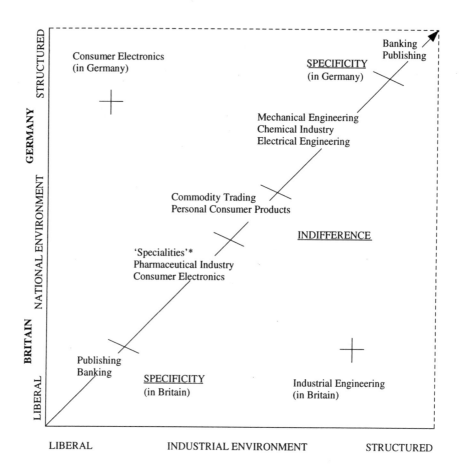

Note:
*Specialities are products which do not reach a stage of mass production, are normally technologically advanced and tend to combine two or more industrial types of input

tion of environments, whereas in Germany it is close to the diagonal line of appropriateness.

Conversely, consumer electronics development and manufacture are far from the optimal line in Germany. They are close to it in Britain, although the British environment is not the only one currently appropriate for this industry. For example, the Japanese success in consumer electronics manufacture benefits from a longer-term and more stable financial basis, but still requires high sensitivity to consumer demands. On balance and compared to Germany, the British combination of environmental features is more appropriate for the fast-developing requirements of this industry.

In addition, Figure 3.1 also shows that individual industries, or types of business, have different levels of sensitivity towards their environment. In our survey, for example, industrial manufacturing displayed a high degree of sensitivity. Consumer manufacturing seems to be less sensitive, and commodity trading shows a very low degree of sensitivity, with the cross-cultural differences being confined to human inputs such as work attitudes and management styles. Although the four dimensions of the environment have effects on the management of all companies, in the less sensitive types of business they have little effect on the quality of output. For this reason such industries can be labelled as *relatively environmentally indifferent*. Additionally, there are industries which are an inherent part of the environment (such as publishing), or even a central part of it (for instance, banking). Such industries are of comparable status in each culture, but their particular products and societal functions change with the nature of the environment. These industries are termed *environmentally specific*. Industries with more central roles in the environment are likely to be more environmentally specific than industries with marginal roles. Thus banking is more environmentally specific than is publishing. In relation to these industries, neither environment could be described as more appropriate.

Table 3.3 shows the distribution of subsidiaries in the sample classified according to the congruence of their industries with the national environment. In the present sample, the German subsidiaries in Britain in industries harmonious with the German environment amounted to 64 per cent of the total of German subsidiaries (29 out of 46). In the sample of British subsidiaries in Germany the companies in these industries amounted to only 38 per cent (17 out of 45). This relative emphasis would suggest that these industries are harmonious with the German environment. They have the resources from their supportive home environment, and the fact that British host environment does not support its home companies allows scope for the German presence.

The British subsidiaries in Germany in the sample in industries harmonious with the British environment are shown in Table 3.3 to be 35 per cent of all British subsidiaries (16 out of 45), while the German subsidiaries in UK in the same group amounted only to 12 per cent of the total (6 out of 46). Again, this disparity would suggest that these industries are harmonious with the UK environment, since they benefit from a liberal environment, and their competitors in Germany do not have the same advantage. Therefore such companies find it easier to establish themselves in the German market.

Table 3.3   *Distribution of subsidiaries in the sample according to the congruence of industries with the national environment*

	Subsidiaries	
	British in Germany	German in Britain
Industries harmonious with the German environment		
Heavy engineering	2	8
Engineering	8	10
Foundry	1	1
Accessories for the Automobile Industry	0	3
Chemical	3	3
Electrical	0	4
Products used in the building industry	3	0
Sub-total	17 (38%)	29 (64%)
Industries harmonious with the British environment		
Consumer electronics	4	1
Information technology (Flexible electronic systems)	2	1
Pharmaceutical	4	2
Specialities	6	1
Trading in building products	0	1
Sub-total	16 (35%)	6 (12%)
Environmentally indifferent industries		
Consumer industries	4	5
Commodity trading	0	1
Transport services	1	0
Mineral extraction	2	1
Sub-total	7 (15%)	6 (13%)
Environmentally specific industries		
Finance	5	2
Publishers	0	2
Sub-total	5 (11%)	5 (10%)
Total (=100%)	45	46

For the groups of industries classified as 'environmentally indifferent' and 'environmentally specific', neither of the environments represents an inherent competitive advantage. As would be expected, they are found to have comparable numbers in both samples.

EXISTING TYPICAL MANAGERIAL CONFIGURATIONS

Our analysis of typical cross-cultural situations shows that the ways in which parent companies and subsidiaries are managed can be classified into a number of configurations. These are based on a combination of three factors:

(i)   Managerial requirements relevant to the needs of an industry.
(ii) Options present in the national environment of the parent.
(iii) Options in the environment of the subsidiary.

Eight types of typical cross-cultural managerial configurations can be recognized. They are:

1. Environmental harmony.
2. Environmental support to the subsidiary.
3. Environmental handicap of the subsidiary.
4. Environmental dichotomy.
5. Environmental handicap of the parent company.
6. Environmental support to the parent company.
7. Relative environmental indifference.
8. Environmental specificity.

These eight configurations are depicted in Figure 3.2.

Figure 3.2   *Cross-cultural collaborative configurations*

HOME ENVIRONMENT	HOST ENVIRONMENT
ENVIRONMENTAL HARMONY National environment supports the requirements of the industry	SUPPORT OF THE SUBSIDIARY Advantage for the parent company over competitors from which the subsidiary benefits; its relative return can be higher than are the returns of the parent company
	HANDICAP OF THE SUBSIDIARY Advantage for the parent company over indigenous competitors; relative returns of subsidiary can be higher than are the relative returns of the parent company, the subsidiary can be 'neglected' (But the structured environment can limit the degree of 'neglect')
ENVIRONMENTAL DICHOTOMY	RELATIVE ENVIRONMENTAL INDIFERRENCE Environment does not have a decisive influence on output (but can reflect on the way how the company is managed)
	HANDICAP OF THE PARENT CO Advantage of domestic competitors over parent company; the parent company has to work harder
Conflict of desirable patterns of behaviour between a company's national and industrial environments = managerial compromise and reduced potential	SUPPORT TO THE PARENT COMPANY BY THE SUBSIDIARY Parent company is handicapped and the subsidiary in the host environment contributes to the operations of the parent company in its home environment
ENVIRONMENTAL SPECIFICITY	
Industries fulfil specific functions for the environment as part of the infrastructure	Lack of demand for standard products but a scope to introduce some products as relatively new in the market

On the left of the figure the four possible situations applicable to parent companies in their home environments are shown – environmental harmony, environmental dichotomy, relative environmental indifference, and environmental specificity. When parent companies in these situations move their operations into a host environment with different characteristics, the emerging situations in relation to their subsidiaries are depicted on the right of the figure. Thus a parent company from a home environment of harmony has two options – support or handicap of its subsidiary. A parent company from a dichotomous home environment needs to work harder. In this situation there are, again, two possible outcomes: support or handicap of the parent company.

Companies in industries of relative environmental indifference need not greatly adjust their activities in relation to their subsidiaries in the host environment. But companies in a situation of environmental specificity tend to find that their standard product range is less appropriate for the requirements of the host market. They tend to use the acquisition of an indigenous company as the vehicle for entering the market.

Illustrations of each of these configurations as found in the present study in relation to German and British companies and their subsidiaries, are now presented and discussed.

ENVIRONMENTAL HARMONY

This is a situation where the national environment supports the requirements of the industrial environment. The actual combination of positions on the dimensions of Table 3.1 is one that caters well for the success of companies in the particular industry. Companies in a harmonious home environment are, on the whole, in a position where their subsidiaries do better than their competitors in a host environment which is not as supportive for the needs of their industry.

Examples relating to German companies

The German environment is of a decisive advantage to the companies in the engineering industry, being distinctly harmonious with that industry's needs. 'Company AA', producing heavy machinery for another basic industry, was established in mining nearly four hundred years ago, at the beginning of the seventeenth century. In line with the economic and technological developments which have taken place since, the company was able to gradually change its shape and product without changing its corporate identity. The German environment protected the company through the many transitions, as well as through more recent changes from state ownership to privatization. The company's UK subsidiary was established five years ago. The subsidiary has had one major customer since establishment, which took 90 per cent of their sales. It takes one year from signing a contract to supply the company's product which has an estimated life of 15 to 25 years. The company believes that its longevity is one of its main competitive advantages in the international market. Customers view the company as reliable and stable, and hence as one able to offer the necessary long-term guarantees and after-sales service.

This example illustrates how a well-structured, supportive and stable environment enabled 'Company AA' to develop into its present form, and establish its specific strength in the international market. In the British environment a company such as this would have been more likely to change its name, product line, corporate identity, and, possibly, become foreign-owned over the years.

Industries which have been shown in the present study to be harmonious with the German environment are shown in Table 3.3. They include sectors such as heavy engineering and the chemical and electrical industries and comprise 51 per cent of the sample (46 firms out of 91).

Typical statements by Chief Executives in these industries reflect this point:

The German joint Managing Director of a German engineering subsidiary 'Company AB' in UK said:

Our main core of components did not change for the last fifty years, but we constantly improve them.

In the chemical industry, the British CE of a subsidiary in Britain, 'Company AC', said:

We have grown faster than anybody else.

(The company has grown five-fold in the numbers of employees in the UK since the mid-1980s, and quadrupled its turnover.)

The German Corporate Director in the subsidiary in Britain of a major German chemical company commented: 'We grew very strongly in acquisitions in the UK.' Referring to the last acquisition he said: 'We have bought it from a larger group, as we could better materialize the potential of that business than the previous owner could.'

In a German electrical and industrial electronics company established in Britain 150 years ago, 'Company AD', the German Chief Executive said:

> We spend 25 per cent of turnover on investment. Partly responsible for this is the German taxation law... From Bismarck's times we try more on *sein* than on *scheinen*. (In translation: *sein* = 'to be', *scheinen* = 'to appear to be'. The statement emphasizes the value of positive achievement, rather than of appearance.)

Examples relating to UK companies

'Company BA' is a British consumer electronics company with completely different environmental requirements. It was established by an entrepreneur 22 years ago. The company's German subsidiary was established four years ago. In the first year the subsidiary had a DM80 million turnover, which grew in the following year to DM135 million and in the third year to DM305 million. In one particularly popular product line the company already has 35 per cent of the German market. According to the German CE, the company's main competitive advantage is, as he put it, '*die geistige Beweglichkeit*', in translation the 'flexibility of spirit' of the company. The term was explained as the parent company's ability to translate new ideas into products on the market from one day to the next. This enables it to generate a succession of advanced product families each with an exclusive status in the market, which have a cumulative effect on sales. The company's product range, which marginally includes some more traditional products and services, has an image of quality in the German market, and of good value for money. By contrast, the parent company according to the German CE of the subsidiary, has an 'absolute Woolworth-image' in Britain.

The example of this company indicates clearly that short product life-cycles and quick reflexes are vital for success in the flexible and fast-moving environment of the consumer electronics industry. 'Company BA's strength internationally lies in a combination of advanced products with speed in their introduction in the market. The same industrial requirements would not find an equally suitable environment in Germany; amongst the company's main competitors in the German market are other Anglo-Saxon and Japanese companies, but not German companies.

Industries which are shown to be harmonious with the British environment are given in Table 3.3. They include consumer electronics, pharmaceuticals (particularly biotechnology) and 'speciality products'. They comprise 24 per cent of the sample (22 firms out of 91).

A 'speciality' is a product which does not reach the stage of mass production, is normally technologically advanced, or even unique, and tends to combine two or more different types of input in the use of materials or expertise. The product may not be typical for the industry of the parent company. Examples include special visual display units using mineral substances instead of electronic displays, special equipment for personal safety and specialist equipment for fire protection.

Typical relevant statements by CEs in these industries include:

The German MD of a company in consumer electronics 'Company BB' summed up his company's position as:

> ... [it] is considered to be amongst the leading manufacturers in Europe, and in the Federal Republic we are at least amongst the leading three. (In relation to one product area, which may be labelled as 'yuppie gadgets', the manager said that the British firm is an unrivalled market leader, having approximately 40 per cent of the German market.)

In a further electronics subsidiary of a British company in Germany, the German Managing Director said:

> For instance in product 'y' the English have 20 years of experience whilst the Germans have only two to three.

One British established pharmaceutical subsidiary 'Company BC' originally used the word *Deutsche* followed by the British name of the parent company as part of its name in Germany. But, as a result of the international recognition of the British parent company, it was decided that it would be in the best marketing interest of the German subsidiary to drop the word *Deutsche* from their name. This was done and now only the British name is used.

These examples illustrate that: *Effective management in harmonious situations is based on expansion through maintaining and further increasing a given competitive advantage in both markets.* This may be done through product development, as well as through maximizing the efficiency of operations. Foreign potential is used where possible to boost performance of the parent company at home.

SUPPORT OF THE SUBSIDIARY

If the parent company's national environment and its industrial environment are in harmony and the subsidiary is in a dichotomous environment, then the parent may choose to support its subsidiary. This is likely to be the case when the business potential of the subsidiary entails good market growth and high returns, and the position of the parent company is reasonably healthy. To such a parent company its home environment gives it an inherent competitive advantage in the subsidiary's dichotomous environment. As the result the returns of the subsidiary in the less favourable environment might well be higher than are the returns of its parent company in its harmonious home environment.

Example relating to a British subsidiary of a German parent company

The British Managing Director in a subsidiary with 27 employees in total of family-owned 'Company CA' in precision engineering said:

> Our main competitive advantage is that we have a lot of innovative products, high quality and good service. In Europe, there is a small market for this product, and there is no British manufacturer. We have a very intensive product development. We think we are going further than the competition. We [the British subsidiary] get very good support from the Germans. Without them we could not do it. We do not write notes. Internal communications are not written. Now we are installing a new computer system. Everything is the same in the company. The different subsidiaries [in different countries] show each other opportunities. In our company we spend a lot on training. ... We were accepted into the family. You get a real job satisfaction, pride in performance. ... We deliberately give an image of a German company. We consistently use the *umlaut* in the name, drive German cars, etc. In our field, it is an advantage.

In the British market this company has a dual environmental competitive advantage. First, the parent company's strengths are drawn from the structured conditions of its German environment. It maintains continuous product and staff development programmes which depend on stable, long-term capital investment. Its competitive strengths spill over to its British subsidiary. Second, the position of its subsidiary is also exceptional. Not only are there no indigenous manufacturers with whom it would have to compete, but the German image is perceived as a competitive advantage in its British industrial market. The subsidiary capitalizes on these circumstances and provides its German parent company with access to the British market with high returns. It makes good financial and managerial sense for the German parent company to support this subsidiary well.

Example relating to a German subsidiary of a British parent company

The German CE of the British subsidiary 'Company DA' in electronics in Germany said:

> Our corporation's strength spans over 100 years, and currently involves 10,000 employees. Traditionally it was associated with military appliances. With the development of electronics it diversified into supplying different industries with computer operated automation systems. Worldwide there are about 30 competitors in our business. We are amongst the top five. Our particular strengths are in the systems developed for the chemical and pharmaceutical industries. Major German chemical corporations are amongst our regular customers. Our product originally involved the complete system: hardware, software, system design, and implementation. But we increasingly specialize towards the service aspect, by purchasing standard hardware from others. It is more profitable than continuing with own full production.

The subsidiary's activities include sales, project work, implementation of software, hardware installation, and maintenance.

About the subsidiary's collaboration with the parent company, the CE said:

> It is brilliant. We have an excellent relationship with our [British] colleagues, which is reinforced through good interpersonal relationships, more so than it is usually the case in German companies. Contacts take place at all levels, at least 60 people here communicate daily, and every day about 20 faxes are sent to Britain and another 20 are received from them. Here [in the German subsidiary] approximately 50 per cent of our software engineers are British. Sometimes they stay for two years, and sometimes even five or 10. We benefit from this because they tend to be experienced engineers and software

specialists. We send our new staff for a short introductory course to Britain. But there are no benefits to the company in keeping the German staff in Britain for extended periods of time. Our regular customers [in Germany] have an excellent relationship with our British colleagues, whether those who are here, or in the parent company. We hold every year in Britain a consumer conference, and major German customers regularly participate at these. Some customers travel to Britain to discuss major projects directly with the engineers in the parent company. The English are very open, and they take care of one another. The good atmosphere shows, for instance, in that regular meetings of friends and former employees are held. Colleagues still meet although they may have moved on elsewhere, as part of their career development.

The situation of 'Company DA' in the German market is of an environmental competitive advantage. The parent company's strengths lie in input for which the liberal British environment is favourable. The British education system encourages, and trains well for skills which are needed in the company's line of business, as discussed in Chapter 5 below. Its main strength in both the British and the German markets is the specialism of the parent company's British staff in computer systems knowledge. The ability of the firm to create individually designed flexible systems leads them to obtain as customers major German companies renowned for their emphasis on the quality and reliability of products and services. The German subsidiary mediates between the parent company and the customers. It assists in arranging their direct interaction on more specialist aspects of business, and provides technical systems support within the market, such as project work, implementation of software, hardware installation, and maintenance. The collaboration between the parent company and the subsidiary is based on the specialization of each towards different aspects of output for the German market. The parent company provides the product, and the subsidiary an efficient technical sales support.

The parent company operates in the British short-term financial environment, and needs to rationalize its operations accordingly. For example, it relinquished its own production of standard hardware in order to increase its financial returns. Although this would be perceived as a business drawback in German terms, it did not negatively effect the British company's overall position in Germany. The collaboration between the parent company and the subsidiary is smooth and effective. The British parent company is in a position to support the German subsidiary well, and finds it worthwhile to do so.

These examples illustrate that: *Effective management in a situation involving the support of the subsidiary is based on maximizing the returns which the parent–subsidiary collaboration is able to generate in the host market.* The parent company's input is typically based on the strengths of its product, and the subsidiary's input is based on accessing and servicing its indigenous market. In this market, the home competitors do not find the same environmental support as is presented to the parent company in its harmonious home environment. In addition, the two examples suggest that this situation offers favourable grounds for good interpersonal relationships between the collaborating British and German managers. In none of the other configurations, whether resulting in an effective business outcome or not, were the work relationships between the British and German staff described so positively.

HANDICAP OF THE SUBSIDIARY

The situation of the subsidiary in a handicap arises when the parent company in a situation of harmony chooses to neglect its subsidiary in a dichotomous environment by limiting its investment. The resulting handicap of the subsidiary may relatively, or in the short term, suit the parent company. In a structured host environment the negative effects on the subsidiary are likely to be limited by the structured host environment.

Examples relating to German subsidiaries in UK

Examples of this situation are given by two engineering companies taken over in the UK by German parent companies. The takeovers occured because the firms were not performing as well in the liberal British environment, as their competitors generally perform in the German environment. Both companies had high expectations from the new German owners since they expected to be treated in the same structured way as German engineering companies. In the event both remained disappointed. Although they were initially 'put back on their feet', they continue to be managed by the new German owners on a short-term profit oriented basis, with a minimum of capital investment. In one of these subsidiaries, 'Company EA', the CE remarked:

> We only have about a quarter of what they [the German parent company] have for instance in production facilities. There is no positive investment programme. They never invest in us, it would be nice if they would.

The Managing Director of a company, 'Company EB', which manufactures parts for car engines, said:

> We did get a large order to run continually for seven years, but our site here is too small. The land opposite [in immediate view of the MD's window] is offered for development. The latest situation is that we would even get a Government grant to develop that land. But the probability is that we [the parent corporation] will not make a positive decision. We will have to double production, and it is already crowded. Not completing the order by ourselves is another alternative.

In the event the German parent company declined to invest in Britain.

The German parent companies in these cases take advantage of the liberal UK environment with the short-term profit option in order to boost their performance in a more regulated German environment. In Germany, companies have to be treated in a structured long-term way. The subsidiaries in the UK, as in the above examples, remain trapped in a handicap due to the differences in the environments to which they belong.

The data suggest that the two examples discussed are unlikely to represent isolated incidents. Further indications of a similar management approach of the German parent companies are given by the perception of subsidiaries in the UK of the amount of capital investment they receive. Out of the 18 heavy engineering and engineering companies in the sample, seven (39 per cent) stated that their German parent companies save money on capital investment in them. None of the engineering subsidiaries indicated that their parent companies invest substantially in their capital equipment.

UK subsidiaries in Germany

There was no clear example of a handicap of the subsidiary amongst the data collected from the UK subsidiaries in Germany. The reason for this may be the protective effect of the structured German environment. But limitations in data collection may also affect this result.

These examples illustrate that: *Effective management in a situation involving a handicap of the subsidiary is based on optimizing the balance between maintaining a competitive edge in the market on behalf of the subsidiary and maximizing the returns which the subsidiary is able to generate for the parent company.*

ENVIRONMENTAL DICHOTOMY

In this situation there exists a conflict of desirable patterns of behaviour between a parent company's home national and industrial environments. The company balances its situation by compromizing between them which entails a reduction of the company's potential. In an ideal situation, subsidiary operations would utilize their indigenous potential, which is complementary to the parent company's own, in order to compensate for this reduction.

Examples relating to German companies

'Company FA' is a German family-owned company in products for home entertainment. It replaced the former German Managing Director of its subsidiary in Britain with the current British Managing Director. Interviewed after one year in post he said:

> Some of the technologies that 'FA' recently brought out were good, but they were not always user-friendly. 'FA' were selling, but not making money. When I took over, we [the subsidiary] cancelled all new 'Product range Xs' [from the parent company], because they did not have the features that every other [brand of that product range] would have had. You cannot sell against the grain.' In relation to the parent company's financial management the MD said: 'FA' is short-term profit oriented. They do not take the long term view. I have not seen anything to indicate this. Our main target is profit, and next year we aim to improve the figure as a percentage of turnover. Basically the Germans [the parent company] have issued a figure on profit and turnover, and ask me to present them with how I am going to achieve it. Our business strategies are balanced between price and volume.

The company needs to find its market share in a competitive international environment which is governed by fast-moving customer expectations. In the last two decades, the industry has changed from electrical to electronic technology. The industry worldwide is dominated by large Anglo-Saxon and Japanese companies which are able to benefit from the short product life-cycles, and which can react swiftly to ever-changing customer demands. These tend to be fashion inspired rather than being quality driven. 'Company FA' is unable to follow a long-term product oriented strategy which is in line with the overall character of the German economy and culture, because doing so would be against the grain of the industry. Limitation of its operations to the German market is not possible due to the well-established international presence in this field in Germany. In fact, for this company the internal pressures of the German environment to conform to certain long-term cultural models represent a trap, and characteristic features, such as German employment laws, technical approval procedures, managerial emphasis on product quality and durability, are a disadvantage. They limit the company's flexibility which is vital for success in this industry. In recent years, the company has gone through several difficult stages but it has been supported by the German infrastructure. As a result, 'Company FA' manages its operations relating to staff and products within the constraints of its environment on a longer-term basis but is financially managed on a short-term basis. The UK subsidiary is managed entirely on a short-term basis.

Another example of environmental dichotomy in relation to German companies is presented by a large corporation, 'Company FB', dealing in, amongst other product lines, building materials. The nature of the business involves buying, processing, and selling a wide range of associated products worldwide. Speed of response to the market and speed of decision-making are important for success. The UK subsidiary's main function is that it is the divisional HQ for the corporation for the product. The main problem in parent company-subsidiary relations from the subsidiary's point of view is the degree of bureaucracy associated with the parent company's style of management. The situation was exacerbated by the large company size. The combination of these factors were slowing down the company's operations which was detrimental to the fast-moving nature of the business. As the solution the corporation was decentralized according to product. This German company underwent reorganization in order to delegate the responsibility for a specific business to its foreign subsidiary whose strengths were better suited to the industry.

Examples relating to UK companies

One large British-owned chemical company, 'Company GA', feels seriously limited in its operations by the short-termism of its financial environment. This is due to the fact that the company needs to conform to the environmental demands of this industry internationally. Long-term management, continual investment, and focus on R&D are essential for retaining a share in the world's chemical markets. For 'Company GA', the UK environment and culture work, to a degree, against the nature of its industry. Since it needs to conform in its internal operations to the short-term requirements of its financial environment in the UK, whilst seeking long-term options for its external operations worldwide, the company operates in an environmental dichotomy.

The situation is nicely illustrated in the statements made by the respondents in the parent company and in the subsidiary. The Corporate Director in the parent company felt that the company's main limitation is the more volatile nature of the UK shareholding. He saw the main advantage of his German competitors as being that their capitalization is a managed one. The manager also felt that the company finds it easier to operate successfully in culturally related markets than in culturally unrelated markets. Referring to the greater product specialization amongst the major players in the industry, he said:

> Crystallization in the chemical industry needs focussing more. Swops have taken place in the 80s. When people do not have money, then rationalization is given emphasis at the bottom of the [economic] trough. But the Germans [the subsidiary] are much less flexible, they are reluctant to get out of anything. They are less adaptable.

The manager gave an example of reluctance to change in the company's German subsidiary. This related to the sale of a marginal production facility in Germany which the subsidiary only agreed to after considerable encouragement from the parent company.

The German manager in the company's subsidiary in Germany said that the company is: '...well accepted and respected in Germany', but he added 'Always the problem is, that we do not have enough money to invest.'

The parent company was at the time undergoing a restructuring which included the sale of a major site in Germany to another corporation. There is a degree of tension between the German subsidiary and the parent company due to the difference in the environments, and the expectations of the German subsidiary. These may be in line with the German companies in the same industry, but are not in the scope of the British parent company, trapped in a national environment which is not supportive to the needs of the industry. The solution is a compromise: the German subsidiary is operationally managed on a longer-term basis than parts of the parent company in the UK. But with regard to strategic management, the German subsidiary has to accept that it is a part of a large group and sometimes decisions need to be taken which appear not to be in the best long-term interest of the German subsidiary.

An example of a British company in a dichotomous situation is 'Company GB'. It produces articles used in the building and associated industries. Unlike the German 'Company FB' discussed above, the nature of this company is that of traditional manufacturing. Raw materials are used for production, and finished products are largely sold from stock. A British Corporate Director in the parent company commented on the company's strength:

> We have overall a very effective R&D programme. Our biggest single income is from our invention of a process from which we get royalties.' But the manager also explained: 'This is a highly capital-intensive business, and the world is in recession [i.e. the industry worldwide]. We try to overengineer. We say that we overengineer because we try to be best. "Think of the cost of failing!" is what we say.

The main function of the German subsidiary is that it has a key market position. The Director added:

> We [the British] accept financial strictures when times are hard. In the UK we have payback in two years because it is a bad time. But the Germans [the subsidiary] would say "You cannot do it." They would insist on year 2000 plus.

The main problem, as perceived by both the parent company and the subsidiary, is the UK short-termism, as opposed to the long-term demands of the industry and of the German subsidiary. As a result, although the parent company has to live on a short-term basis, it endeavours to manage its subsidiary on a longer-term basis.

This situation was confirmed by the German Chief Executive of the subsidiary. The parent company judges performance according to such financial indicators as turnover per employee, in which the German subsidiary is below the level reached in most other subsidiaries. In spite of this, the subsidiary tended to get allocated substantial amounts of investment by its parent company.

'Company GB', therefore, boosts its performance through a strong German manufacturing subsidiary covering the company's interests in the German and other important markets of Europe. Additionally, the parent company clearly realizes the importance of a long-term investment-intensive management for the industry, and concentrates some of its own energy into its subsidiary which is situated in an environment well suited to the needs of the industry.

These examples illustrate that: *Effective cross-cultural management in a dichotomous situation is primarily aimed at utilizing foreign subsidiary potential which is complementary to parent company potential.*

HANDICAP OF THE PARENT COMPANY

A situation of the parent company in a handicap arises when its environment and the industrial environment are in a dichotomy, and the subsidiary, which is in a harmonious environment in relation to the industry, has to be managed incongruently. For the parent company from a dichotomous home environment, the host environment of the subsidiary, which is harmonious to the industry and from which the home competitors benefit, presents an added inherent competitive disadvantage. Such situations put additional requirements on the parent company.

Examples relating to German parent companies of UK subsidiaries

An example of this situation is given by a German company 'HA' in information technology. The company was originally established in mechanical engineering. Due to technological developments within the industry and in order to survive, the company has had to change to electronics in the last ten years. The company has a well-known name of a traditional German engineering manufacturer, and the German management perseveres to maintain that reputation through offering quality hardware and proven reliable information systems. But whilst their product seems acceptable in Germany, it was found to be inadequate for the market requirements of the UK, other countries of Europe and elsewhere. The solution implemented by the parent company was to allow the subsidiary to provide their own custom-made designs. As a result, the company's products consist of standard packages sold in Germany and individual flexible designs sold in the UK.

The German CE of the subsidiary in Britain noted:

We are in a field where we rub shoulders with the Japanese who tend to go for low cost. We cannot compete with the Japanese on price. We have a market oriented product. We offer a Total System Solution to the customer. Our sales account for 66 per cent of our business, whilst looking after the products represents the remaining 34 per cent. We invest mainly into people, expertise and specialisms which are our main assets. We are operating independently [from the German parent company] within the limitations of the plan, and guidelines of the corporate structure. As long as we produce profit we are left alone. ... The Germans [parent company] do not give us support and help easily. But they do know our problems. Our environment is different. Faster, almost unpredictable. They are too slow for us, although being thorough, methodical and reliable. We need flexibility and speed which earn us our results and profit. The German attitude is really defeating the object.

In addition, the subsidiary, which is not large, was made responsible for other European markets on behalf of the parent company. It looks after Italy, France and Spain, because the demands associated with the industry in these countries are believed to come closer to the options offered by the British subsidiary, rather than those of the German parent company. The company's fate changed from near failure to clear success in those markets. The perception of the problem and the initiative for the necessary change came from the subsidiary, and was initially opposed within the parent company. But in the event the parent company used foreign potential in the form of knowledge and skills less readily available to it, to compensate for its handicap in the UK and other related markets.

In the current study, other activities of British subsidiaries complementing the handicap of their German parent companies with UK potential include:

- Flexible and non-standard designs (in particular in information technology).
- R&D for hi-tech industry and less traditional technical areas.
- R&D in the pharmaceutical industry.
- Management of fast-moving businesses (in particular in strategic management).
- Marketing in the UK and other related markets.
- Sizeable domestic market for suitable German products.
- Access to other markets culturally related to Britain.
- Low-cost manufacturing in some traditional industries.

German parent companies are aware of the potential present in the UK for complementing their own performance. For instance, unlike the engineering subsidiaries in UK who felt underinvested, none of the German subsidiaries in UK in the industries harmonious with a liberal environment claimed to be underinvested or neglected.

Examples relating to British parent companies of German subsidiaries

An example of a British company in a handicap is the long-established traditional firm in the machine tool industry, 'Company IA'. The German Managing Director in this company's subsidiary in Germany said:

> IA was in Germany already 38 years ago. Their strength was in quick reactions to individual requirements.

The German subsidiary, which is small and was further reduced in the previous year from 35 to 28 employees, provides sales and service for the parent company's products in the German market. The main problem from the German subsidiary's point of view is UK short-termism coupled with a lack of understanding in the parent company about the needs of the German market. The manager said:

> We belong to a large concern that is profit oriented. They are not inter-ested in long-term company investment and involvement.... We lost the time in England in developing new technologies. If you go back 40 or 50 years we were ahead in the machine tool industry. But since then they were dreaming and sleeping, others went with the future. English companies lose market share and hold their profit. Now we are behind 20 years, and we have lost the trust of the customers. That is a more difficult situation than starting from scratch. The problem is that when we started the 'Company IA' name was good, only later we have lost a good name, and you cannot change that now.

The solution which the subsidiary is attempting to implement is that of offering special custom-made supply and service deals in order to retain the remaining customers. 'Company IA's' main competitive disadvan-tage in Germany is insufficient new product development due to the parent company's lack of capital resources. Indeed, it was recently taken over by a large US conglomerate. This manager blamed the subsidiary's problems on the management style of the parent company. But that is affected by the pressures on the company for short-term results. Thus the external environmental restrictions (national and corporate) on the UK company reflect on its subsidiary in Germany.

It is clear that the industrial environment in which this company oper-ates requires an unconditional long-term management approach. For a company in this industry to survive in Germany, it requires a steady level of capital investment. This would maintain continuous improvement in

products leading to a strong market position and a good long-term reputation. The subsidiary of 'Company IA' is not in a position to effectively
compensate with its operations in the German market for the handicap of
its parent company. The subsidiary does not have a sufficient degree of
autonomy and vertical integration. As a result of the handicap of the
parent company, as well as the corporate weakness of the subsidiary, the
outlook for the company's future as perceived by the German manager
looks very bleak. The situation is made worse through the fact that the
parent company has become part of a conglomerate and has to contend
with an industrially heterogeneous owning environment indifferent to its
specific industrial needs. The subsidiary is clearly in a trap, unable to
obtain the resources it needs in order to perform well for the parent
company, and the parent company is trapped in its corporate and
financial environment. Neither is likely to survive.

In the current study, other activities of German subsidiaries complementing the handicap of their British parent companies with UK potential include:

- Efficient manufacturing in traditional industries, engineering in
  particular.
- Efficient management of standard industrial operations.
- R&D in traditional manufacturing areas.
- Sizeable domestic market for suitable UK products.
- Access to other markets culturally related to Germany.

British engineering companies appear to be aware of the importance of a
structured management approach for their industry. They also realize that
this approach is required for a presence in the German market, and that a
successful German subsidiary could provide support to the parent
company on the basis of the returns generated in Germany. Therefore,
British companies endeavour to manage their subsidiaries in Germany on
a longer-term basis compared to the standards for the industry in the UK.
For instance, the CE of one car manufacturing subsidiary, when asked
what is done with the profits generated in Germany, pointed out that

> We have made so much loss in Germany, that it will be no problem if
> we make a profit in the next two to three years.

His answer illustrates the longer-term commitment of the British parent
company in the German market. But those UK companies which are seriously struggling for their own survival may simply not be able to afford
the luxury of a long-term investment in their subsidiary.

These examples illustrate that: *Effective management in a situation involving a handicap of the parent company is based on building up a strong subsidiary with a high degree of operational autonomy and vertical integration.* Through maintaining a close strategic link with the parent company the subsidiary is in a position to compensate within its harmonious environment for some of the shortcomings relating to the parent company's dichotomous environment.

SUPPORT TO THE PARENT COMPANY BY THE SUBSIDIARY

In this situation the parent company is handicapped and the subsidiary in the harmonious host environment contributes to the operations of the parent company in its dichotomous home environment. The support may take the form of complementary production, or a financial subsidy.

Example relating to British subsidiaries of German parent companies

The British subsidiary of 'Company JA', which is a large German pharmaceutical company, was given the exclusive corporation-wide responsibility for a major hi-tech 'speciality' product line. The British CE, a member of the parent company's main board, explained that the quality of research in Britain and its efficiency were responsible for this decision. The subsidiary's main strength is drawn from the availability in this field of British scientists with exceptional qualifications. Since the research does not involve experiments with animals or humans, and does not entail environmental pollution, the different British regulations on these issues were not a factor in this decision. The CE said:

> We are the only makers of [product A] here in Britain. We have patented products in many areas where there is no direct equivalent.

But the interpersonal relations between the British and German managers are not without problems. In this respect the CE commented:

> Our [the subsidiary's] line of business involves a lot of politics. There is always some pressure that investment should remain in Germany. The jealousy amongst the managers is shown at the middle management [level], rather than at the top. There is a lot of mistrust, and it is often easier to speak to top people in Germany than to our opposite numbers.

Example relating to German subsidiaries of British parent companies

The large German subsidiary of 'Company KA', which manufactures engine parts for the automobile industry, has total operational autonomy. It uses all the advantages of its environment to build up its own identity and has a good market share. The subsidiary is responsible on behalf of the UK corporation for certain lines of business, looks after other territories culturally related to Germany and is a profit centre. But, whilst the collaboration is highly efficient, cross-cultural human relations are far from smooth. At the core of the disharmony is the fact that the German managers do not understand the constraints put on the industry and the parent company by the UK environment. They blame any shortcomings on the 'managerial incompetence' of the UK managers. Indeed, the Personnel Director showed his frustration and ignorance of the environmental constraints by referring to the parent company top managers as '*Die Englische Idioten*'. The situation is exacerbated by the fact that the German managers are aware that the German subsidiary plays an important role in contributing to the parent company's overall performance.

These examples illustrate that: *Effective management in a situation involving the support of the parent company by the subsidiary is based on encouraging an operationally strong independent subsidiary able to contribute financial resources to it, or produce outputs on its behalf.* The complementary outputs will subsidize the shortcomings of the parent company. But compared to other situations, this configuration may promote less harmonious interpersonal relationships between the collaborating British and German managers.

RELATIVE ENVIRONMENTAL INDIFFERENCE

In this situation the managerial requirements of the industry are environmentally indifferent. The differences in the environments reflect only on the way the company is managed, but do not have a decisive influence on the company's output. The parent company and the subsidiary are managed on the basis required by their respective environments.

Examples of relative environmental indifference in UK and Germany

A pure case of an environmentally indifferent industry is commodity trading. Its operations are global with standard products. The UK branch of 'Company LA' is a subsidiary of the German office, but they are both in US and Dutch ownership. And although cultural differences show in human interactions, there is no substantial difference in operations or performance between the UK and the German offices. Both are vertically integrated to a similar degree. Their responsibilities are territorially defined. In relation to commodity trading, the clearly defined nature of the business makes it largely independent of the environments in which the firms operate. This independence is due to three characteristics:

- specific rules and conditions applying to operations, and their speed
- bulk character of product movements
- global participation

These three elements make commodity trading fully international. Most other industries tend to be cross-national: that is, each nation imparts, to a degree, features of its own culture on the way in which operations are executed.

Consumer goods manufacturers offer another example of companies in a situation of relative environmental indifference. These are companies producing goods for personal consumption, such as food, clothing and tableware. None of them felt limited themselves, or through their subsidiaries, by the nature of either of the environments in which they operate, nor did they believe that one of the environments was better suited for their industry's needs than the other.

But, unlike commodity trading, in these industries there is a certain secondary element of cultural dependence. It does not show as much in industrial operations, as in the buying patterns of consumers. Different markets display different culturally related product preferences (cf. Chapter 4). These cross-cultural differences need to be addressed by companies, either through offering product portfolios adjusted to the different demands in the host market, or through an appropriately varied marketing approach. The present study found that the problem of understanding relevant market differences in relation to consumer goods appears to be more frequent among German companies in relation to the UK than vice versa. The following examples describe relevant situations involving German subsidiaries in UK.

In the sample, three out of the five German subsidiaries in the consumer goods industries shown in Table 3.3 had quality products which did not sell in the UK owing to differences in the buying patterns between the two countries. The strategy adopted was to increase the autonomy of the subsidiary to allow it to select its own product range and to do its own marketing differently from the parent company. In all three cases, the results took a U-turn from near failure to clear success in the UK market. In each case, the initiative for the change came from within the subsidiary, and was accompanied by initial opposition in the German parent company. In two of these cases the changes also involved the replacement of the German CE of the subsidiary by a British national.

These examples illustrate that: *Effective cross-cultural collaboration in the indifferent situation is based on efficient communication and task co-ordination in order to capitalize on an optimal combination of the different potentials. In consumer goods industries, differentials in market demands need to be typically addressed as a priority through using marketing expertise and understanding from the host environment.*

ENVIRONMENTAL SPECIFICITY

The industries in a situation of environmental specificity are an inherent part of the environment, fulfilling specific economic and social functions for other industries as part of their infrastructure. As the result of such close ties, the products and operations of these industries have historically developed into a form best suited to cater for the specific needs and expectations of each society. In the UK and German environments, by definition, these environmentally specific industries differ considerably. Companies in a situation of environmental specificity are likely to encounter a distinctly limited demand for their standard products in the host environment, since they are likely to be perceived as inappropriate. But there may be scope to introduce certain relatively new products in the host market.

Examples of UK and German companies in environmentally specific situations

Banking and insurance are clear examples of environmental specificity. The roles and typical strengths of the British and German financial institutions differ. Both are equally developed and sophisticated in relation to their own environments.

In the liberal UK environment, financial services are seen as an industry which has the right to operate on the same basis as any other industry. This means that it is expected to cater primarily for its own survival and profits. As a result, UK financial services are more flexible and individual, offering products such as credit cards, and non-standard insurance. According to a German manager in a UK bank, 'Company MA', the German banks are far behind the UK banks technically, and in terms of know-how in these fields. But one German interviewee in a UK bank 'Company MB' also felt that:

Many of the city transactions involving buying and selling are just speculations in which a few can become rich, but not the country. People make decisions based on wishful thinking. The culture here is generally to pay late.

The manager continued, referring to Germany: 'In Germany people strive for safety. There is a developed fixed rate finance market, and people pay on time.'

To a greater degree than in Britain, the German finance industry is characterized by such activities as: greater consideration given to the non-financial potential of a company in relation to loans; less willingness to call in receivers as soon as financial liabilities exceed current assets; the granting of unsecured company bank loans; and a more supportive export credit finance system.

Similarly, in relation to the insurance industry a German manager in a German insurance company in the UK, 'Company MC', said:

In Germany the approach is very technical. In Germany they have long books. 'Sorry, it is not in the book' the German would say. In Germany we employ a large field of engineers who carry out crash tests, etc. The British are very flexible, they have it in their stomachs. The nature of our business has a very strict legal background, we have to have standardized products. All foreign companies entering Germany have a difficult life, except the Swiss.

And a British respondent in a UK insurance company, 'Company MD', said:

Our main asset is our flexibility. We write individual policies for individual clients.

A British manager in a German insurance subsidiary in UK, 'Company ME', also felt that

the UK financial industry is international, whilst the German is more domestic.

The main problem as perceived by the UK and German companies and subsidiaries in relation to their respective markets is the lack of demand in the host markets for the parent companies' products, and the degree of 'resentment' in accepting the services and products of the host companies. For example, four out of 5 UK financial subsidiaries in Germany in the study named 'establishment in the host market' as their main target – even though one of them has been operating there for 71 years!

It is clear from the above comments that the main societal function of the finance industry in a structured environment such as Germany is to serve the specific needs of the home economy. In the liberal UK environment, the finance industry is expected to develop and offer products for the home, and potentially other markets, on a profit based, self-developing basis.

In publishing, 'Company NA' is an example of a company in an environmentally specific situation with a different managerial outcome from those in the finance industry. The corporation is managed as a joint venture. The top 'say' in the management alternates at regular intervals between the UK and Germany. As a result, the strategic management of the corporation is a functional combination of both management styles. But the end-result does not entail a reduction in the sum of the two individual potentials. On the contrary, it is synergistic: The German input supplies stability, and the British shrewd financial management. Unlike the example of the banking institutions, it is able to encompass the specificity of both environments in its two separate and distinctly different companies, each catering for the relevant needs in their own environment. The corporation, which operates across continents, also uses its British and German market understanding to advance in other culturally related markets.

Both the British and German parts of the company have full operational autonomy from the other. The subsidiary of this corporation in the UK is the only large company in the sample (that is, those with over 500 employees) which did not have a single German among its 1000 employees. The environmentally determined differences become utilized through the division of the corporate strategic tasks using the different strengths of each part. Distribution, for instance, according to the UK CE is incomparably more efficient in the German company. And whilst the German top management are interested in some operational aspects of the management of the companies in the UK as well as in Germany, the British top management concerns itself only with the financial aspects of the German part. However, despite this and other differences in management between the two parts, neither's overall performance could be described as superior to the other.

It would appear from this publishing example that there are four conditions characteristic for cross-cultural success in the situation of environmental specificity. These are:

1. A high degree of vertical integration of each part.
2. A low degree of operational dependence between the parts.
3. Clear definition of respective markets, with corresponding product lines.
4. Corporate management able to accommodate the specific needs of each part.

These examples illustrate that: *Effective cross-cultural co-operation in the situation of environmental specificity is directed at seeking relatively new opportunities in the host market. Alternatively, a more comprehensive function in the host market can be successfully sought through joint activities with established home companies.*

Figure 3.3 summarizes the effective strategies for all eight configurations.

Figure 3.3 *Effective cross-cultural management strategies*

HOME ENVIRONMENT	HOST ENVIRONMENT
	SUPPORT OF THE SUBSIDIARY Maximising the returns which the parent-subsidiary collaboration is able to generate in the host market
ENVIRONMENTAL HARMONY Expansion through maintaining and further increasing a given competitive advantage in the market	**HANDICAP OF THE SUBSIDIARY** Optimising the balance between maintaining a competitive edge in the market and maximising the returns which the subsidiary is able to generate for the parent company
ENVIRONMENTAL DICHOTOMY Utilising foreign potential which is complementary to own potential	**RELATIVE ENVIRONMENTAL INDIFFERRENCE** Efficient communication and task co-ordination in order to capitalize on an optional combination of the different potentials / **SUPPORT OF THE PARENT COMPANY BY THE SUBSIDIARY** Encouraging an operationally strong independent subsidiary able to contribute financial resources to the parent company or product output on its behalf
	HANDICAP OF THE PARENT COMPANY Building up a strong subsidiary with a high degree of operational autonomy and vertical integration
ENVIRONMENTAL SPECIFICITY Recognising and respecting the different nature of the host market and utilising foreign potential to market suitable products, and/or to enter into joint activities with established companies in the host market	

CONCLUSION

This chapter has identified typical strengths and weaknesses of companies engaged in Anglo–German business collaboration. The eight configurations elaborated vary in relation to the different industries' home environments and their foreign subsidiaries' host environments.

Companies interested in exploring the opportunities which operating in the German or British environment presents can learn from these successes and failures. By assessing their position in relation to the eight configurations, they can identify and avoid some of the typical pitfalls. They will also be in a better position to take advantage of the potential growth opportunities highlighted in the examples. These options will be examined in more detail in Chapter 8 below.

4 Cultural Influences on British and German Marketing

'The German consumers take pride in being able to buy expensive. The British will brag about having bought cheaper than their neighbour did.' — German Chief Executive of a German subsidiary in Britain

'Their [German] marketing sounds like a learned academic journal. The British tend to look for buzz words.' — British Chief Executive of a German engineering subsidiary in Britain

In relation to cross-cultural business collaboration, marketing may be seen as the means of communicating market related values to different cultures and their markets, and identifying and encouraging cross-cultural market complementarity. The nature of the British and German economic and cultural environments leads to basic differences in their approaches to marketing. The recognition of these differences is a condition of success in Anglo–German business collaboration. This chapter examines some of the problems entailed by the lack of recognition of this divergence.

ENVIRONMENTAL CHARACTERISTICS OF MARKETS

As discussed in Chapter 3, there are large variations between Britain and Germany along the four basic environmental dimensions of Table 3.1, viz: stability, industrial infrastructure, speed of managerial response and broader cultural environment. The market related aspects of these dimensions are shown in Table 4.1.

The degree of stability offered by the environment is affected, for instance, by the prevailing type of ownership. Stability can be lower, as in the UK (stock market equity), or higher, as in Germany (bank equity and credit finance). The impact of these differences on the nature of the market causes varying degrees of emphasis between the two countries on 'value for money' orientation *v.* quality orientation; more lease contracts *v.* more direct capital investment; and so on.

The industrial infrastructure can be better or less well developed. Britain's less well-developed infrastructure is characterised, for instance,

Table 4.1   *Market related environmental characteristics in Britain and Germany*

Liberal (UK)	*Structured (Germany)*
Stability	
Low	*High*
Entreprise oriented	Production oriented
Value for money orientation	Quality orientation
'Cheap' is product advantage	'Expensive' is product advantage
Return on capital employed	Long term reliable performance
More lease contracts of machinery	More direct capital investment
Industrial infrastructure	
Less well defined, largely optional	*Well defined, largely normative*
Output less subject to control by the infrastructure	Output more subject to control by the infrastructure
Changing machinery only after breakdown	Changing machinery for higher efficiency
Hi-tech awareness (electronics and 'gadgets')	Advanced technology awareness (machinery and process)
Price elasticity	Price inelasticity
Speed of managerial response	
High	*Low*
Emphasis on flexibility	Emphasis on efficiency
Emphasis on market strategy	Emphasis on sales
Focus on product function	Focus on product performance
More user-friendly aware	Less user-friendly aware
Fashion influence high	Fashion influence lower
Broader cultural environment	
Less predictable and volatile	*More predictable and organized*
Lower technical awareness	Higher technical awareness
Home seen as enterprise (with higher home ownership)	Home seen as investment (with lower home ownership)
Personal enjoyment important	Prestige and status important
Mass markets	Market segmentation
Marketing function high status	Marketing function underdeveloped and low status
Less 'Buy British'	More 'Buy German'

by lower corporate taxation, higher distribution of profits to shareholders and voluntary, low-status trade associations. For the market, this results in a lower degree of constraints put on the outputs, with the market willing to accept more frequent changes in product functions (such as an interest in electronic gadgets) with lower emphasis on quality and durability (for instance, the replacement of production machinery only after breakdown). This approach entails an emphasis on price elasticity. In Germany, the well-defined infrastructure is shown by the higher levels of corporate taxation, lower distribution of profits to shareholders, and statutory high-status trade associations. These impact on the market by imposing more output constraints; insistence on longer lasting efficiency of original purchase in production machinery; and a high value put on quality with its resulting price inelasticity.

The facilitated speed of managerial response is higher in the UK, and lower in Germany. Amongst the factors influencing it are, for instance, greater management concern with strategy *v.* greater management concern with operations. It leads to a differing emphasis on market strategy *v.* sales volume and there is a higher fashion influence in relation to technical products in Britain but a lower influence in Germany.

The broader cultural environment can be less predictable and volatile, as in Britain, or more predictable and organised, as in Germany. The volatility is the result of factors such as the free enterprise system, while the organised environment is influenced by the social market economy. The impact on the market of these differences is considerable. The purchasing attitudes and buying patterns of customers in the UK are also different from those in Germany. The characteristic differences include the lower concern with technical efficiency in Britain as against the higher awareness of it in Germany, and the British emphasis on personal enjoyment of the product as against the importance of the prestige and status which it may bring.

There is also less emphasis on 'buying British' in Britain compared to the German pride in buying German products in Germany. Another aspect was summed up neatly by the German manager of a subsidiary in Britain:

The German consumers take pride in being able to buy expensive. The British will brag about having bought cheaper than their neighbour did.

And the British Chief Executive of a German subsidiary felt:

The British see their household as an enterprise.

The UK buying pattern was described by several managers in subsidiaries in Britain. Five Chief Executives (3 British and 2 German) characterised it as a tendency to 'buy cheap'; five managers (all British) as a tendency to 'buy value for money'; and eight CEs (7 British and 1 German) as following the 'current mass market'. And in relation to industrial purchases, the choice for British companies is often similarly defined by the short-term character of their financial environments.

The British enterprise orientation may lead to the expectation of wider product varieties in the market compared to Germany. But this is not the case. The mass marketing available to large companies tends to be based on economies of scale, and not on product uniqueness. Smaller independent manufacturers who may be able to offer additional, and more sophisticated, product varieties tend to be weaker in their capital base. Because of the high costs, they can rarely afford involvement in major marketing and advertising activities. Since the competition amongst the major market suppliers in Britain is not primarily product based but enterprise oriented, this limits product choice in the market. In Germany, the business infrastructure (banking, trade associations and local community) allows the independent producer to better withstand the competitive pressure. The resulting German market segmentation supports a greater proportion of medium sized family firms, leading to greater product variety. However, the structured nature of the German market means that all competitors strive for a high quality of product as the main competitive advantage, with less emphasis on price or 'value for money'.

The aspects of the British market listed in Table 4.1 are interrelated. The lower stability of the British market requires a higher speed of managerial response and a less well-defined industrial infrastructure. So 'enterprise oriented management' is congruent with 'more lease contracts'; as is 'marketing function being of high status' with 'mass market' and 'lower technical efficiency awareness'.

The British approach to marketing, therefore, is built on the idea of multiple choice criteria in a market of lesser product variety. The competitive advantage of a product is in its specific mix of benefits as perceived by each customer. It is assumed that different customers are looking for different advantages. Price and appeal are recognised as equally worthy of consideration as quality and performance. Marketing activities are aimed at influencing customer choice not only through rational argument, but also through emotional reaction. This approach, as part of the British economic environment, can be characterized, using the terms adopted in Chapter 3 as a *liberal* concept of marketing. It leads to increased sophistication in the marketing function.

By contrast, the higher stability of the German market encourages a well-defined, largely normative industrial infrastructure which tolerates a lower speed of managerial response. Here 'production orientation' fits well with 'more direct capital investment'; and 'focus on product performance' with 'price inelasticity' and 'lower fashion influence' in technical products. The traditional German attitude to manufacture is thus one of ensuring high value-added products, high technology, and continuous technical innovation. This implies that there is no need to attempt to influence the market by secondary means over and above what may, in German terms, be perceived as an obvious and natural choice of 'the best'. Since a choice between products is made on a perfectly rational basis it is 'the only correct choice'. So advertising should solely be concerned to present the appropriate technical information on the product (cf. Lawrence, 1980). This approach, as part of the German economic environment, can thus be characterized, using the terminology of Chapter 3, as a *structured* approach to the market. In it, the concentration is on selling techniques, distribution channels and export procedures. The marketing function in Germany remains underdeveloped.

These cultural differences in market approach have resulted in a relative British strength in marketing activities, and a relative German strength in servicing the market. The cultural characteristics of the market in each country also determine the expectations of that market in regard to foreign inputs. Comparing these national differences in terms of the demand for, and supply of, products in the market, it is clear that the supply activities typical for Britain do not fit well with the nature of the demand in Germany, and vice versa. For example, the German quality orientation and underdeveloped marketing function make it difficult for German firms to operate successfully in the British mass market, where cheapness is a product advantage and where generating an appropriate market image is likely to be the vehicle for success. Similarly the British 'focus on product function', and 'creative' marketing approach fits uneasily with the German market expectation of long-term reliable performance and established company reputation. *This cross-cultural incongruence of supply and demand is at the core of all market related problems in collaboration between the two countries.*

COMPETITIVE ADVANTAGES OF BRITISH AND GERMAN PRODUCTS

British and German firms are attracted to operate in each other's markets for two basic reasons. Firstly, the British and German markets are large ones. Secondly, they are in strategically important locations. Germany is seen as facilitating British access to Eastern Europe, while Britain facilitates German access to other English-speaking countries. When operating in a culturally different country, firms may expect to find that an identical product would present different benefits (or disadvantages) to the host market. This is because the specific mix of product advantages in a particular market stems from its national economic and cultural characteristics. As described in Table 4.1, these are very different in Britain and Germany.

To test this proposition, all managers in the present study were asked to specify what they see to be the main competitive advantage of their company's product. Table 4.2 shows that the nature of the British and German competitive advantages in their subsidiaries' host markets differs considerably. The results show important contrasts which reflect the differences between the two cultures.

The British strength in the German market is based on the advantages of products with new functions. Almost half of the replies regarding British products referred to this aspect (47 per cent), whereas there was a much smaller proportion of such replies regarding German products (18 per cent).

The first competitive advantage given is that of 'unique product', and 11 per cent of British subsidiaries in Germany give this reply. So also did 7 per cent of German subsidiaries in Britain. But it would appear that there are differences in what is considered unique in the two countries. For instance, the products which German companies considered unique included a particular brand of saloon car, and a particular make of an industrial sewing machine. In contrast to these, the unique products of the British companies included an apparatus based on digital technology in an area where only mechanical instruments were used; a new type of a drug for the treatment of previously untreatable conditions; and the effective use of physical reagents in a biological area where only chemical reagents were used. The examples suggest that 'higher performance' is regarded as a unique characteristic in Germany, whilst only a 'new function' is regarded as unique in the UK. This difference again reflects the importance of the value of higher performance in the German culture.

The further British competitive advantages mentioned are: product range (new, more comprehensive); know-how; and the managerial flexibility of the company. This last refers to the ability of the company to respond to the changing requirements of the market by bringing out new products with non-standard or non-traditional product functions as required. The six mentions of British company flexibility are characteristic. (In contrast, no German subsidiary gave 'flexibility' as its main com-

Table 4.2 *Main competitive advantage of UK and German subsidiaries in their host markets*

	No of subsidiaries	
	UK in Germany	German in UK
Competitive advantage		
New functions		
Unique product	5	3
Range of product	6	5
Know how	4	0
Flexibility of the parent company in responding to the market	6	0
Sub-total for 1–4	21 (47%)	8 (18%)
Higher quality		
Advanced technology offered	3	7
Quality and service	6	10
Total customer technical service	0	2
Reputation	0	5
Sub-total for 5–8	9 (20%)	24 (52%)
Others		
Marketing by subsidiary	0	3
Price	0	3
Quality of subsidiary staff	0	1
Financial strength of company	3	3
Geographical location	1	1
Distribution	1	0
Low labour costs	1	0
No competitive advantage perceived by the subsidiary	1	0
Missing data	8 (18%)	3 (7%)
Total	45 100%	46 100%

petitive advantage. Indeed, as Table 4.3 below shows, in 13 subsidiaries in Britain there was reference to a lack of flexibility on the part of their German parent company as a limitation to performance in the UK market.) Such a combination of advantages suggests that *market driven innovation* is the key force for product change in British companies. This may be seen as congruent with the relevant options in the liberal UK environment.

The group of competitive advantages labelled 'higher quality' typically represents German strength in the UK market. Over half the replies for German products (52 per cent) quoted this aspect compared with only 20 per cent for British products. The advantages given are: advanced technology; quality and service; total customer technical service; and reputation. They show that German strength in the UK market is built on offering improved quality of existing products and services in the market. Such a combination of strengths suggests that *technology driven innovation* is the key force for product change in German companies. This may be seen as congruent with the options in the structured German environment.

TYPICAL PROBLEMS IN RELATION TO MARKETING COLLABORATION

From the above data it would appear that the traditional German approach to the market is focussed on one 'P': the Product. But in Britain, the concept of marketing relates to four 'P's: Product, Price, Place, and Promotion. While the Germans, by focussing only on the product, have become masters at *Technik,* the British (as part of the Anglo-Saxon culture) have developed a whole range of marketing activities including market research, promotion, advertising and public relations.

In the open-ended part of the interview, issues of marketing were frequently raised by the managers as examples of the differences between the British and German approaches. Table 4.3 shows that 82 per cent of the problems of the German subsidiaries in the UK are due to marketing (32 out of 39). Whereas 82 per cent of the problems of the British subsidiaries in Germany are concerned with sales (27 out of 33). The nature and frequency of these problems are in line with the different market approaches predominantly followed in Britain and Germany.

As Table 4.3 shows, the key problem of German subsidiaries primarily concerns the fact that different British market preferences require a different marketing approach. Typically, the problem may be formulated as: 'When the Germans invent something that is good in their own market, they automatically assume it must be wanted in every other market'. The managerial attitude of the German parent companies, in effect, *negates* the function of marketing. The core of the problem is that the structured approach of German companies is incongruent with the liberal expectations of the British market.

Table 4.3 *Market related problems of British subsidiaries in Germany and German subsidiaries in Britain*

Nature of the problem experienced	Subsidiaries	
	British in Germany	German in Britain
Marketing problems		
1. Different customer preference requiring a different product portfolio than offered by the parent company	3	5
2. Lack of flexibility on the part of the parent company in accommodating to different customer preferences	1	13
3. Different marketing approach is required in the host market than that pursued by the parent company	2	14
Sub-total	6 (18%)	32 (82%)
Sales problems		
4. Efficiency of parent company–subsidiary communications in relation to customer and market issues of the subsidiary	4	1
5. Different product specifications, due to product regulations or market standards	8	3
6. Different market infrastructure, e.g. in relation to suppliers, agents, distributors, approval procedures	15	3
Sub-total	27 (82%)	7 (18%)
Total (=100%)	33	39

The key market related problem of British subsidiaries in Germany, shown in Table 4.3, primarily concerns areas such as market procedural differences, technical product specification and efficiency in delivery. Typically, it may be formulated as: 'The British do not understand how the German market works.' The nature of this problem is not related to the marketing function itself, but to the operational management of sales, the required technical standards, and the higher level support services which go with it in Germany. The core of the problem is that the liberal approach of British companies is incongruent with the structured expectations of the German market.

THE MARKETING SKILLS OF BRITISH AND GERMAN MANAGERS

In this context there would be expected to be considerable differences in the marketing approach of British and German companies and the marketing skills shown. Table 4.4 illustrates these differences as seen by the managers interviewed.

In general, British managers are regarded as having well-developed marketing skills and market understanding (38 mentions in total). The German managers, with only 3 such mentions, are in general not considered as highly competent marketers. Indeed, they are regarded as having insufficiently developed market understanding and skills (49 mentions in total, compared with only 14 mentions of British managers' inadequacies in market approach). Typical statements made in the interviews were:

The Germans are poor marketers [and] They bash the technology drum.

In contrast it was repeatedly felt that

The British have a natural flair for marketing.

All sales and marketing managers when entering a new market in a different culture face the formidable task of understanding the differences between their home and host markets. As would be expected, both British and German managers are regarded as having a lack of understanding of the different nature of the host market. Table 4.4 shows 14 mentions of this problem regarding British managers. Similarly, there are 19 mentions of the problem in regard to German managers. Therefore, a learning process is necessary. Example 8 in the Appendix shows that this acquisition of market understanding can take a well-established company as long as two years. Twelve interviewees felt that the British managers have an understanding of the differences; 2 felt that German managers understood the differences.

Indeed, some managers felt that being good marketers is the main natural business asset of British managers. The good marketing skills of the British were commented on by 13 managers, but not a single interviewee, whether in the UK or in Germany, felt able to say the same about the Germans.

In contrast, interviewees felt that the overall level of sophistication of German marketing is lower than that of the British. There were 17 mentions of low degree of sophistication of German marketing, whereas no managers made this comment about British marketing. Typically, it was felt that the middle aged and older generation of managers in German

Table 4.4 *The marketing skills of British and German managers*

	Subsidiaries		Parent companies		Total
	UK in Germany	German in UK	UK	German	
In relation to British managers					
Good marketing					
Understanding of differences between British and German markets	0	10	2	0	12
Good marketing skills	0	11	1	1	13
High degree of sophistication of marketing	1	9	3	0	13
Total 1–3	1	30	6	1	38
Poor marketing					
Lack of understanding of differences between British and German markets	13	1	0	0	14
Poor marketing skills	0	0	0	0	0
Low degree of sophistication of marketing	0	0	0	0	0
Total 4–6	13	1	0	0	14
In relation to German managers					
Good marketing					
Understanding of differences between British and German markets	0	2	0	0	2
Good marketing skills	0	0	0	0	0
High degree of sophistication of marketing	0	1	0	0	1
Total 1–3	0	3	0	0	3
Poor marketing					
Lack of understanding of differences between British and German markets	1	16	1	1	19
Poor marketing skills	0	12	1	0	13
Low degree of sophistication of marketing	2	13	2	0	17
Total 4–6	3	41	4	1	49
Total of all mentions	17	75	10	2	104

companies, simply do not understand marketing. One British interviewee having worked for many years in Germany said:

Most managers in Germany do not know what marketing is.

Another interviewee in Germany acknowledged that

Marketing is new in Germany.

The reasons for the difference lie in the traditional German approach to business. In Germany, marketing is primarily aimed at highlighting different product characteristics, and hence its message tends to be explicit. The German target audience is expected to be less receptive towards those elements of advertising which may not be supported with a clear rational argument. The technically better educated Germans are, on the whole, also better equipped to receive, and to benefit from the more detailed technical product information, than would be the case in Britain.

A British CE summed up the differences in the typical marketing message in Germany and Britain as:

Their [German] marketing sounds like a learned academic journal. The British tend to look for buzz words.

In Britain, marketing, through advertising and public relations, is accepted as a form of popular entertainment. This shifts the emphasis from technical accuracy to the art of delivering the message, which itself becomes increasingly implicit. Sophisticated visual and sound effects are widely used. This can be seen as associated with the, commonly noted, greater British flair for 'creativity' in management activities, as discussed in Chapter 6 below.

On the other hand, as Chapter 6 also notes, the Germans were equally regularly seen as being very methodical, analytical, and effective. These cultural characteristics can be linked with excellence at the sales functions. In the interviews mentions were made of German skills in sales operations such as forecasting and planning, and negotiating, completing and servicing deals.

CROSS-CULTURAL MARKETING PROBLEMS IN DIFFERENT INDUSTRIES

As established in Chapter 3, there are considerable differences between industries in their cultural requirements for efficient operation. Industries which are harmonious with the German structured environment will be expected to have different market related cross-cultural problems when operating in the liberal British environment compared with those industries which are dichotomous with the German environment. A similar variation would exist for those harmonious or dichotomous with the British environment.

The distribution of all market related problems according to industry and country is shown in Tables 4.5 and 4.6. Only those industries in which such problems were reported appear in the tables. The industries where no problems were reported are included in 'Other'. The distribution shows considerable variation according to industrial sector. A simple index of problem intensity can be calculated by dividing the number of problems raised by the number of subsidiaries in each industry. This index is shown in the final column of the tables.

As Table 4.5 shows, German subsidiaries in Britain have a greater problem intensity in those industries which are harmonious with the British environment, rather than in those which are harmonious with the German environment. The maximum problem intensity occured in relation to the consumer electronics and flexible electronic systems with 3.5 problems per company. This compares with only 0.4 per company in heavy engineering, which is harmonious with the German environment. On the other hand, the British subsidiaries in Germany, as shown in Table 4.6, experience a greater problem intensity in those industries which are harmonious with the German environment (for instance, 1.5 in heavy engineering). This compares with a lesser problem intensity in those industries which are harmonious with the British environment (for example, 0.3 in 'specialities').

In the case of British heavy engineering in Germany (problem intensity of 1.5), an industry harmonious with its host environment, subsidiaries are disadvantaged in their market whilst their home competitors have the advantage of their environment. Thus British heavy engineering is handicapped in Germany from two points of view: Firstly, it is in an extremely competitive market where home producers have the advantage of harmony, and the market in this industry is thus used to very high technical standards. Secondly, the market is used to German selling techniques (Appendix, Example 7, 'Company IA'). A similar argument applies to German consumer electronics in the UK. These subsidiaries are handicapped by an extremely competitive British market used to high standards, promoted by British marketing techniques (Appendix, Example 1, 'Company FA').

On the other hand, minimum problem intensity occurs in those industries which are harmonious with respect to their parents' home

Table 4.5 *Market related problems of German subsidiaries in Britain*

	No of firms	Marketing problems			Sales problems			Problem total	Problems per firm
		No. 1	No. 2	No. 3	No. 4	No. 5	No. 6		
Industries harmonious with the German environment									
Heavy engineering	8	–	3	0	–	–	–	3	0.4
Engineering	10	–	4	5	1	–	1	11	1.1
Electrical	4	–	1	1	–	–	–	2	0.5
Other	7	–	–	–	1	–	–	0	0
Sub-total	29	–	8	6	1	–	1	16	0.6
Harmonious with the British environment									
Consumer electronics and flexible electronic systems	2	1	1	2	–	2	1	7	3.5
Products for the building industry	1	–	1	1	–	–	–	2	2.0
Other	3	–	–	–	–	–	–	0	0
Sub-total	6	1	2	3	–	2	1	9	1.5
Environmentally indifferent									
Consumer industries	5	4	2	4	–	–	–	10	2.0
Other	1	–	–	–	–	–	–	0	0
Sub-total	6	4	2	4	–	–	–	10	1.7

Table 4.5 *Continued*

	No of firms	Nature of market-related problem						Problem total	Problems per firm
		Marketing problems			Sales problems				
		No. 1	No. 2	No. 3	No. 4	No. 5	No. 6		
Environmentally specific									
Finance	2	–	1	1	–	1	1	4	2.0
Other	3	–	–	1	–	–	–	0	0
Sub-total	5	–	1	1	–	1	1	4	0.8
Total problems	46	5	13	14	1	3	3	39	0.8
		Total marketing = 32			Total sales = 7				

Table 4.6 *Market-related problems of British subsidiaries in Germany*

| | | Nature of market-related problem | | | | | | |
| | | Marketing problems | | | Sales problems | | | |
	No of firms	No. 1	No. 2	No. 3	No. 4	No. 5	No. 6	Problem total	Problems per firm
Industries harmonious with the British environment									
Consumer electronics and flexible electronic systems	6	–	–	1	1	–	1	3	0.5
Specialities	6	–	–	–	–	–	2	2	0.3
Other	4	–	–	–	–	–	–	0	0
Sub-total	16	–	–	1	1	–	3	5	0.3
Harmonious with the German environment									
Heavy engineering	2	–	–	–	1	1	1	3	1.5
Engineering	8	1	1	–	1	4	4	11	1.4
Products used in the building industry	3	–	–	–	–	–	1	1	0.3
Other	4	–	–	–	–	–	–	0	0
Sub-total	17	1	1	–	2	5	6	15	0.9
Environmentally indifferent									
Consumer industries	4	2	–	1	–	–	2	5	1.3
Other	1	–	–	–	–	–	–	0	0
Sub-total	5	2	–	1	–	–	2	5	1.0

Table 4.6 Continued

	No of firms	Nature of market-related problem						Problem total	Problems per firm
		Marketing problems			Sales problems				
		No. 1	No. 2	No. 3	No. 4	No. 5	No. 6		
Environmentally specific									
Finance	5	–	–	–	1	3	4	8	1.6
Other	2	–	–	–	–	–	–	0	0
Sub-total	7	–	–	–	1	3	4	8	1.1
Total problems	45	3	1	2	4	8	15	33	0.7
		Total marketing = 6			Total sales = 27				

environment but dichotomous with respect to their subsidiaries' host environment. Thus, British consumer electronics in Germany and German heavy engineering in Britain have an environmental competitive advantage, since their parent companies operate in environments harmonious with their industries. They can take advantage of the less competitive situation of the indigenous suppliers for whom their environment is dichotomous. In addition, the German host market seems receptive towards the marketing approach generally adopted by the British companies, and the British host market responds well to the selling approach generally adopted by the German companies. This is exemplified by the minor nature of the few complaints occuring in these industries. (Appendix, Example 6, 'Company AG' in relation to German heavy engineering in Britain and Example 11, 'Company BA' in regard to British consumer electronics in Germany.)

In the consumer industries which are classified as environmentally indifferent in the tables, the national environment is of little importance for the industry's operations. It does not present a decisive competitive advantage for design and manufacturing (Appendix, Examples 2, 'Company LB', and 3, 'Company LC'). But in these cases, when moving into an export market, differences relating to customer preferences become pronounced, and tend to represent a problem (problem intensity 1.3 for British subsidiaries in Germany and 2.0 for German subsidiaries in Britain).

The marketing approach must therefore close the gap between the products and the market expectations, by adjusting the products or influencing the market's preferences through advertising, or by a suitable combination of both.

The highest potential for market related problems occurs in environmentally specific industries. This is because both their products and operations are designed to suit specific environments. In the case of the financial industry the problem intensities were high (1.6 for British subsidiaries and 2.0 for German subsidiaries). Whilst in other industries a mere adjustment to the product may suffice in order to satisfy the culturally distinctive demands of the host market, in the financial industry the differences are so great that, typically, a different product range will be required. Thus the marketing director of one of the two German financial subsidiaries in the sample in Britain ('Company ME' in Chapter 3) pointed out:

> All products offered in the UK market are designed for the UK market. We do not sell any German designed products, as they would be uncompetitive in the UK market.

Similarly the problems caused for British financial subsidiaries in Germany were underlined by one German manager. He commented that his British subsidiary's main competitors are not domestic ones, but other foreign financial institutions, and that the industrial clients of all non-German banks in Germany represent only about 3 per cent of the market.

SOME TYPICAL PROBLEMS OF GERMAN SUBSIDIARIES IN THE UK MARKET

Within the general framework discussed above, we now consider some of the typical marketing problems raised by the managers: first of German subsidiaries in Britain and then of British subsidiaries in Germany.

While British consumers are generally happy with the quality and reliability of the German products, there are two typical problems of servicing the UK market. The first is the way in which products are presented (literature and advertising, Table 4.3, 14 mentions) which, in relation to consumer goods in particular, is frequently overtechnical.

The second is the lack of willingness of German parent companies to accommodate customer required adjustments to their standard products (Table 4.3, 13 mentions).

This form of problem appears to be particularly pronounced in regard to the smaller-sized subsidiaries of traditional family-owned German companies (e.g. Appendix examples 2, 'Company LB' and 3 'Company LC'). This suggests that German paternalism with its conservative approach to product development is typically unable to accommodate the degree of flexibility in product design and marketing methods which successful cross-cultural marketing requires. In these situations, it would make managerial sense to give a subsidiary sufficient autonomy to use its knowledge of its own market, in order to implement the parent company's foreign operations in such a way as required by the host market. But, as discussed in Chapter 7, in no less than eight of the German subsidiaries (17 per cent of the sample) it was stated that their parent companies simply 'dump' goods for sale on them, without considering their appropriateness for the UK market. This problem may well be exacerbated by the more autocratic style of management in the German companies, as discussed in Chapter 6 below. (No British subsidiary in Germany complained about goods being 'dumped' on them by the parent company, perhaps because of the more open style of British management, referred to in Chapter 6 below.) But adjustments in market approach do take place leading to the success of German companies.

These typically happen as the result of pressure for change from the subsidiary after overcoming initial opposition from the parent company (Appendix, examples 1–3).

In engineering, including heavy engineering, the importance of a British style of marketing approach with its emphasis on image and flexibility reduces even in the UK market. Any problems focus on establishing an understanding on the part of the German suppliers of the different business needs of their UK industrial customers. These are largely due to differences in the economic environment in the UK, compared to Germany: that is, there is a stronger pressure to keep expenditure on capital equipment low. Seven companies in engineering and heavy engineering are shown in Table 4.5 to experience the problem of a lack of willingness by the parent company in accommodating to different customer preferences (Table 4.5 Problem No. 2). However, most of the subsidiaries in this industry did not report these problems (15 out of 22). This suggests that they are likely to be generally satisfied with the market approach of their German parent companies.

The low proportion of problems per company in engineering shown in Table 4.5, suggests that the German market approach is on the whole appropriate for marketing engineering products not only in Germany, but also in the UK. Of the five mentions of a different marketing approach being required in the UK market in engineering, none came from heavy engineering. Typically, the problems related to the marketing of consumer durables (see, for example, Appendix Example 4, 'Company AE').

SOME TYPICAL PROBLEMS OF BRITISH SUBSIDIARIES IN THE GERMAN MARKET

British subsidiaries face a different range of market related problems. Typically, they are not those of marketing in the British sense. Only two managers in British subsidiaries found their parent company's marketing approach or advertising techniques not to be appropriate for the German market (Table 4.6, Problem no. 3). Thus the primary problems are sales problems due to a lack of understanding of the host market as Table 4.3 shows (27 mentions). They primarily relate to the provision of a technical service to the market and to the inappropriateness of British technical standards for the product.

A frequent problem (Table 4.6, 8 mentions) are the different German standards, particularly the DIN specifications ('*Deutsche Industrie Norm*' i.e. the German equivalent of the BSI standards). This problem tends to be exacerbated by a lack of interest, as perceived by the subsidiaries, of some British managers in learning more about the specific differences of the German market. One German CE in a company producing industrial equipment felt that, since the British tend to detach themselves from the rest of Europe by always referring to the 'UK and the Continent', this attitude makes an understanding of other markets more difficult for them. A similar comment was made in a company providing products used in the building and associated industries. The respondent felt that if the British managers identified themselves more with the German, and also the European market, it would enable them to understand other markets better. Items mentioned as influencing market behaviour in Germany were differences in law, taxation, and *Mitbestimmung* (co-determination). The existence of these constraints is also an indication of the protective attitude of the structured environment towards traditional German industries in their home market. But adjustment to the German market does take place. For example, 'Company GC' learned from its initial difficulties and eliminated them through appropriate changes to product and market policy.

In consumer electronics, however (Examples 10 and 11, 'Company BD' and 'Company BA'), the problems experienced are minor. In the six UK subsidiaries in this industry in the sample, only three mentions of any problems in the German market were reported. This suggests that for this industry, harmonious as it is with the British environment, the British market approach can also be effective in Germany.

CONCLUSIONS

The activity of marketing is an area in which the fundamental difference between the British and the German business related cultures shows very clearly. Because the nature of marketing lies in communicating culturally related values between companies and their broader cultural environments, this activity reflects cross-cultural differences more readily than most other managerial functions. Hence, the British marketing approach reflects the liberal nature of its broader cultural environment, whilst the German marketing approach has developed as required by the structured production-oriented German environment and culture.

The effective achievement of cross-cultural market activity is a key to success in Anglo–German business collaboration. But the differing nature of the markets of Britain and Germany tends to be underestimated, or even overlooked, by parent companies in Germany and Britain. As a result, they fail to adapt the marketing approach of their own culture for the market requirements in the other. Since a universal approach, equally suitable for both markets is unlikely, success is often achieved only through cross-cultural trial and error.

But improvements can be made through a collaboration between parent companies and their subsidiaries in developing a culturally aware market approach. As presented in this chapter, such a strategy would be tailored to the liberal marketing environment in Britain with its emphasis on consumer choice, marketing image and value for money; or to the structured market environment in Germany with its lower price elasticity, emphasis on continuous technical improvement, and company reputation. This implies that, on the whole, German firms should adapt to the UK market by recognising the worth of appropriate marketing activities in it, whereas British firms in the German market should become more technically and market service oriented. In such a situation, cross-national market activities can become an effective tool for international market integration.

APPENDIX: EMPIRICAL EXAMPLES OF MARKET RELATED PROBLEMS

Table 4.7 lists the examples referred to in this Appendix. It gives the type of market related problem reported, classified according to Table 4.3.

German subsidiaries in the United Kingdom

Example 1: Consumer electronics (problem refs 1, 5, 6)
'Company FA' (referred to in Chapter 3, p. 49) is a German family-owned business in the home entertainment industry in a situation of environmental dichotomy. The British CE of the UK subsidiary who took over from his German predecessors said:

> Because they [the German managers] did not do so well in the UK, they tended to forget it [the British market]. If they had listened to the UK, they would have avoided problems in the UK and some other countries. My predecessors always knew that they would go back to Germany. They did not bother greatly to understand the market, and to stick out for it. They took anything that the parent company shifted on to them. When I took over, we cancelled all new 'As' [a product], because they did not have a feature that every other competitor would

Table 4.7 *Overview of the examples of the market related problems of German subsidiaries in Britain and British subsidiaries in Germany*

No.	Company	Marketing problems			Sales problems			Problem total
		No. 1	No. 2	No. 3	No. 4	No. 5	No. 6	
	German subsidiaries in Britain							
1	'Company FA'	*				*	*	3
2	'Company LB'	*		*				2
3	'Company LC'	*	*					2
4	'Company AE'			*			*	2
5	'Company AF'			p*				p1
6	'Company AG'		*					1
	British subsidiaries in Germany							
7	'Company IA'				*	*	*	3
8	'Company GC'	*					*	2
9	'Company MA'				*			1
10	'Company BD'				*			1
11	'Company BA'			p*				p1

Note: (* = problem, p* = potential problem)

have had. The feature was fashionable, and was demanded in the UK. You cannot sell against the grain.

The CE felt that people in Britain tend to insist on features of equipment which are broadly popular, but without questioning what actual benefits can be derived from them:

The German manufacturer aims to produce goods of exceptional performance, rather than copy the fashionable gimmicks of mass producers ... In some products nobody in the world has the same technology. It is German quality and engineering combined. But some of the technologies were not always user-friendly. The UK market did not get excited. The UK market is dominated by major chain stores. They have a name for destroying technology. They go for large volume, and the Japanese sell large volume for low margins. Now I choose my own product range, and my own exclusive retailers, and we are doing better.

But the regulatory nature of the structured German environment has its market drawbacks in relation to Britain. The CE said that if the parent company agreed to participate in mail order sales in the UK, it would increase its British market share considerably. But owing to the product guarantee laws in Germany which can not be satisfied through mail order in Britain, the German parent company refuses to enter this type of business in the UK.

Example 2: Consumer goods for personal consumption (problem refs 1, 3)
'Company LB' is a family-owned business in the specialised food industry in a situation of environmental indifference. The British MD of the UK subsidiary, who took over from his German predecessors, said:

> For the first five years the subsidiary was just an extension of the German company in the UK in terms of products, coverage of the trade, selling techniques and management style. In fact, the total activity amounted to 'sales' managed by the Germans, and was totally unsuccessful. Legally it was a company, but run as a sales office, because the German MD at the time did not know anything else. His previous position was that of a regional sales manager.

With the change of the MD from a German national to a British national experienced in the field and familiar with the UK market, the company's fate changed. The MD in collaboration with the German parent company developed products specifically designed to suit the British market. They adapted traditional British taste to the currently fashionable image of 'Continental' products. The CE felt that one of the reasons behind the German company's success was that its products represented the image of 'being Continental' more genuinely, than similar products of UK companies merely labelled as 'Continental'. Currently two out of the three Company best sellers in the UK market were products adapted for that market. The subsidiary is developing market volume through private labels, but is also establishing its own niche market through a British TV advertising campaign.

The problems of this company were overcome by the parent company giving sufficient autonomy to the subsidiary and showing flexibility in accommodating to different customer preferences in the UK market.

Example 3: Kitchen furniture (problem refs 1, 2)

The family-owned 'Company LC' makes kitchen furniture, and is thus in a situation of environmental indifference. The British CE of the subsidiary said that:

> ...only now do they [the parent company] start listening more to what we have to say. They have very strong people on the design side, but in marketing they are not as strong as we are. We could do with things that are more appropriate for the British market. Our second best seller does not sell in Germany, and the Germans want to take it out of the range. Every year we have to battle for it.

The main problem for this subsidiary is different customer preferences in the British market. The continued inflexibility of the parent company in acknowledging these differences makes the problem a persistent one.

Example 4: The automobile industry (problem refs 3, 6)

'Company AE' is a major German car manufacturer in harmony with its home environment. The British Marketing Director of its subsidiary in Britain said:

> In volume, the UK is the fourth biggest car market in Europe, which is unique to the extent it is a company car market [i.e. a different market infrastructure is used]. The Germans [the parent company] very strongly pressurise with regards to the [sales] targets. Although they recognise the problems, they believe that things will only go well if they exert excessive pressure. We tell them 'Please leave us to do the job and we will do it for you.' In comparison with the Continental market it is a more emotional market, and less technical and logical in purchase decisions. We [the British subsidiary] are doing better with the product in the UK than the parent does in its home market in Germany. We have complete autonomy in running our internal affairs, but there is a trend to Europeanization which does not work well in the UK. In terms of marketing they [the parent company] push towards the Pan-European style, but that is not effective. Ultimately the parent company compromised, and allowed the leading markets, such as the UK, to develop their own marketing/sales approach. The smaller countries then take over [the marketing approach] from the big ones, where there is a cultural relationship. For instance, our marketing is extended to New Zealand, the German one to Switzerland, French to Luxembourg, etc. Our success reflects our long-term marketing effort. The result is a much stronger image of the product here [in UK] than anywhere else in the World.

'Company AE' thus originally attempted to centralize its marketing internationally. Large German companies attracted to the idea of European market integration, typically attempt to achieve this through, as they fashionably call it, 'Pan-European marketing'. But in their understanding that usually amounts to German marketing throughout Europe. Such a market approach does not work in the UK and in other markets culturally unrelated to Germany. But when this parent company allowed diversification of marketing styles, the subsidiary succeeded in combining the benefits of the German product, renowned for its quality and reliability, with the benefits of its sophisticated marketing approach designed to appeal to the specific expectations of British customers. In this case the combination of German production and British marketing brought synergistic results in the UK and other markets culturally related to Britain.

Example 5: Light engineering (potential problem ref. 3)
'Company AF' is in a fast-moving engineering sector associated with the automobile industry in a harmonious situation in relation to the German environment. The British CE of the subsidiary paid a tribute to his German colleagues:

> It is good that they are very proud to supply their products. When something goes wrong, they can organise themselves over the weekend in order to put things right. They do care for quality... It was difficult to market German products after the War. But now they have a proud place in the market.

This acknowledgement came despite the fact that the subsidiary of 'Company AF' has one of the highest number of complaints in the sample about its relations with the parent company. Critical comments were raised by the subsidiary on issues which include: a 'technocratic and illogical' company structure, lack of autonomy for the subsidiary, and German 'obsession with detail'.

Commenting on marketing in Britain, the CE said:

> All the marketing stuff is produced in Germany. Ours is only a translation. We hope for media advertising, and therefore the German material may be inappropriate in the future.

This company's success in the market depends very strongly on technical specifications, reliability, and support services. Market presentation and price of product are likely to take a secondary place in purchase considerations of its corporate customers.

Example 6: Heavy engineering (problem ref. 2)

'Company AG', in heavy engineering, is in a situation of harmony with its home environment. In the UK it sells machinery for the food and other industries. The British CE of the subsidiary noted that the German managers in the parent company 'find it hard to adapt to the demands of the customer', are inflexible, and are viewed by the customers as 'arrogant'. But in relation to marketing the CE said:

> We do not do our own marketing material. It comes translated from Germany. We are very pleased with the literature they put out. It is excellent. Advertisements are pretty good, and well laid out.

British subsidiaries in Germany

Example 7: Machine tools (problem refs 4, 5, 6)

> 'Company IA' is in the British machine tools industry in a situation of dichotomy in its home environment which entails a 'handicap of the parent company' in the German market (cf. Chapter 3, p. 55) The German MD of the German subsidiary said:

> 'IA' was in Germany already 38 years ago. Their strength was in quick reactions to individual requirements. ...But now our flexibility is low, and we are in a big recession. We do not have money. We belong to a large concern that is profit oriented. ...We are unable to keep delivery dates, and we are losing customers. Today we send a fax [to the parent company] requesting an offer tomorrow, and you have to wait for two weeks. We do not develop new technologies. ... Others went with the future. ...The problem is, that when we started the 'Company IA' name was good, only later we have lost a good name, and you cannot change that now. ...With a German name it would be somewhat easier. (The solution which the subsidiary is attempting to implement is that of offering special custom-made supply and service deals in order to retain the remaining customers.)

This subsidiary has market related problems in Germany of a complex nature largely as a result of the position of its British parent. They show on three levels: mismatch in market approach, inadequate product development and specifications, and lack of efficiency in supply. The subsidiary is not in a position to compensate for the shortcomings of the parent.

Example 8: Automobile industry (problem refs 1, 6)
'Company GC' is a British car manufacturer in a situation of dichotomy
with its home environment. Its German subsidiary sells cars in Germany,
but its German competitors have the advantage of a situation of harmony
within their home environment. The British manager of the subsidiary
explained the market by saying:

> I think that in business life one has to spend some time in a certain
> position, before one understands things correctly. What buttons one
> has to push, and what reactions are to be expected. The first two years
> in Germany we did not take the correct courses of action. But now we
> have found the correct way, and we have started on the way to success.
> We have changed our marketing policies and our dealer policies. Our
> cars are a little more expensive, and we have now goals for specific
> product mixes. For instance, two or three years ago we were selling
> 'Car M' as a cheap car, below 10,000 DM. But later we started experi-
> menting with a wooden dashboard, wider tyres, and other minor
> details which distinguish our car from other makes. Naturally, the
> price has gone up as well. For instance now we are selling 'Car M'
> 60–65 per cent dearer. That means 75 per cent more money, and we
> doubled the turnover. That means more cars, and more contribution
> per car. We have added special interest to the model. It is almost a
> curiosity. An interesting car.

The market related problems of this subsidiary initially consisted of a
lack of understanding of the differences between the British and German
markets. This was shown in relation to the supplier infrastructure, and
through the underestimation of the differences in customer product preferences. The German car market is dominated by major German car
manufacturers who traditionally compete on the quality and reliability of
their products, with a lesser emphasis on price. It would have been more
difficult for the British subsidiary to compete with its British product
solely on quality. The development of a 'curiosity' product allowed the
company to establish itself in a specific niche in the market. As the
parent company was flexible enough to give sufficient autonomy to the
subsidiary to accommodate the market differences in Germany, the initial
problems of this subsidiary were overcome.

Example 9: Financial services (problem ref. 4)
'Company MA' is in a situation of environmental specificity, typical for
the financial services (Chapter 3, p. 60). The company appropriately
recognised the need to offer a different product portfolio in Germany and

the subsidiary was given a high degree of autonomy to develop its own portfolio. But there is a lack of effective communication, and managers in the parent company are not fully aware of the differences.

The British CE of the subsidiary explained that some managers in the parent company are ignorant of the subsidiary's product portfolio and assume it to be the same as their own. They have therefore made referrals of customers who are seeking services which the German subsidiary does not offer.

This problem is a manifestation in relation to market issues of the lack of efficiency in parent company–subsidiary communication.

Example 10: Consumer electronics (problem ref. 4)
The consumer electronics 'Company BD' is in a situation of environmental harmony in Britain. The managing director of the subsidiary in Germany said that initially, the subsidiary sold from stock in Britain, but experienced a problem of delays in the supply of goods to Germany. In order to alleviate the problem, the subsidiary started buying products from the parent company in order to be able to deliver from stock in Germany. Following this change the performance of the company in the German market is described as very successful.

Example 11: Consumer electronics (potential problem ref. 3)
'Company BA', in consumer electronics, is in a situation of harmony with its home environment in Britain (Chapter 3, p. 42). It sells identical products in the German and UK markets. But whilst the same product sells in the UK with the image of being 'cheap', in Germany it sells with the image of 'quality and value for money', but does not claim to be 'cheap'. For this reason the German subsidiary cannot use translations of the firm's British marketing literature. It produces its own films, brochures, and even photographs of the products in order to communicate the different image.

The MD of the subsidiary said that whilst 'Company BA' has the reputation in Germany of offering quality products which represent value for money, it has 'an absolute Woolworth image' in the UK. The interviewee explained that using the image of quality and service 'as a hotline to low prices' is not acceptable in the German market.

This example indicates clear market differences between UK and Germany. First, the overall level of product development and quality in this industry is higher in the UK compared to Germany, since a cheap UK product passes as a quality product in Germany. Second, buying patterns are different. Although German consumers' needs may well be satisfied with a 'cheap' product, they still insist on buying a quality product, regardless of price. The British parent company respects these market differences which do not represent a managerial problem. The collaboration between the British parent company and the German subsidiary was described as an exceptionally successful one.

5 Qualifications and Skills of British and German Management: The Views of the Managers

'The point is in the purpose of education. Here [in Britain] it seems to be a value in itself. In Germany it is to become good businessmen tradesmen, etc. Training and education should be one thing, as it is in Germany, and not separated as it is here.' — British manager in a subsidiary in Britain in engineering

'With education lasting this long, to 27, 28, and around 30 with PhDs, a young person gets used to receiving information only. By the time they get the opportunity to generate or create information, they no longer have the courage, and may not even know how to do it.' — German manager in a subsidiary in Britain in finance commenting on the German system of higher education

The educational system is a central institution in every developed society. It is an important cultural element which both reflects and perpetuates values. The quality of education also has an impact on labour performance, which is a readily observed factor of industrial performance. Attempts to explain the differences in the economic performance of Britain and Germany in recent decades have focussed on education, in particular in relation to vocational qualifications (see, for instance, Lawrence, 1980; Prais, 1981; Lane, 1989; Randlesome *et al.* 1993). Often these educational comparisons are made only in relation to formally defined structures since the relevant information is in most cases available in written form. Aspects such as educational curricula, hierarchies of examinations, and options in routes to gaining qualifications, are considered as contributing strongly to better German economic performance.

Far fewer authors have undertaken a comprehensive analysis of the values which underpin the two systems, since this requires a wider cultural understanding of both countries (see Lane, 1994). But conclusions drawn in regard to the economic impact of education without a proper

consideration of the broader cultural environment are likely to be mis-
leading. The relationship between education and economic performance
must be viewed systemically. An educational system cannot be regarded
as an independent factor which can be transplanted from one environment to another with the same effects. Rather each element of culture
must be seen in context, since the impact it has will be crucially affected
by the whole societal system of which it is a part.

AN ENVIRONMENTAL FRAMEWORK FOR EDUCATIONAL
COMPARISONS

In Chapter 3, four dimensions were suggested to characterize environmental differences. These were stability, speed of response, industrial
infrastructure, and broader cultural environment. The British and German
environmental characteristics along these dimensions were labelled as
'liberal' and 'structured' respectively. These same dimensions are now
used in Table 5.1 to present a framework for understanding the educational differences between Britain and Germany, and to structure the previous literature on German and British educational comparisons (Lane,
1992, 1994; Lawrence, 1980; Randlesome *et al.*, 1993)

Table 5.1 suggests the impact of each dimension on the factors which
shape education in the British and the German environment. Each of
these is now discussed in turn.

Differences in *stability* show in attitudes to company training. This
entails investment in people which requires a longer term view in relation to financial returns. Therefore, in Britain the tendency to shorter
term management based on more immediate financial returns, means that
training is of lower priority in the company. Lane (1994) believes that
employers in Britain are inclined '…towards skill poaching rather than
towards sustained training effort'. By contrast in Germany, where there is
a tendency to longer-term management, company training is likely to be
given higher priority (e.g. Randlesome *et al.*, 1993). In addition, the
closer link between qualifications and existing employment opportunities in Germany leads to a greater continuity of employment (Lane, 1992,
Stewart *et al.*, 1994). The situation is reversed in Britain, where official
qualifications are no guarantee for career success. Progress is more likely
through change of employer, rather than continuity of employment.

The *industrial infrastructure* plays an important part in shaping the
system of education. Lower corporate taxation in Britain, allowing
greater distribution of profit in dividends, encourages the lower priority
given to training noted above. In Germany, higher corporate taxation

Table 5.1 *Contrasting UK and German environmental characteristics in relation to education*

UK	Germany
Liberal	*Structured*

1. Stability

Low	*High*
Training of lower priority	Training of higher priority
Career progress more likely through change of employer resulting in 'skills poaching'	Continuity of employment resulting in investment in people

2. Industrial infrastructure

Less well-defined, largely optional	*Well-defined, largely normative*
Management education detached from technical training	Management education incorporated in technical training
Technical research of lower status and less industry-linked	Technical research of high status and industry-linked

3. Speed of managerial response

High	*Low*
Management education emphasises strategy	Management education emphasises operations

4. Broader cultural environment

Less predictable and volatile	*More predictable and organized*
Free enterprise (low cohesion of different educational institutions with overlaps)	Social market economy (high cohesion of educational institutions with co-ordinated responsibiliy)
Education is independent from industry (entailing high status differential in relation to educational institutions)	Education is vocational in overall character (entailing low status differential in relation to educational institutions)
Decline of traditional apprenticeships	Emphasis on vocational qualifications
Lower proportion of graduates (achievement important for professional status)	Higher proportion of graduates (formal qualifications important for professional status)

combines with lower distribution of profits to encourage a higher amount of investment in training.

The greater concern with profit and marketing in Britain has resulted in *management education* becoming largely independent from the management of production. In Germany, by contrast, management education has remained production linked. Furthermore, the fact that British trade associations and Chambers of Commerce are voluntary, and have a low status and low involvement, precludes them from playing the active and important part in vocational and management training that their equivalents in Germany do (Bennett *et al.*, 1993).

The lower *status of technical research* in Britain, compared with scientific research in non-manufacturing areas, means that less money is spent on it and fewer results can be obtained and put into practice. In Germany, the status of industry is higher and so is that of industry-linked technical research. More takes place and a higher proportion of its results get put into practice, faster (Lawrence, 1980; Lane, 1989).

The differences in facilitated *speed of managerial response* in Britain and Germany are reflected in the nature of the business education being offered for would-be managers. In Britain it focuses on profit, the key nature of the marketing function and the necessity for a strategic approach. In Germany, efficient operations through planning and appropriate procedures are emphasised.

The *broader cultural environment* accommodates and influences the previous three dimensions, and has a decisive influence on the entire system of education. The principle of *free enterprise* in Britain applies to a considerable degree in education. Industrial organizations in Britain have a limited degree of contact with education. Lane (1989) describes the resulting British system of vocational education as: 'It is felt that there exists a confusing variety of training and validating bodies, that there is a wasteful overlap between them and insufficient continuity between different levels' (p. 63), and Lane (1994) concludes: 'Organizational division and weaknesses of capital, as well as ideological predispositions, have thus militated against the development of self-administration on the German model.'

Industrial self-regulation in Germany enables a closer dialogue between education, industry, and any other relevant regulatory bodies (e.g. Chambers of Commerce) to take place. In the more structured German environment, all these institutions co-ordinate their demand and output, and so work towards ensuring an optimal fit of education to the demands of industry. The main characteristics of the resulting vocational educational system in Germany were described by Lane (1989) as: 'Vocational education has been shaped in a corporatist manner, with the state and the two sides of industry cooperating. The strong guiding role of the state has meant that vocational education is conducted in a highly standardized and formalized manner throughout the country' (p. 63).

In the more liberal British environment, *education is independent from industry*. Educational institutions are likely to follow the market principle of supply and demand in relation to the courses and subjects which they offer. Accordingly, the choice of a course of study is more likely to be guided by more general influences such as tradition, fashion trends, social status of the subject, in addition to a rational assessment of options in education against options in employment. In Germany, the demand for education is monitored and co-ordinated with existing opportunities more closely (including apprenticeships, both industrial and commercial, conducted at companies with attendance at a technical college; the distinctive presence of technical school at middle level; specialized technical universities, and so on). 'The German graduate has much less freedom of choice than his British opposite number; the German to a much greater extent chose his career when he decided what to study. ... everyone knows "the way it is" and this reflects in low enrolments (proportionally) in subjects with limited occupational outlets...' (brackets as in original, Lawrence, 1980, p. 63).

The *decline of traditional apprenticeships* in Britain compared to Germany, which has taken place in the recent decades, was documented by Prais (1981). Based on the OPCS figures for Britain, general Household Surveys (1974–8), unpublished tabulations, and for Germany on *Microzensus* (1978), unpublished tabulations, Prais has shown that at the intermediate level, that is, non-graduate qualifications including apprenticeships, in Britain the proportion of labour with this level of qualifications was only about a half of that in Germany. In manufacturing, in Britain 28.7 per cent of the labour force attained this level of education compared to 60.8 per cent in Germany, and in non-manufacturing the figure was 30.7 per cent in Britain, compared to 59.4 per cent in Germany (p. 48, Table 1).

Although it is generally believed that the qualifications gap between Britain and Germany is considerable, particularly in engineering and at the graduate level (see Lawrence, 1980), Prais (1981) found that the percentages of *graduates* in the existing labour force compared by industrial group were similar in Britain and Germany. For instance, in 1978 there were 3.3 per cent of persons with stated university level education employed in manufacturing in Britain compared with 3.5 per cent in Germany (note that the British sample included members of many professional institutions who may not have been required to attend full-time university education). Even in relation to engineering, the difference was not great: 3.8 per cent in Britain compared to 4.4 per cent in Germany.

This finding goes against the generally accepted views, but two questions may be raised: First, to what degree did the subjects of the qualifications gained correspond to those ideally required by employing industrial groups in Britain and in Germany? Did an equal proportion of those graduates in, say, the chemical industry have a degree in chemistry in Britain as they had in Germany, or did perhaps a larger proportion of the British graduates in the chemical industry have a degree other than one specific to their job, such as in history or geography? In a situation where the demand for education and job opportunities are to a considerable degree left to follow the market principle of supply and demand, as in the liberal British environment, a lower proportion of appropriate qualifications is to be expected. And second, what was the calibre of applicants for the subjects associated with traditional manufacture in Britain compared to Germany? In Britain, unlike Germany, manufacturing related subjects, being of lower status, are likely to attract a lower calibre of talent and abilities than those of the socially higher status disciplines.

In summary, it would appear that the German environment facilitates considerably better conditions for the development of good vocational training compared to Britain. But an important question for further research is whether this superiority applies to all areas of industry. It may be that a more contingent approach to the differences in education between liberal and structured environments is required. This would involve examining different industrial sectors to see whether greater reliability or greater flexibility would be required for success in them. The present study explores the views of managers on these differences.

THE PRESENT STUDY

In relation to education, the standard opening question asked in the present study was whether the interviewee saw a difference in the education of British and German managers (Question 19). In most interviews conducted by the British team the topic developed into a conversation in which answers were followed up by the interviewer with more detailed questions as appropriate. In total, 266 mentions of education related issues were made by the 99 interviewees who participated in the study. The majority of the mentions were collected by the British team (250 mentions), against only 16 mentions collected by the German team. This disproportion indicates a difference in the focus of the interviewing conducted by the two research teams.

With regard to the nationality of the respondent, the interest in educational differences appears to be reasonably balanced. The 46 managers of British nationality volunteered 155 mentions, while the 48 German managers volunteered 110. One mention was made by one of the five other nationals.

QUALIFICATIONS OF MANAGERS

The frequency of mentions of education in relation to cross-cultural staff management issues highlights the importance of managerial qualifications in Anglo–German business collaboration. Although as part of the interview managers had the opportunity to raise any issues of interest, no one raised, for instance, personnel selection procedures, or personnel assessment as an important issue in relation to staff performance. The standard part of the interview contained questions on whether the subsidiary (or parent company) has a defined career structure, and an appraisal system. Typically, these questions produced only short answers consisting either of 'yes', 'no', or 'we are developing it'. No one extended these topics into a discussion. But, in many cases, as soon as educational differences were mentioned, an interested reaction from the manager followed, and a discussion on the topic of qualifications ensued.

Table 5.2 shows the frequency of the mentions of qualifications by the managers. They are listed under 'strengths' and 'weaknesses' in relation to the British and German systems of education. The table demonstrates that the managers subscribe to the view that there is an overall greater appropriateness of German qualifications for existing staff requirements. The total of British strengths is only 33 mentions against 98 mentions of weaknesses. But the total of German strengths is 104 mentions against only 31 mentions of weaknesses.

Thus, in general, the opinions shown in Table 5.2 support most of the well-rehearsed findings in the literature. It is felt that German staff are considerably better technically qualified than their British counterparts. There is a higher number of managers with degrees and further degrees in Germany compared to the UK. The emphasis in these higher degrees is on technical specialisms and management functions associated predominantly with economic and legal qualifications. The main overall strength of German vocational training is in its system of apprenticeships, which encompasses a comprehensive range of training and skills. It supplies adequate middle-level qualifications to most industrial and administrative sectors. The match of qualifications with existing

Table 5.2   *Frequency of mentions of issues relating to strengths and weaknesses of education in Britain and Germany according to company*

No. of mentions of qualifications and skills made by managers in:	Subsidiaries		Parent companies		Total
	British in Germany	German in Britain	UK	German	
In relation to German education					
Strengths					
Apprenticeships of advantage	1	9	0	0	10
Middle business qualifications adequate	2	9	1	0	12
Good practical experience	0	16	1	0	17
Good planning skills	3	8	1	1	13
General level of qualifications high	2	19	2	1	24
Management training good	0	3	0	0	3
Adequate technical qualifications	2	18	4	1	25
Total strengths	10	82	9	3	104
Weaknesses					
Education lasting too long	2	7	1	0	10
Over qualifications for functions	3	1	1	0	5
Lack of practical experience	2	2	2	0	6
Inadequate technical qualifications	0	0	1	0	1
Management training less good	0	3	0	0	3
Lack of computer understanding	1	5	0	0	6
Total weaknesses	8	18	5	0	31
Total in relation to German education	18	100	14	3	135
In relation to British education					
Strengths					
General level of qualifications good	4	2	3	1	10
Good computer understanding	0	5	0	0	5
Adequate technical qualifications	2	4	1	1	8
Management training good	2	1	1	0	4
Good practical experience	2	2	2	0	6
Total strengths	10	14	7	2	33
Weaknesses					
Apprenticeships missing	2	11	0	0	13

Table 5.2   *Continued*

No. of mentions of qualifications and skills made by managers in:	Subsidiaries		Parent companies		Total
	British in Germany	German in Britain	UK	German	
In relation to British education (weaknesses cont.)					
Middle business qualifications missing	5	5	2	0	12
Lack of practical experience	0	12	1	0	13
Inadequate technical qualifications	1	11	3	0	15
Poor planning skills	2	3	0	1	6
General level of qualifications low	4	15	2	0	21
Mismatch of higher qualifications	1	2	1	0	4
Management training too general	1	3	0	0	4
Company education programmes due to subsidiary staff incompetence	n/a	10	n/a	0	10
Total weaknesses	16	72	9	1	98
Total in relation to British education	26	86	16	3	131
Total of all mentions	44	186	30	6	266

employment opportunities facilitates a higher overall operational efficiency in the German enterprise.

The managers feel that the lack of traditional apprenticeships in UK presents a problem of shortage of qualified staff, in particular in the industrial sector. As a result, middle-level qualifications are inadequately represented, and some are missing altogether. For example, there is an absence of middle-level business administration qualifications within the British vocational education system. While the level of higher education is good, it would be desirable to improve the match between education and the employment requirements of industry.

But if we consider the range of categories, the table also shows that the overall potential based on the strengths and weaknesses of both educational systems is regarded as much more balanced than is generally supposed. Five categories of British strengths were mentioned against 9 British weaknesses, and 7 categories of German strengths were mentioned against 6 German weaknesses. British strengths included reference to the level of general qualifications and of a high level of computer understanding, together with good practical experience and management training. German weaknesses included education being overlong with consequent lack of practical experience, and overqualification for functions.

Seven managers with first hand experience of both countries (3 British and 4 German) felt that the overall strengths and weaknesses of the educational systems were equally balanced. A typical comment is that of a German Chief Executive in an engineering subsidiary in Britain, who compared the education of the managers in the subsidiary to the managers in the German parent company by saying:

> German education is very good. But being a student for so long [in Germany] does not give you much for your self-confidence. Brits are more go-getters. There are some strong people in Britain who have more drive.

Table 5.3 shows the same data analysed by the nationality of the respondent, rather than by the country in which the company is located. It is significant that the perceptions of both nationalities about the two systems of education and their effects are similar. For instance, not only Germans tended to view the British level of technical qualifications as inadequate (4 mentions) but even more British nationals took the same view (11 mentions). Similarly, not only British managers believed that German education lasts too long (6 mentions), but some German managers thought so too (4 mentions).

GERMAN STRENGTHS AND BRITISH WEAKNESSES

The views of managers on the different strengths and weaknesses of the British and German systems of education in their environments are analysed in Table 5.2. To a considerable degree, the 104 German strengths and the 98 British weaknesses are opposites, emphasising the contrasts between the two countries. They relate primarily to aspects of vocational training and technical qualifications, and are illustrated below by quotations from the interviews.

VOCATIONAL TRAINING AND TECHNICAL QUALIFICATIONS

The bond between industry and education in Germany, as discussed above, has meant that a strong system of vocational training has become the societal backbone of the entire educational system (German strengths, item 1: 10 mentions of apprenticeships being of advantage).

Table 5.3 *Frequency of mentions of issues relating to strengths and weaknesses of education in Britain and Germany according to the nationality of the respondent*

No. of mentions of qualifications and skills made by managers of:

	British nationality	German nationality	Other nationality	Total
In relation to German education				
Strengths				
Apprenticeships of advantage	6	4	0	10
Middle business qualifications adequate	4	8	0	12
Good practical experience	12	5	0	17
Good planning skills	8	5	0	13
General level of qualifications high	15	9	0	24
Management training good	1	2	0	3
Adequate technical qualifications	21	4	0	25
Total strengths	67	37	0	104
Weaknesses				
Education lasting too long	6	4	0	10
Over qualifications for functions	3	2	0	5
Lack of practical experience	5	1	0	6
Inadequate technical qualifications	1	0	0	1
Management training less good	3	0	0	3
Lack of computer understanding	4	2	0	6
Total weaknesses	22	9	0	31
Total in relation to German education	89	46	0	135
In relation to British education				
Strengths				
General level of qualifications good	3	7	0	10
Good computer understanding	3	2	0	5
Good degree level technical qualifications	5	3	0	8
Management training good	2	2	0	4
Good practical experience	5	1	0	6
Total strengths	18	15	0	33
Weaknesses				
Apprenticeships missing	6	7	0	13

Table 5.3 *Continued*

No. of mentions of qualifications and skills made by managers of:

	British nationality	German nationality	Other nationality	Total
In relation to British education (weaknesses cont.)				
Middle business qualifications missing	3	9	0	12
Lack of practical experience	8	5	0	13
Inadequate technical qualifications	11	4	0	15
Poor planning skills	2	4	0	6
General level of qualifications low	12	8	1	21
Mismatch of higher qualifications	0	4	0	4
Management training too general	1	3	0	4
Company education programmes due to subsidiary staff incompetence	5	5	0	10
Total weaknesses	48	49	1	98
Total in relation to British education	66	64	1	131
Total of all mentions	155	110	1	266

This is particularly felt in the German subsidiaries in Britain (9 cases) when compared to the lack of British apprenticeships. In addition, 12 mentions of middle level business qualifications in Germany being adequate are mentioned (German strengths: item 2). By contrast, in British conditions education is considered to be largely independent of industry. As a result, general education has developed but vocational education has remained underdeveloped (British weaknesses, item 1: 13 mentions of apprenticeships missing, of which 11 were made in German subsidiaries in Britain).

The British Chief Executive of a division of a large German industrial conglomerate with divisional headquarters in Britain, felt:

Germany is 20 years ahead of Britain. Training is excellent, and I tried to bring it into the UK. In the UK there is no common training system. Here if we have a recession, the first thing we cut is training. But sometimes we come across people who are overtrained and are not getting satisfaction out of their job. The German dual system [i.e. learning and working at the same time] is brilliant. That apprenticeship system is preparing for life.

The British Marketing Director in a subsidiary in Britain in engineering stated:

> The point is in the purpose of education. Here [in Britain] it seems to be a value in itself. In Germany it is to become good businessmen tradesmen, etc. Training and education should be one thing, as it is in Germany, and not separated as it is here.

The British Chief Executive of a German subsidiary in Britain in pharmaceuticals, discussing the importance of appropriate qualifications for economic performance, expressed his belief that it is the confrontational nature of British politics which precludes longer term rational measures being taken about education, and confines a government to taking only popular measures in these areas:

> British politicians have the choice of losing votes, or the Economy, and they choose the votes.

And the British Managing Director in a German engineering subsidiary in UK made this typical comment:

> The old education system here was better. We had apprenticeships. Unified education meant levelling down. "Give everybody a chance" is a nice idea, but it lowered the standards.

The 12 mentions of middle level business qualifications being missing in Britain (British weaknesses, item 2) come equally from 5 German subsidiaries in Britain, as well as 5 British subsidiaries in Germany and 2 British parent companies. The most comprehensive assessment of this weakness was given by a German Chief Executive in a German engineering subsidiary in Britain who commented:

> The main difference [in qualifications between Britain and Germany] is in clerical staff. Businessmen in Germany are trained in a more broad fashion. Broad aspects of business life, accountancy, trade law. They know the product, organizational aspects, commercial arithmetic. They are able to work out percentages, interest rates, etc. very fast and accurately. The British managers would use a computer to work out percentages. If I was to employ someone in Germany I would know that he had an all-round understanding of an organization. In Britain people have a first-class understanding of business if they studied economics, but those more clerical have not. Here [in Britain] the person

is doing things without understanding and making decisions although they know very little – or less than they would be expected to know in Germany.

The 17 mentions of the Germans having good practical experience normally means that German trainees are seen as better 'organizational all rounders' (German strengths: item 3). This was said to apply both in areas of technical apprentices having an understanding of the business, and business apprentices having an understanding of production. Both are believed to have a sound understanding of the basic principles behind the functioning of an organization, which gives them the benefit of seeing their own place as part of one of the functional units within the whole organization. The role of *Meister*, the equivalent of a British senior supervisor but much more highly technically qualified, is a classic example of such a combined technical, production, business, pedagogic and all-round function.

The clear division in Britain between education and work is regarded as the main cause of the British shortcoming in vocational training, seen by a lack of practical experience through apprenticeships (British weaknesses, item 3: 13 mentions). As a consequence of this division, a lack of attention is given to 'less fashionable' technical subjects in Britain. 15 managers felt that there are inadequate technical qualifications (British weaknesses, item 4) and certain traditional manufacturing areas simply fall out of the British system of higher education. A clear example of this was given in a foundry where the British manager, commenting on the differences in the qualifications between the British and German managers in the company, said:

They [Germans] go through a University level education within foundry technology. They are much better qualified. We do not have a UK equivalent, which is wrong. We do not get equal quality on the shop floor.

The frequent mentions of adequate technical qualifications in Germany are linked to engineering subjects in particular (German strengths, item 7: 25 mentions). For example, the German Chief Executive of a large German engineering and electrical company said:

The German engineer is better educated. The German school system is target oriented. The British 'equality' in education has brought the standards down.

Similarly, the British Managing Director of a car accessories manufacturing subsidiary in Britain said:

> Germans tend to be better qualified right across the board. It is the attitude more than training. They are committed.

Education in Germany is associated with an accent on planning. Thirteen mentions (German strengths, item 4) of the Germans having good planning skills were made. The value of 'uncertainty avoidance', which Hofstede (1980) has suggested is strong in the German culture, is likely to more easily allow the development of a planning approach to future activities compared with the British culture which is characterised by attitudes of greater tolerance of uncertainty. The application of planning is of greatest benefit in technical subjects and areas of work involving predictable and quantifiable outcomes, e.g. traditional manufacturing, stock control, distribution. These areas are well developed in Germany, and familiarization with a planned approach to work is made an integral part of the German vocational training. A British manager in an engineering subsidiary in Britain acknowledged that:

> Having learned to plan from the Germans was of a substantial benefit to us [the subsidiary].

The greater tolerance of uncertainty in the British culture does not require a similar emphasis on planning, but it facilitates a better exploitation of new opportunities. The balance of the strengths and weaknesses of both approaches was commented on by a British Chief Executive of a large German chemical subsidiary in Britain, who said:

> I reckon that the Germans plan so carefully that they find it difficult to adapt to circumstances, whilst the British are so sure that they are flexible that they forget to plan.

The strength of the German vocational training is also reflected in the relatively high expectations of Germans in relation to their subsidiaries. 21 interviewees (British weaknesses, item 6) named the generally low level of qualifications in the UK as a managerial problem. Of these managers, 12 were British, 8 German, and 1 other national. 24 managers indicated a superiority of the German system (German strengths, item 4). Of these managers, 15 were British and 9 German nationals. The highest level of appreciation of German education is in the German subsidiaries in UK with 19 mentions of superiority of the German system (German strengths, item 5) coupled with 15 mentions of the inadequacy of the British system (British weaknesses, item 6).

As the result of discrepancies between required and available standards of qualifications 10 German subsidiaries in Britain (British weaknesses, item 9) indicated that they need to run company education programmes to improve the degree of technical competence of their UK employees. Of these 10 companies, 7 were in the engineering industry, 2 in the chemical industry and one in building materials. This suggests that the German subsidiaries which need to run education courses to improve the technical competence of their British staff are those industries which are successful and well developed in the German environment, but are less successful in the UK environment. No companies felt that the skill available in Britain in industries to which the British environment is favourable (such as consumer electronics) may not be adequate.

A mismatch of education with actual employment is more frequent in Britain than in Germany. Four managers (British weaknesses, item 7) indicated a mismatch in qualifications of professionals compared with the requirements of their currently-held positions in their company in the UK. Among the examples given were a former geography teacher and an English literature graduate employed as merchant bankers. Whilst this is likely to entail an initial lack of particular specialisms, the problem was not seen as a fundamental weakness in relation to overall competence amongst British professionals.

In summary, the current data thus confirm the general perception of the superiority of German vocational training to that in Britain. But this perception does not apply to all types of skills. It applies primarily to practical skills, and middle-level qualifications associated with traditional manufacture. Indeed, good vocational training is felt to be Germany's major contribution to a combined Anglo–German potential. It compensates for the British weakness in the same field. These views exemplify the influence of the environment on the nature of training and education. The structured German environment with its concomitant structured system of education prepares well for work in areas which require 'structured knowledge' – that is knowledge, qualifications and skills which tend to concentrate on the acquisition of information that is predictable, is likely to be quantifiable, and can be tested in practice. Such knowledge is especially appropriate in the more traditional areas of work, and in technical areas, in particular. Industries covering these areas, it has been suggested in Chapter 3, are harmonious with the German environment.

BRITISH STRENGTHS AND GERMAN WEAKNESSES

The 33 mentions of British strengths and the 31 mentions of German weaknesses in Table 5.2 mainly stress opposite characteristics. They relate primarily to three areas: (i) qualifications in specialized and fast-developing areas, (ii) length of time spent in graduate education; (iii) management education and training.

QUALIFICATIONS IN SPECIALIZED AND FAST-DEVELOPING AREAS

In relation to skills associated with some of the faster developing industries, the dissatisfaction with British education diminishes. As discussed in Chapter 3, consumer electronics can be considered to be comparably as strong in Britain as traditional engineering is in Germany. It is not surprising then, that five managers (British strengths, item 2) in German subsidiaries in Britain stated that the British have good computer understanding. One German Chief Executive felt that:

> The British take to computers like duck to water,

while six managers indicated that the Germans tend to have less well developed computer skills (German weaknesses, item 6).

The British Chief Executive of a German subsidiary of a publishing company commented:

> They [specialists in the German parent company] have the formal education but not quite the flair. We have developed a computer system relating to our customer base which would be flexible. It may be monthly, weekly, or daily, and we divided it into 5 'quarters'. All of our competitors operate on a four-quarter basis. 5 'quarters' have been shown to be an advantage. But their [the parent company's] computer systems were so rigid that it took them £2 million and two years in time to get four or six 'quarters', but still not five! And they are still working on it. If you build a flexible system, then changing is easy. But the Germans never thought of flexibility.

Similarly, a British manager in a specialised engineering company managed as an Anglo–German joint venture commented:

We [the British partner] have a totally integrated manufacturing system computerwise. It is probably the most advanced system in the country. We have done a lot of work with the DTI. Our German company is not so advanced in its computer systems. For instance, we can get an order through our system so that components are moved out of the shop in less than 24 hours. In Germany it can take up to two weeks for the paperwork to move through the system. Now we are actually educating them on the techniques, the computer systems that are available, the internal communications. One always has this impression that German companies are very advanced in terms of their systems. But our experience is that they are not so.

A British manager in a German subsidiary commented:

Our German colleagues like computers, have many of them, and they are of the latest design. But the programmes they use are old fashioned and cumbersome. They [German managers] insist on the latest technology in computing but do not have the skills to benefit from it.

As the examples illustrate, the lack of computer understanding and skills tends to be associated with a lack of flexibility and 'creativity' at work amongst the German managers, as discussed in Chapter 6. Another skill which is commonly believed to be superior in the UK compared to Germany is that of marketing, as discussed in Chapter 4.

In university education, British standards, even in technical fields, were seen as very good (British strengths, item 3). One British CE in a German engineering subsidiary maintained, in relation to technical qualifications, that:

German advanced education is not as good as the British best.

In two specific cases it was felt that it is the poor availability of highly qualified people in Britain that is a problem, but not their quality. For example, in one major engineering subsidiary, the German CE felt that, out of five board members who are German expatriates, only two would ideally be required to be of German nationality. The remaining three were there as necessary German substitutes for staff that were hard to recruit in the UK.

Even the tendency to separate education from employment, resulting in a greater degree of mismatch between qualifications with currently held jobs, was not seen overall as an negative feature by the managers. None of the four managers who mentioned the issue believed that it results in actual longer-term professional inadequacy amongst the British managers. Indeed, the respondents believed that changing fields broadens and improves people's horizons and their professional competence.

The fairly strict matching of education with future professional life in Germany was believed to be the reason behind the 'tunnel vision' and excessive risk avoidance of German managers as discussed in Chapter 6. This tends to be exacerbated through the fact that, compared to the British, the German graduates acquire managerial experience later in their life.

Thus the German lack of experience (German weaknesses, item 3) tends to be associated with senior management and marketing skills, rather than technical expertise, and two major aspects of German education are highlighted as contributing factors: (i) the general trend in German education to produce technical specialists rather than people with broader managerial expertise and experience; and (ii) the fact that the education of German graduate managers lasts too long (German weaknesses, item 1).

For example, a British manager in a German engineering subsidiary in Britain commented:

> The administrative managers in our [parent] company have a more extensive training in financial management than in the UK and concentrate on it. They are highly trained in the engineering field. But they have less practical experience across the board.

LENGTH OF TIME SPENT IN GRADUATE EDUCATION

While not a single manager mentioned examples of mismatching qualifications in Germany, the shorter time necessary to obtain professional qualifications was seen as a British strength when compared to Germany. It allows for the acquisition of earlier and more comprehensive managerial experience. Ten managers (German weaknesses, item 1) felt that German education lasts too long. The German Chief executive of a German subsidiary in mineral extraction in Britain said:

> When you get a graduate geologist in Germany he will be 25–27 years old. He would have studied for 5 years, and after that he is expected to do military service. Here somebody is lucky to have 4 years of studies in geology, be finished at 22, and have 5 years experience by the time he is 27.

Asked whether he felt that as a consequence of the longer preparation the German specialist may be, perhaps less experienced, but on the whole better qualified than his British counterpart, the manager replied:

> I do not see a big difference in qualifications or performance between British and German managers.

And the German Chief Executive in a German subsidiary in Britain in finance commented:

> With education lasting this long, to 27, 28, and around 30 with PhDs, a young person gets used to receiving information only. By the time they get the opportunity to generate or create information, they no longer have the courage, and may not even know how to do it. By the time you are 30, it is time to think of a pension plan, not to start professional life.

As the result of the greater societal emphasis on acquiring specialist degrees in Germany, formal qualifications are important for professional status. One British CE in a German electrotechnical subsidiary said:

> The Germans [in the parent company] are much more concerned with academic qualifications. Just as long as someone has so many letters to his name, they are not concerned with experience. We [in the British subsidiary] find the development of skills which may not be based on academic qualifications, important. But in our parent company academic qualifications are a better means to a career than what you really can do. The German nation is obsessed with good academic qualifications.

And the German Managing Director of a British financial subsidiary in Germany felt:

> Here [in Germany] there is a higher proportion of people with university education. We are more theoretical. We see all the 'dangers'. But to what benefit? The British are more pragmatic.

Indeed, the supply of well-qualified job seekers in Germany appears to be outgrowing the availability of matching employment opportunities. Five managers (German weaknesses, item 2) indicated that they have German staff in their company who are overqualified for the functions they perform. Of these five managers, 3 were British and 2 German nationals.

MANAGEMENT EDUCATION AND TRAINING

After qualifications in specialised and fast-developing areas, management education and training were seen as the main areas of British strength.

The difference in the perceptions of what 'management' should be about has historical roots. Early industrial managers in both countries were equally involved in the production and sale of goods. But later, business development in Britain and Germany took different routes. Britain managed her empire not just in terms of administration, but also as a worldwide business venture. London was the first capital of world finance and the British entrepreneur was much more inclined to see an industrial venture as a means to an end (Lane, 1992). In the liberal British environment, business education gained independence from the management of production, and became relatively well developed.

By contrast, Germany's foreign market activities concentrated on the export of manufactured goods, and Germany became the world's largest exporter. The attention of the German business managers, often owner-managers, was therefore focused on quality and performance of the product, and production. The additional skills required in Germany concerned: (i) the promotion of technical goods by demonstrating their quality and performance, and (ii) the establishment of reliable distribution and maintenance support systems. Such sales activities remained closely linked to technical specialisms. Business education therefore remained production based with a second focus on purchasing, sales and distribution, rather than business and marketing (cf. Chapter 4 for differences in the German and British approaches to marketing).

British managers, as Lawrence (1980) has pointed out, are much more likely to see themselves as generalists rather than technical specialists. The four mentions of management training in Britain as being good, primarily related to general management skills (British strengths, item 4). On the other hand, the three mentions of management training in Germany as being good emphasised the worth of specialist knowledge in management (German strengths, item 5).

The business values of the past continue to be culturally perpetuated in both countries as statements made by German and British managers illustrate. One respondent (German, early post-war generation, engineering company) said:

> The term 'Management' should be eradicated. What is a manager? Someone who sits, and pulls a few strings. People should be doing something.

A British corporate director in a German chemical subsidiary in UK with many years of experience in Germany gave his view that:

> In Britain the book-keepers are running the show. This goes back to the Empire; there was no competition. In Germany, the wealth creators are the most rewarded – the scientists, technicians and engineers. Second are the distributors of wealth. Administration are only third. In England it is exactly the reverse. Historically the top three were: the administrator of the Commonwealth, the officer in the army and the minister. The place of the army officer was taken by the financial people in the City.

And the British Chief Executive in a German heavy engineering subsidiary in UK said:

> The administrative managers in our company [the parent company in Germany] have a more extensive training in financial management than in the UK, and they concentrate on it. General managers tend to be highly trained in the engineering field with less practical experience across the board.

The German Managing Director in a German heavy engineering subsidiary in UK commented:

> We [Germans] have well developed costing systems. It is something very product oriented. English have not got a clue about costing. They make a decision by just looking at a cylinder. Here [in Britain] people make a quick decision that suits them, regardless of other departments.

The comments refer to the fact that most Germans employed in engineering are likely to have appropriate engineering qualifications in addition to business qualifications. In Britain, even in engineering, business managers are primarily expected to have business experience, rather than engineering qualifications.

Thus four opinions were given that management training in Britain is too general (British weaknesses, item 8). Three mentions on this issue came from German managers and one from a British manager, who briefly commented:

> British management training is very unstructured. They acquire less formal skills.

Indeed, the six mentions of the British having good practical experience (British strengths, item 5) primarily relate to practical managerial, rather than technical, experience.

The perception of German management training being less good (German weaknesses, item 5) appears to be associated with the more senior managerial positions, not with middle management. Again reference is made to German education lasting too long and being too technically orientated. A British CE in a German subsidiary in consumer goods said:

> They [the German parent company] have an awful lot of doctors and economists, but no practical experience. Their high-ranking managers study until they are 26–28. They may have fairly senior jobs by the time they are 35. But when I was that age, I had already had 15 years of experience. It comes down to their centralization. They do not have experience of what real life is. All is corporate planning and controlling. They have the intellect, but not the knowledge based on experience, the understanding of the market, etc. The quality of people on the main board is not as high as I expected.

With the internationalization of business and the growing globalization of the larger German corporations, the need for a more entrepreneurial understanding of business even in Germany has become evident. Whilst the traditional orientation to product and technical specialisms may still largely apply to German business education, and to the older generation of German managers, with the younger generation, and the larger German corporations, the attitude is gradually changing. As Randlesome *et al.* (1993) noted 'a more generalist approach to management education and development has now become desirable'.

Nowadays German managers are increasingly aware of the changes that take place in the world's markets, and of the new challenges which this presents for management in Germany. But because there is a lack of an appropriate German business education, the companies and the managers increasingly look towards business education from the Anglo-Saxon countries, particularly MBAs. Additionally, four German managers made the point that management experience from Anglo-Saxon countries in particular is considered highly beneficial to career prospects in the larger German companies.

These findings suggest that the main British strengths are concentrated around knowledge and skills associated with new and faster developing areas of work, and business management as different from production management. These strengths are primarily built on a higher degree of 'creativity' and flexibility in managerial decision making.

EFFECT OF ENVIRONMENT ON STRENGTHS AND WEAKNESSES OF EDUCATIONAL SYSTEMS

Table 5.4 summarizes the strengths and weaknesses of the British and German systems of education as based on the views of the respondents. It reflects the impact of the different systems on management. The most distinct German strength is seen by the managers to be in the area of vocational training in relation to traditional industries, whilst the most distinct British strength is seen to be in the potential for new creative input in the faster moving industries and areas of knowledge relevant to them.

The educational aspects listed in the table are interrelated in each country. For example, in Germany formal qualifications are important for status, and more people study for longer. One of the consequences is that a proportion of the labour force becomes overqualified for their jobs. Too extensive and highly specialized education not only produces exceptional expertise in individual fields, but may also entail the 'tunnel vision' which is sometimes described as 'professional deformation'. The high vocational competence and longer period of study develop better analytical skills with attention to detail. This reflects in a willingness to take calculated risks, but also in a reluctance to take advantage of uncalculated opportunities which are intuitively thought to be advantageous.

In contrast, because in the British managerial system achievement is a more important basis for promotion than qualifications, employees are more strongly motivated to take on earlier professional responsibility. This is likely to include taking entrepreneurial opportunities, which may at times include taking personal initiatives which would be considered excessively risky from the German point of view. The British emphasis on achievement and personal initiative can also detract from concentration on specific detail. One German respondent, when commenting on the differences between the British and the German management approach, pointed out that: 'The devil is in the detail'. But the emphasis on initiative and creativity carries a potential for developing new skills (such as flexible information systems), as opposed to traditional ones.

In general, it thus appears that the weaknesses of each system of education are produced as the inevitable side-effects of the system's strengths. So in Germany high specialist expertise brings with it the possibility of 'tunnel vision', and in Britain, emphasis on results obtained flexibly entails the risk of lack of attention to detail.

Table 5.4 *The strengths and weaknesses of the British and German systems of education*

Britain	Germany
Environment: Liberal	*Environment: Structured*
Strengths:	
Good professional flexibility	Good vocational competence
Strong on creative innovation	Strong on technological innovation
Earlier professional responsibility	More people study longer
Emphasis on financial business results	Emphasis on operational efficiency
Potential for speciality skill	Developed traditional skill
Management experience important	Work experience important
Taking entrepreneurial opportunities	Accepting calculated risks
Good on initiative	Good on attention to detail
Weaknesses:	
Separation of education content and work	Danger of 'tunnel vision'
Tendency to mismatch of qualification with job	Tendency to over-qualification
Excessive initiative	Excessive risk avoidance
Lack of attention to detail	Attention to petty detail
Tendency to compromise on quality	Tendency to overengineering (in relation to non-German markets)

DOES THE ANSWER TO BRITISH ECONOMIC PROBLEMS LIE IN TRANSPLANTING THE GERMAN EDUCATION SYSTEM TO BRITAIN?

Because national economies depend heavily on the output of manufacturing industry, the German system of education is economically effective. As Lane (1989) puts it: 'The strengths of German manufacturing enterprises are widely seen to emanate from two core institutional complexes – the system of vocational education and training and the system of industrial relations' (p. 298). Britain, on the other hand, has '... a system which, despite the early development of industrialism and material prosperity, has been inadequately oriented towards the needs of industry and poorly adapted to develop the human resources necessary for a high level of performance among managers and employees at all levels' and

'"Practical men" and status lenders still have a strong weight among managers today, and among those with professional management skills, generalists predominate while engineering skills remain weakly represented' (Lane, 1994).

Hence, Lane suggests that for Britain to improve her industrial performance, lessons from the German example should be learned: 'The necessary transformations of British industrial structures and practices need to be initiated or powerfully stimulated by the state.' Referring to features of German business organization, Lane (1989) comments: 'No doubt they would be adapted to what is possible and acceptable in the British context' (p. 297).

The current study suggests that sufficient recognition of the different nature of British education with its own strengths in fast-developing areas of knowledge needs to be made. The interrelated nature of elements in an environment, including the British one, casts doubt on the effectiveness of introducing German-style vocational education, even in an 'adapted form' in Britain.

It may be asked, however, whether British industrial development could benefit from the introduction of particular features of the German system of education? This policy might involve, for instance, a wider introduction of apprenticeships or the establishment of middle-level qualifications in those industries to which the British environment is favourable, such as consumer electronics or biotechnology. The German apprenticeship system is built on the structured nature of the relationships between a whole number of participating institutions in government, industry and education. In order to introduce aspects of it in Britain, several features of the British educational and industrial infrastructure would have to be made less liberal and more structured according to the German model.

But, as discussed above, a distinctive charateristic of those industries harmonious with the British environment is fast development. They have better grounds for flourishing in the UK environment precisely because it is liberal. Establishing set apprenticeships for these industries according to the German model would slow down the pace of development, and the competitive edge gained through speed of response and flexibility may well be lost. The conclusion regarding the possibility of introducing a German style of education into Britain has to be that the nature of the environment and the nature of education with all their strengths and weaknesses are interlocked in all major aspects. Whilst the benefits of German education for German industry are clear, in a different environment the same outcome cannot be expected.

It thus appears unlikely that Britain would benefit from the German style of education without becoming more 'like the Germans' *in toto*.

CONCLUSION

The options in the German educational system structure and channel human resource potential. The options in the British educational system give liberal opportunities for the development of individual flair and scope. The effect of the former is the optimal match of vocational qualifications with existing requirements in industrial employment. The effect of the latter is a high degree of work-related flexibility and managerial creativity. They are not just different; they are, to a considerable degree, antagonistic. It is doubtful whether an environment exists which can facilitate both sets of benefits equally. As discussed in Chapter 8, this very limitation gives scope for Anglo–German business co-operation.

6 Organizational Behaviour in British and German Firms

'The Germans are better prepared for working. They do not think as much as the British; they just do what they are told. But it works better than here, where everybody thinks and does the wrong thing.'—British Managing Director of a German subsidiary in Britain in non-manufacturing industry who has many years of experience of a comparable position in Germany

'The British aim to be flexible, to do things in the last minute, to be creative. They can do that because in the UK things are organised only to 75–80 per cent. In Germany everything is 120 per cent organised.'— German manager in a German parent company

In recent decades, the German economy has clearly outperformed most other countries of Europe. Germany's success has been built around efficient organization of manufacture and its main strength has been in traditional engineering. The whole social infrastructure of Germany, as discussed in Chapter 3, has been considerably fashioned to suit the requirements of industry; for example, the banking system, the system of vocational education, and the new graduate's job opportunities are all well integrated. This institutional cohesion and support of the environment underpins German industrial success, which could not have occurred solely through effective management.

The nature of the social environment in which a company operates has a major impact on the nature of its organizational behaviour. By organizational behaviour we refer to the structure and functioning of organizations and the behaviour of groups and individuals within them (Pugh, 1990). The structured nature of environmental relationships typical for German industrial culture crucially affects the style of management, the attitudes to work and the interpersonal relationships associated with work activities in Germany. Similarly, the liberal social environment of Britain, with its greater individualism and contractual nature of relationships, strongly affects British organizational behaviour.

PREVIOUS FINDINGS ON ORGANIZATIONAL BEHAVIOUR IN BRITAIN AND GERMANY

The organizational behaviour of British and German companies has been the subject of a number of Anglo–German studies (e.g. Child and Kieser, 1979; Stewart *et al.*, 1994). In addition, organizational behaviour has been examined in studies of large numbers of national work contexts which include Britain and Germany (e.g. Hofstede, 1980). There have been a variety of findings but two major streams can be identified with distinctly diverging conclusions. The fundamental difference in the conclusions reached may have been affected by the differing nature of the samples studied and of the main methods of data collection.

STUDIES OF SPECIFIC ANGLO–GERMAN COMPARISONS

The first stream is represented by studies which aim to conduct specific Anglo–German comparisons. They were originated in Britain, and their findings were published there. This stream primarily relies on qualitative research based on interviews from a limited sample in each country, general observation, and library research. Amongst the authors represented are: Millar (1979), Lawrence (1980), Stewart *et al.* (1994), Lane (1992, 1994). In the interviews by Lawrence (1980), primarily Germans in Germany are questioned on how they see themselves and this is then related to the way the British in Britain see themselves. In the interviews by Millar (1979) and Stewart *et al.* (1994) what Germans in Germany said about themselves was compared to what the British in Britain said about themselves.

Millar (1979) studied one company operating in both Germany and Britain in an industry associated with engineering. She asserts that, in relation to their company, the German respondents were '...found to have a more personal feeling, "rather than thinking of oneself it is more like a big family..."' (p. 28).

Lawrence (1980) finds that : '...industry is more domesticated, less alienating, in Germany than in America...' (p. 103) He states that 'It is a reasonable inference that German managers are ambitious, but it is noticeable that they do not have very much to say about their ambitions. ... Parallel to this German disinclination to discuss personal career ambitions goes what might be termed a diminished consciousness of status' (p. 108), and the author continues: '...qualificational differences seem to inspire relatively little envy among German managers.' Lawrence terms this situation 'harmonious heterogeneity' (p. 112). He further found that the German managers were unlikely to point at differences between their salaries (p. 108). In regard to criticism in relation to work performance in German, companies Lawrence suggests that: 'One has to have a good case for imputing dereliction of duty to the victim, but if one has, then it is possible to ignore status and hierarchy and open fire' (p. 117).

Lawrence's main area of investigation in Germany seems to have been the management of production, and the majority of companies mentioned in the book are in mechanical engineering. The results of both Millar and Lawrence are thus influenced by the limited nature of the industrial base of their units of observation.

However, the study by Stewart *et al.* (1994) is based on a comparison of three companies in Britain and three in Germany, matched by industry, that is, the brewing industry, the insurance industry and the construction industry. It examines only middle management, and thus primarily concentrates on operational aspects of management. The strategic aspects and those aspects of vertical managerial relationships towards the top of an organizational hierarchy are not considered.

Stewart *et al.* acknowledge that: 'A comparative study of managerial behaviour must recognise that individual behaviour is shaped by national culture' (p. 11). They found that: 'A key difference between the German and the British managers interviewed was the way the Germans associated work with fun. ... It was evident from the interviews that the German managers enjoyed working hard, liked their jobs and saw work generally as a pleasure' (p. 183). The authors further report that their 'findings suggest that we need to reconsider the view that German management is autocratic ... since all employees "buy into" the idea that organizations should be task oriented, there is less of a need to handle others with "kid gloves"' (p. 193). In relation to Britain the authors refer to Laurent (1989) : '...managers view their organization primarily as a network of interpersonal relationships between individuals who get things done by influencing and negotiating with each other...' (p. 197). But in comparison with the previously discussed studies of Millar and Lawrence, Stewart *et al.* (1994) recognise that: 'It seems clear that any cross-cultural comparison must be muddied by contextual and organizational differences' (p. 150).

Lane (1992) whose work is primarily based on library research, refers to the British and German business systems as 'polar opposites in all their fundamental components' (p. 92). She points out that: '...the productivist ethos of the German firm suffuses all hierarchical layers and acts as an integrating mechanism, the British predominantly financial orientation fails to provide such a common focus' (p. 86). In her subsequent work, Lane (1994) maintains that: 'Given the strong individualism in

British culture, both inter-personal and group relations are calculating, low trust relations, described variously as "arms-length" or "minimum involvement relations" (p. 5) ... Subordinates generally show a sceptical mistrust towards those occupying positions of authority' (p. 6).

In relation to organizational behaviour in Germany, Lane (1992) stresses that: '... German firms lean more towards a limited communitarianism and a willing acceptance of some regulatory frameworks' (p. 76). She further considers the 'reconciliation of family control and modern business organization' to be responsible for the fact that in Germany '...bureaucratic management tradition, associated with high level of education, integrity and a sense of duty and accountability, checked fraudulent activity and thus lessened the fear of passing control to non-family middle managers...' (1992, p. 77).

Lane (1989) also suggests that Britain is likely to look to the German example in the systems of vocational education and training and industrial relations. Referring to the need for new industrial relations structures in Britain which might be beneficial to both sides, she believes that 'It might be possible to achieve such mutually beneficial results by the introduction into the British system of industrial relations of a body akin to the German works council' (p. 300). Lane (1994) develops the ideas maintained by this stream of studies, and suggests that the nature of management in Germany as distinct from Britain, results in higher moral standards amongst companies and individuals.

Table 6.1 summarizes the conclusions of this stream under three characteristic aspects of organizational behaviour: management style, work attitudes and interpersonal relationships. As the table shows, these studies found organizational behaviour in Germany to have many positive aspects when compared to Britain. But the studies focussed on such parameters of organizational behaviour, as the degree of expressed 'conflict', or 'joy of work' as presented to external observers visiting the company. This approach has several limitations.

First, generally speaking, people being interviewed, or under observation, feel the need to display the positive aspects of their circumstances. Second, the pressure to show these positive aspects is greater in situations where the observer is external to the group. In the case of Millar (1979) and Lawrence (1980) in Germany, that meant not only being external to the companies, but also being viewed as a foreign visitor. Third, this same pressure is greater in cultures where high performance, collective responsibility, and personal blame are strong. These characteristics are more emphasized in the German than the British culture. But such differences in context were not adequately recognized by the studies, and were not discounted in the interpretation of the data. As the result, data from Britain

Table 6.1 *Organizational behaviour in Britain and Germany as characterized by authors of specific Anglo-German comparisons*

Britain	Germany
Management style	
Individualistic financial approach without a common focus	Collectivistic production approach providing a common focus
Work attitudes	
Tasks negotiated through interpersonal relationships	Overall task orientation justifies the use of authority
Working hard is less fun	Working hard is more fun
Higher sensitivity to wage differences	Lower sensitivity to wage differences
Interpersonal relationships	
'Less like a family'	'More like a family'
Professional envy more likely	Professional envy less likely
More status-conscious	Less status-conscious
Less forthright in personal critism	More forthright in personal critism
Low trust and 'calculating'	High trust and 'integrity'

and Germany were interpreted on a basis which assumed their meanings to be common for both countries. This was done despite a recognition of the many differences between the cultures of the two countries.

STUDIES OF LARGER SCALE SAMPLES

In contrast, the second stream of studies primarily refers to quantitative empirical data from larger scale samples which were obtained mainly through questionnaires. Amongst the authors representing this stream are Child and Kieser (1979), Hofstede (1980), Noelle-Neumann and Struempel (1984). Apart from their use of quantitative data, the studies representing this stream are diverse, but they conclude that the existing higher degree of institutionalization of management in Germany is *not* accompanied by a correspondingly higher degree of harmony in interpersonal relationships, nor a more committed work attitude on the part of employees.

Child and Kieser (1979) conducted an Anglo–German management comparison based on 82 British companies and 51 West German companies. They found that German companies were more centralized than British ones, and that German managers tended to have a lower job mobility. In this respect reference to the German term *Sitzfleisch*, translated as the ability to 'sit it out' is made. German managers were also found to experience considerably more routine in their work; 'their activities follow a less varied programme and involve less novel problem solving and application of new skills and techniques' (p. 68). 'The data imply that German departmental managers have a greater dependence on the personal decisions of top managers … as opposed to their position being formally and "objectively" defined in a somewhat legal-rational manner' (p. 68). Furthermore, 'The level of job satisfaction *expressed* by German managers is higher'. But 'This higher level of job satisfaction *is not a consequence of lower conflict* or a greater feeling of competence among German managers … most authorities would accept that the level of satisfaction with jobs is a function of how compatible those jobs are with the expectations of their incumbents. The higher job satisfaction of German managers therefore suggests that the limited authority and variety which tends to characterise their jobs is accepted as legitimate' (pp. 68–9, italics added).

Hofstede (1980) carried out a cross-cultural survey involving IBM subsidiaries in 40 different countries. He aptly compares the German style of management to a 'well oiled machine', and the British to a 'market place'. Hofstede recognises that in relation to industial democracy the first dimension involved is Power Distance. But whilst in his empirical measurements the Germanic culture scored lower in Power Distance, Hofstede confirms that a stronger push towards *formal* participation (for example through workers' councils or boardroom representation) generally takes place in the larger power distance cultures. The author says: 'All forms of industrial democracy are in themselves ways of reducing power distance. …the ideological statement that "Employees in industry should participate more in the decisions taken by management" meets with stronger endorsement in *larger* power distance cultures; it seems that the ideological statement acts to some extent as a compensation for what happens on the pragmatic level' (p. 268, italics as in original). 'In … German speaking countries … we should find more stress on formal legally determined participation [*Mitbestimmung*]' (p. 269). So, in effect, Hofstede suggests that the lower power distance scores obtained in Germany are the result of the 'legal push' towards formal participation without which Germany would be characterized by higher power distance values. It is clear that Hofstede does not equate a higher degree of institutionalization of work relations in Germany with a greater underlying harmony in interpersonal relationships.

Noelle-Neumann and Struempel (1984) studied the impact of work development on enjoyment of work in Germany, but referred to large scale international, as well as German national statistical data. On the basis of the international survey 'Jobs in the 80s', carried out in Britain, Germany, USA, Sweden, Japan and Israel, their study concludes that the British workforce has a stronger work ethic than the German one.

In answer to questionnaires, only 42 per cent of Germans stated that they fully devote themselves to their jobs and often do more at work than they are asked to, compared to 66 per cent of the British. This stated commitment was associated with being prepared to make personal sacrifices for work. But 41 per cent of Germans indicated that they only do what they are asked to do at work, compared to 30 per cent of British. This German stated preference for less initiative at work was associated with the avoidance of 'being accused of anything' (Table 10.1, p. 186).

The study also showed that with German workers there is an emphasis on reward through pay, coupled with a sensitivity to existing differences in pay amongst them; for example 51 per cent of the German work population believe that better ability at work is not reflected in better pay (Tables 2.7, 2.11 and 4.17). Noelle-Neumann and Strümpel (1984) do not present comparative data for British workers on this indicator.

On the theme of *Mitbestimmung* there was found to be little difference between Britain and Germany: 20 per cent of Germans felt able to agree with the statement that 'I can fundamentally influence decisions which can affect me', compared to 22 per cent of the British; and 22 per cent of the Germans agreed with the statement that 'I have no influence on decisions that are made', compared to 20 per cent of the British (Table 6.10).

As is the case in other European countries, all population groups in Germany (but most notably men) were found in the Noelle-Neumann and Strümpel study to perceive a decline in the enjoyment of work since 1962 (Table 2.9, p. 42). The problem is addressed in their study and, amongst others, the following suggestion is made: '…it is possible that an unfortunate institutionalisation of the work environment precludes certain groups from participating in the elementary experiences of the production sphere, and then perhaps energetic steps should be taken in order to remove such barriers' (p. 153, translated by DEG).

The conclusions of this stream of studies are summarized in Table 6.2 under the same three headings as Table 6.1. These studies do not on the whole find organizational behaviour in Germany to be more positive than in Britain. German management styles when compared to British ones are found to be characterized by a higher degree of institutionalization, with higher centralization, more formalized duties, and greater dependence on superiors. The institutional embeddedness of the framework of relationships results in a lower degree of manifest problems (cf. Hofstede's 'well oiled machine') but this smooth appearance does not necessarily entail happier interpersonal relationships for the employees. Thus job satisfaction is subject to limited job authority and variety, rewards are primarily sought through pay rather than the job itself, and so on.

In general large-scale questionnaire surveys are in a position to offer more objective data. Compared to smaller and limited surveys the likelihood of a bias in the sample is reduced, whilst there is the ability to offer personal anonymity to the respondents. But despite these strengths, this approach, too, has several limitations. The major drawback is that the use of questionnaires does not offer flexibility during data gathering. The questionnaire is standard and fixed in the preparatory stage of a survey, but an interviewer can bring forward additional points of interest as they arise during data collection. New characterizations can be spotted and

Table 6.2   *Organizational behaviour in Britain and Germany as characterized by authors of studies of larger scale samples*

Britain	Germany
Management style	
Low institutionalization of work environment	Danger of overinstitutionalization
Less centralized	More centralized
Management resembling a 'market place'	Management resembling a 'well oiled machine'
More novel problem solving	More routine
Work attitudes	
Lower expressed job satisfaction due to higher expectations of job variety	Higher expressed job satisfaction due to lower expectations of job variety
Higher work ethic	Lower work ethic
Employees emphasizing obligations	Employees emphasizing rights
Emphasis on 'interesting work'	Emphasis on 'good pay'
Lower sensitivity to wage differences	Higher sensitivity to wage differences
Lower personal dependence on superiors	Greater personal dependence on superiors
Higher job mobility	Lower job mobility
Interpersonal relationships	
Some degree of conflict present	Some degree of conflict present

developed by experienced interviewers in conversation with the inter- viewees. So the interview method is a more appropriate tool for exploratory surveys involving less well-defined or more novel areas of study. Good interviews can bring more insightful results.

COMPARISON OF THE TWO STREAMS OF STUDIES

A comparison of Tables 6.1 and 6.2 shows that there is agreement between the two streams on the nature of the differences in management styles in British and German firms. Both find the British approach more individualis- tic and the German approach more institutionalized. But there is a clear dis- agreement between the findings of the two streams on the nature of work attitudes and interpersonal relationships in the two countries. An example is the direct disagreement between the conclusions on attitudes to pay by Lawrence (1980) and Noelle-Neumann and Struempel (1984). There is a clear difference between the conclusion of 'work being fun' and the empha- sis on pay with a sensitivity to wage differences between employees.

The value of the German style of industrial relations is clearly seen differently by authors within the two streams. Within the first stream in Britain the positive implications of the German system of formal partici- pation is highlighted and suggestions for its application to Britain are made (see, for example, Lane, 1989). Within the second stream in Germany the worth of the German system is seriously questioned, and the advantages of the system are balanced against its drawbacks (for instance, Noelle-Neumann and Strümpel, 1984).

Unlike the first stream, comparisons within the second stream of studies interpret organizational behaviour in Britain and Germany in rela- tion to the differences in work environment, such as employer–employee relationships in the two countries. For example, in Child and Kieser (1979) the degree of expressed job satisfaction is interpreted in the light of the differences in work expectations in Britain and Germany. Thus comparative studies of organizational behaviour within the second stream appear to take greater account of differences in the nature of the social environment as described in Chapter 3.

In view of the very divergent conclusions of the two streams of previ- ous work in organizational behaviour, research to explore further the issues raised can be usefully organized to test the following propositions:

1. Management style
The management style in German firms is more highly institutionalized than in British companies.

2. Work attitudes
This institutionalization is associated with a greater degree of com-
mitment in work attitudes on the part of managers and employees in
German than in British firms.
3. Interpersonal relationships
This institutionalization and commitment entails a lower degree of
conflict, and is accompanied by greater harmony in interpersonal rela-
tionships at work.

The current study tests these three propositions with empirical data from
Britain and Germany. The work environment plays an important role in
shaping organizational behaviour. The differences found, therefore, will
be interpreted in the light of the differences in the British and German
environments, as discussed in Chapter 3.

Considering the strengths of both the interview and questionnaire
methods, it would appear that a potentially useful approach would be to
combine some of the benefits of both. This could be achieved by:

(i)   Using the interview method on larger scale samples.
(ii) Asking questions so phrased that the interviewees are less likely
      to be reluctant to give their views because these may go against
      the public image pursued by their employers, or the image gener-
      ally perceived as 'appropriate' in the culture.

This is the approach taken in the present study.

THE PRESENT STUDY

The present study attempts to address the issues raised above and to
explore whether the higher institutionalization of organizational behaviour
in Germany entails a lower degree of conflict and alienation in that country
compared to Britain. It examines whether German work processes are
accompanied by more harmony in interpersonal relationships, as suggested
by the first stream of studies, or not as suggested by the second stream.

There are two innovative aspects to the current study. The first stems
from the fact that a much larger sample across a range of industries was
investigated. As the details given in Chapter 2 show, in 99 firms in both
countries, the chief executive or other senior manager participated in a
wide-ranging interview covering these topics among others. Thus both
the difficulties of generalizing from a small number of firms which
characterizes the interviewing approach of the first stream, and the rigidity

of the questionnaire approach of the second stream may be considerably reduced.

The second innovative aspect, as discussed in Chapter 2, stems from the fact that interviewees were not asked to talk about themselves, but to focus on their work relationship with their British and German partners. This gave them the opportunity to raise different topics of interest involving Anglo–German collaboration.

In relation to organizational behaviour, the interview contained a number of open-ended questions as described in Chapter 2 and listed in the Appendix at the end of that chapter. Questions were asked, such as:

'What was the first thing you (or your colleagues) had to learn in your current position or when you first became involved in Anglo–German business co-operation?' and 'What took you longest to get used to?' (questions 20–23 in the schedule)

In reply to these general open-ended questions the interviewees raised the specific issues discussed below.

THE RESULTS OF THE PRESENT STUDY

As was shown in Chapter 2 (Tables 2.20 and 2.21), topics of organizational behaviour are amongst the main concerns of managers involved in Anglo–German collaboration. They formed 35 per cent of all topics raised in the interviews, that is 578 mentions. Table 6.3 analyses the frequency of mentions of these issues under the headings of Tables 6.1 and 6.2. Management style was the most frequent issue raised by both British and German managers in answer to the open-ended questions given above (315 mentions). Interpersonal relationships were the next most frequent with 172 mentions, followed by work attitudes with 91 mentions. As the table shows, all the issues generated both British and German managers' comments on British and German organizational behaviour.

The comments of the managers on all these issues will now be examined in order to evaluate the propositions given above. Each of the issues will be further analysed into topics and examples given of the statements made.

1. Management styles

The items covered under this issue concern 'creative' or 'non-creative' approaches to management, taking or avoiding initiatives, following a

Table 6.3 *Organizational behaviour issues**

	re British	re Germans	Total
Management style			
by British	61	140	201
by Germans	65	44	109
by other	4	1	5
Sub-total	130	185	315
Work attitudes			
by British	19	25	44
by Germans	25	21	46
by other	1	–	1
Sub-total	45	46	91
Interpersonal relationships			
by British	16	94	110
by Germans	32	26	58
by other	4	–	4
Sub-total	52	120	172
TOTAL	227	351	578

*Number of mentions by nationality and regarding nationality
(99 managers: 46 British, 48 German, 5 other nationality).

disciplined or an undisciplined approach to problems, superficiality or thoroughness in work, and associated topics. The data, given in Table 6.4, refer to what is perceived as the radically different styles of British and German managers. Examples of the comments made by the managers illustrate the differences.

British management style
Comments about the British style emphasize a creative approach to work (71 mentions). But this is coupled with a view of the lack of a disciplined approach to problems (47 mentions). This characterization is commonly offered by both British and German managers. Very few comments are made of lack of creativity (7 mentions), and no one suggested that the British managers had a disciplined approach to the execution of tasks.

The creativity of the British in relation to management is particularly associated with their tendency to 'take the initiative'. One German manager in a subsidiary in Britain commented:

Table 6.4 *Management style**

	British	German	Other	Total
British management style				
Creative approach to work				
Creativity present	24	7	0	31
Taking initiative	15	8	0	23
Seeking own initiative	5	4	0	9
Tendency to generalize	2	5	1	8
Total creative approach to work	46	24	1	71
Lack of creativity				
Avoiding initiative	0	7	0	7
Tendency to follow procedure	1	4	0	5
Total lack of creativity	1	11	0	12
Disciplined approach to work				
Discipline present	0	0	0	0
Undisciplined approach to work				
Lack of discipline	8	12	1	21
Lack of preparation for meetings	2	6	1	9
Superficial in work	3	9	1	13
Over-optimism in reporting	1	3	0	4
Total undisciplined approach to work	14	30	3	47
German management style				
Creative approach to work				
Creativity present	0	0	0	0
Lack of creativity				
Creativity absent	26	6	0	32
Avoiding initiative	17	7	0	24
Too little initiative	10	1	0	11
Avoidance of generalizations	3	1	0	4
Tendency to follow procedure	30	8	1	39
Total lack of creativity	86	23	1	110
Disciplined approach to work				
Good discipline	11	2	0	13
Thorough at work	16	9	0	25
Well prepared for meetings	6	3	0	9
Concentration on petty details	19	7	0	26
Total disciplined approach to work	52	21	0	73

Table 6.4 *Continued*

	British	German	Other	Total
German management style				
Undisciplined approach to work				
Not thorough at work	2	0	0	2
Total undisciplined approach to work	2	0	0	2

*Mentions by managers.

> Whilst specialists here are quite willing to cross the demarcation line and use initiative, their counterparts in Germany will follow the procedure. To get any answers always takes longer in Germany.

Another German manager in the financial industry said:

> The British are more risk-minded. But we must not underestimate their accuracy. They are only not making such a point of it. We, the Germans, are making it a trademark. It comes more naturally for them.

Typical comments made by German managers about British managers' lack of discpline at work included:

> In Britain people like to make decisions even if they know very little.

> The British do not like to make joint decisions but their own, which is frustrating.

> Everybody wants to be a manager, and no one wants to work.

> The standards of presentation are low, reports are scribbled on a piece of paper, rather than having a proper format.

The British 'overoptimism in reporting' can be illustrated by the following two comments. A German Chief Executive in a German engineering subsidiary in Britain noted:

> People here [in Britain] are sometimes too optimistic about the real potential which we can achieve. I trusted my managers in Germany to make the right decisions. I learned that I have to be more critical here.

And the same point was alluded to by a British Chief Executive of a German heavy engineering subsidiary in Britain, who said:

> Customer names need to be included in the sales forecasts for credibility.

The examples suggest that the comments on creativity relate primarily to the fact that, in the British culture, management is seen as a more attractive and more rewarding contribution to work than is the execution of operations. This attitude has, again, a clear association with the British managers seeking opportunities for, and taking, initiatives. It results in less attention being given to detail. The following extract from an interview with a British CE of a German subsidiary in Britain is an example:

> The way they [the Germans] do business is different. Rules are laid down. It can be frustrating as hell. Rules, if they do not work, have to be disobeyed. Our sourcing man in Germany is constantly moaning and groaning about us [the British].

German management style

Comments on the German style of management overwhelmingly stressed the opposite aspects. It is particularly striking that not a single mention of the Germans being creative was made either by a British or a German manager, whilst there is such an overwhelming agreement on the creativity of the British style. German managers are regarded as lacking creativity, tending to follow procedure and avoiding taking initiatives (110 mentions). German managers, however, are widely considered to take a disciplined approach to work, be well prepared for meetings and be good on detail (73 mentions). There were only two comments that they were not thorough at work.

One British MD in non-manufacturing industry, with many years of experience of an identical position held in Germany, commented about the differences between the British and Germans in relation to creativity and initiative:

> The Germans are better prepared for working. They do not think as much as the British, they just do what they are told. But it works better than here [in Britain] where everybody thinks and does the wrong thing... You cannot give a task to the Germans, only instructions. They are not geared to problem solving, they are clerical people.

Another British manager, also with long-term experience in Germany, felt:

> The Brit will think positively, creatively, and the German will say 'Give me negative reasons why I should not do it my way, anymore.' The approach is totally different in areas less easily quantifiable.

And a third British manager qualified the above difference: 'The fundamental difference is that they [the Germans] are very logical, methodical, and analytical. We have a different approach. Germans always go from '1' to '2' to '3' to '4'. If we [the British] can jump it, we would try to go to '4' directly. Germans would go from '1' through the complete succession just to prove themselves.'

A German manager in a German parent company, when asked what was the first thing he had to learn when he first became involved in Anglo–German co-operation, replied:

> The British aim to be flexible, to do things in the last minute, to be creative. They can do that because in the UK things are organised only to 75–80 per cent. In Germany everything is 120 per cent organized. But the British and the German make quite a good team. They combine organizational skill with improvization.

And the same German view on the planning approach pre-empting creativity was endorsed by a German manager in a German subsidiary in Britain, who said:

> We are for precise planning, then you are not so creative.

The above lack of initiative needs to be seen as associated with 'good discipline' on the part of the Germans (13 mentions). One British CE in a German engineering subsidiary in Britain said:

> They [the Germans] are regulated by the clock. Discipline makes formidable characters. They are self-opinionated. There is only one way of doing things – the German one. They fight quite easily. They try to dominate you, but you need to be hard and establish that you have an opinion and it is valid. They have an undoubted obsession with detail. Their discipline is bureaucratic, they follow the pattern. Everything is standardised in Germany. There is no freedom in doing things. There is a blind obedience towards superiors with a great respect for authority. They can be very petty or very generous. They are best together when on the factory floor solving problems on the customer premises.

And a British manager of another engineering subsidiary said:

> If, in a prestigious project technical problems occur, they [the German partners] can mobilise all of their potential over the weekend to put it right. In this respect they are brilliant.

The differences between the British and the German styles in relation to creativity coupled with the German discipline were summed up neatly by a British Chief Executive of an Anglo–German joint venture, who said:

> In general terms the Germans are much more methodical. They never give up. They carry on until they solve the problem. The British are much more creative. We [the British] have ideas, and the Germans help us to put it into a framework. They are good on framework, but short on ideas.

Differences in management style

Table 6.4 shows that data given by interviewees of both nationalities is congruent. For instance, not only did the British managers see themselves as having a creative approach to work (46 mentions in total); this view was also shared by the Germans (24 mentions in total). Similarly, the view that German managers lacked creativity was expressed by both British managers (86 mentions in total) and German managers (23 mentions in total). No interviewees, of either nationality, volunteered a statement that British managers lacked a creative approach to work, or that German managers were creative in work. A similar congruence is displayed in relation to the lack of discipline of British management compared to the discipline shown by German management. Indeed, the German discipline is emphasized more strongly by the British managers than by the Germans themselves (52:21). Additionally, Table 6.6 shows a striking agreement between the managers of both nationalities on the British managers' lack of identification with their current employers (British: 15, Germans: 20), compared to German managers' corporate identification (British: 18, Germans: 16). The British and the German interviewees were thus in clear agreement about the main characteristics of British and German management.

However, there is also a marked tendency to highlight one's own nationality's strengths as against one's partners' weaknesses. Thus the creative approach to work was emphasized as a British strength more often by British interviewees than by German, as shown in Table 6.4. But when commenting on British weaknesses, the German managers saw the British lacking a disciplined approach much more frequently than the British managers (30:14). The pattern is repeated in relation to German weaknesses. Many more British managers commented on the German tendency to follow procedure and avoid initiative or creativity than German managers (86:23).

When it comes to German strengths, however, this pattern seems to be broken. British managers highlight their German partners' strengths more than the German managers themselves. For instance, more British managers mentioned German thoroughness than German managers (16:9), and more commented on the good discipline (11:2) of German management. These strengths, so clearly related to the high economic achievement of German firms, appear to have impressed themselves on British managers.

The examples illustrate that the British 'creative approach' is closely related to the British 'lack of discipline'; equally the German 'good discipline' is accompanied by 'lack of creativity'. Depending on whether one thinks in British or in German terms, the terms 'discipline' and 'creativity' can be easily interchanged. The characteristics of the British 'creative undisciplined' management style are facilitated by a liberal institutional employment framework and work culture as discussed in Chapter 3. The German 'disciplined uncreative' management style is equally facilitated by the German structured employment environment and work culture. A cultural difference is manifest in that, whilst 'creative' behaviour is likely to be viewed more positively in Britain, it is the 'lack of discipline' interpretation which is more likely to be emphasized in Germany.

These data concur with the findings of previous authors on the performance orientation of German management. They confirm the findings in the literature which compare German work discipline to British lack of discipline (Millar, 1979; Lawrence, 1980; Lane, 1992). Just as with the German emphasis on planning (cf. Chapter 5), these characteristics can be associated with the difference between British and German culture with regard to 'uncertainty avoidance' (Hofstede, 1980). The higher German score on this dimension may entail a preference for discipline over 'creativity'. But there has been little emphasis in the literature on the managerial effects of a greater toleration of ambiguity in a culture. This study suggests that in Britain, this lower level of uncertainty avoidance brings benefits by way of a more flexible approach to management, and a more 'creative' approach to problem solving, both of which are less constricted by constraints of bureaucracy and tradition.

It is clear from the above examples that the German 'lack of initiative' is the other side of the coin from the German tradition of 'discipline'. Since in the German culture discipline is given a high emphasis, it assists in perpetuating existing values and practices. By implication this reduces scope for individual creativity and managerial innovation. But it is important to emphasize that it does not reduce the scope for technological progress if the latter is attributed a high value by the structured industrial environment. Technologically innovative progress is likely to be incremental rather than radical and its success depends on the availability of long-term stable capital input, including investment in human resources. Thus high discipline with a lower degree of managerial creativity may be a good basis for advance in technological innovation, as the German achievement suggests.

2. Work attitudes

The issues covered here concern presence or absence of commitment to work content, and identification with current employer or lack of it. The data, given in Table 6.5 and Table 6.6, refer to what is perceived as the different approaches to work and employment of British and German managers. Examples of the comments made by the managers illustrate the differences.

Commitment to work content
On the subject of 'commitment to work content' the same attitudes, both positive and negative, are attributed to British and German managers with about the same frequency, as Table 6.5 shows.

British commitment to work content
The British commitment to work is noted by the British managing director of a German subsidiary in the furniture industry who commented:

Table 6.5   *Commitment to work content**

	British	*German*	*Other*	*Total*
British management commitment to work content				
High commitment to work content	3	0	0	3
Lack of commitment to work content	1	5	0	6
German management commitment to work content				
High commitment to work content	5	0	0	5
Lack of commitment to work content	5	0	0	5

*Mentions by managers.

Here [in Britain] people work overtime if necessary. They [Germans] start at 8.00 and go home at 16.30. They do not have the work ethic that the British people have. The Germans work more efficiently but they do not work longer, and in a quite inflexible way.

A British manager in a parent company in Britain made a wider comment on his experience with German managers:

Modern Germans do not work as hard as we do. They are more efficient. But they are getting lazier. They are going to have major problems. We can see.

But British lack of commitment is noted by the British Managing Director of a German subsidiary manufacturing accessories for the car industry in Britain:

We [the British] have no discipline in the home, school, no national service. It was a sad day when they dropped it. We find it difficult to conform in the workplace.

And the German Chief Executive in a British engineering subsidiary in Germany noted:

The quality of management in the industrial sector is lower [in Britain] than here [in Germany]. That shows right through from commitment to work to know-how. The British agree to do something, but subsequently fail to do it. If one exercises pressure on them, they complain. Privately the British are more pleasant.

German commitment to work content
In the current study, references to the Germans 'working hard' have come from managers in German family-owned businesses. A British manager in a German family-owned company in the electronics industry felt that his German colleagues:

Do work hard, whilst not limiting work to defined working hours.

A British manager in a German family-owned pharmaceutical subsidiary in Britain commented:

The Germans are very proud of what they achieve. They are committed to work. Perhaps they could enjoy themselves a little more.

On the other hand, rather different comments come from managers in the more impersonal large German corporations. The British Chief Executive of a German subsidiary in Britain of a large pharmaceutical company commented:

> Many UK people think that German business is super-efficient. I believe it is very effective because German companies take a long-term view and are consistent and reliable in what they do. But they are not as hard-working as many people in this country believe that they are.

Similarly a British Managing Director of a British subsidiary of a large German engineering corporation stated:

> The company had a bad time, but they [the Germans in the parent company] all went on holiday. Everything dies in July–August. They are not commited, particularly at management level. They are ace clock watchers. We work long hours as a small organization, but we cannot contact them outside their working hours. I have the feeling that there has been in recent years, a change in culture in Germany. First there was the generation of hard workers, but the current generation has become lazy.

Almost the same perceptions about the Germans were echoed by two other British managers. The managing director in a German heavy engineering subsidiary in Britain said:

> Most people have forgotten the myth about hard-working Germans. They are not there very often.

And another British manager in a German subsidiary in Britain concluded:

> Intelligent Germans are quite idle.

In summary on this topic, it would appear that managers in both British and German subsidiaries find inadequacies with their collaborating partners in regard to commitment to work content.

Identification with current employer
The topics covered under this issue are concerned with interest in work achievements or the lack of it, the presence or absence of personal

identification with the company, an 'entrepreneurial' attitude to the job or the belief in job continuity as an asset. Table 6.6 shows a wide difference in the interviewees' perceptions of British and German managers' identification with their current employers.

British identification with current employer
The British identification was typically described as an 'entrepreneurial attitude to employment', and was mentioned 12 times. A manager with

Table 6.6 *Identification with current employer**

	British	*German*	*Other*	*Total*
British identification with current employer				
Identification with current employer present	0	0	0	0
Lack of identification with employer:				
Lack of interest in work achievements	1	2	0	3
Entrepreneurial attitude to work	6	6	0	12
Lack of personal identification with company	4	8	0	12
Lack of continuity	4	4	1	9
Total lack of identification with current employer	15	20	1	36
German identification with current employer				
Identification with current employer present:				
Pride in work achievements	6	2	0	8
Non-entrepreneurial attitude to work	5	5	0	10
Personal identification with company	6	6	0	12
Continuity an asset	1	3	0	4
Total identification with current employer	18	16	0	34
Lack of identification with current employer:				
Lack of personal identification with company	2	0	0	2

*Mentions by managers.

such an attitude to work chooses to stay in existing employment only until a more interesting, or a better paid, job becomes available elsewhere. A suitable change of a job is considered at all times. This approach reflects the underlying shorter-term contractual attitude of the British to their employment.

A German employer's point of view can be illustrated with the following observation about the British made by an older generation German Chief Executive in a German engineering subsidiary in Britain:

> Here in Britain people are not concerned about the state of their factory. Even if they have nothing else to do, they prefer to just sit around doing nothing. In Germany an engineer would pick up a broom and sweep the floor or polish the bench if he saw it was not clean and if he had the time to spare. German people see the factory as their other home, the British just work there.

Another German respondent in an engineering company in Britain felt:

> People here are not feeling responsible for the company. They just do their job.

These statements by the interviewees seem to contradict the findings by Noelle-Neumann and Struempel (1984) who refer to large-scale data which show that German employees are less willing to make a personal sacrifice for work compared to the British employees. The difference may be due to the anonymity of the questionnaires used. In the more structured German environment the displayed degree of attention to a job may not fully reflect the degree of personal commitment.

German identification with current employer
Table 6.6 shows that the respondents recognized a high degree of identification with their current employer on the part of German employees. A total of 34 mentions covering personal identification with the company, non-entrepreneurial attitude to work, pride in work achievements, and continuity as an asset were given. By contrast there were only two mentions of the lack of such identification. A German manager in a German parent company commented:

> In the UK people are not so faithful to the company. They do not have the same loyalty and relationships as we know it. The commitment is not so serious. There [in the British subsidiary] are more problems in business; we need to constantly check and emphasise accuracy.

A German Chief Executive in a German engineering subsidiary in Britain, who had previously been responsible for the same parent company's Austrian subsidiary, was asked what are the company's main internal limitations. He replied:

> The average duration of employment is lower in Britain than in Germany. As soon as the sales people are successful, they want to become managers, and go elsewhere. Whilst our average employment is 15 to 20 years in Germany, it is on average four to five years in Britain. Quality of technical sales staff is well below the Continent. We have to spend a lot of money with new staff on training.

The examples illustrate that the higher degree of identification with the current employer in Germany is associated with lower job mobility of employees compared to the British. It combines with a greater personal dependence of German employees on their employers, and a higher degree of centralization (cf. Child and Kieser, 1979) to encourage work discipline. But a greater emphasis on hierarchy can lead to more competitive and professionally defensive interpersonal relationships at work.

For example, a British Chief Executive of a German heavy engineering subsidiary in Britain said:

> They [the Germans] make errors, but they are horrified to admit them. If something goes wrong with the delivery, they say to the customer: 'We have never seen it before', and it's a lie. Once I had an enquiry for a prestigious project, and I sent them a fax saying that we need to employ a first-class engineer for this project. The fax was intercepted by someone in the office and sent back to me with the following message: 'Sorry, we employ here only second-class engineers.' Obviously, they were sensitive to the comment to which I had not attached any personal meaning, but which they saw as questioning their competence.

Such examples suggest that the German higher degree of identification with their current employer tends to lead to a higher efficiency in operations whilst entailing a high degree of work team integration. But it need not lead to smoother interpersonal relations with people outside the culture as the above example illustrates.

The structured nature of the German environment, as discussed in Chapter 4, encourages a cohesive employer–employee relationship. For employees, existing career constraints limit possible changes of employers. For employers, structured employment conditions and practices require them to invest in their workforce. Thus, there are pressures from both sides of industry to encourage employee loyalty.

These pressures apply particularly strongly to employers well integrated into the German social system. The attitude to employment in those companies operating in Germany which are external to the system, such as British subsidiaries in Germany, is not the same. These companies are expected to tailor the technical and legal aspects of their operations to the requirements of the German market. But they depend managerially and financially on their British parent companies. Thus, not being fully integrated into the system, they do not receive the same protection and institutional guarantees, formal and informal, about accepted standards of conduct as fully integrated German companies. Therefore, employee loyalty is left to be more subject to individual choice. Examples suggest that the loyalty of German employees to their British employers under these conditions is not always the same as generally found in Germany.

Two clear examples of a difference are given by the experiences of two British parent companies in the financial sector in regard to the German managing directors of their German subsidiaries. One of the British managers said:

> Our first German MD left 'by mutual agreement'. In selecting his clientele he pursued his own personal interests which were not in line with the interests of the company. German moral standards do not seem to be as high as here. Our experience with the Germans is that they are not very trustworthy as employees or customers. Perhaps as business partners on a good exchange basis they may apply different standards.

The second British parent company also had to change the MD of their subsidiary on similar grounds, that is personal abuse of company position. The coincidence that these extreme cases both developed in the financial sector may relate to the fact that the German financial sector is organized in a very different way from the British sector. In addition to a small number of leading banks, there is also a large number of regional banks. Personal relationships as a part of financial relationships are seen as very important. Consideration of a loan may well be based on personal trust, rather than on securities, as would normally have to be the case in Britain (Lane, 1994). In the British liberal environment the lending bank needs to safeguard its interests; effectively, it has to rely on securities. In Germany, such trust is facilitated through the guarantees and the support given both to the lenders and borrowers by the structured environment. As Lane (1992, p. 69) points out: 'Banks own substantial amounts of industrial equity, as well as acting as proxies for small investors. ... Groups of banks have acted as "crisis cartels" to assist in the restructuring of traditional industries...' The British financial institutions in Germany are more marginal in relation to this system. At the same time, the nature of their dealings has to retain the form, based on personal involvement which is standard in Germany. So whilst the employing British financial institutions are less involved and less protected compared to German home standards, their employees in Germany enjoy a higher degree of personal freedom in decision making compared to British standards. The emerging imbalance between less security to the employer and more freedom to the employee presents scope for pursuing personal interest by the employees, in some cases over and above the interests of their employers.

3. Interpersonal relationships

The issue of interpersonal relationships is the second most popular in the number of comments made by the managers. It refers to the degree of social openness or social distance exhibited by British and German managers. Important component topics include: verbal expression whether people speak bluntly or in nuances, easy-going or confrontational behaviour, socializing or the lack of it at work, and democratic or autocratic attitudes. Both British and German managers find that there are very considerable differences between the managerial cultures in these respects.

Verbal expression in communication
The contrast of the British and German cultures reflects very clearly in the perceptions by collaborating managers about the ways their foreign partners communicate. As Table 6.7 shows, German managers are regarded as blunt speaking whereas British managers are considered to talk in nuances and hidden meanings. There also appears to be general agreement that British managers have a sense of humour, whereas German managers do not. On all these topics of verbal expression, there is consensus from managers of both nationalities. No interviewee suggested, for example, that German managers exhibit a sense of humour at work.

The characteristics of a language encapsulate the characteristics of a culture. The German language relies on more precisely defined attributes of pronunciation, grammar and syntax, whilst English is more flexible. It could be said, in the terms introduced in Chapter 3, that the nature of German is more 'structured', and the nature of English is more 'liberal'. For instance, in German few words have several meanings, whereas in English multiple meanings are normal.

Table 6.7 *Verbal expression in communication**

	British	German	Other	Total
British verbal expression				
Talking in nuances and hidden meanings	2	6	1	9
Sense of humour	6	5	1	12
German verbal expression				
Blunt speaking	7	4	0	11
Addressing coleagues by title and surname	6	1	0	7
Absence of sense of humour	11	4	0	15

*Mentions by managers.

But sometimes such cultural characteristics can become confused with character interpretations in relation to the Germans and the British, and may result in distinct negative stereotypes about each other. Thus, for example, mention of the British talking in nuances and hidden meanings included a comment from a German manager in a subsidiary in Britain who had previous experience of working in Texas:

> Some people [in Britain] have to change their attitudes. A Texan knows everything, but accepts the straightforward approach. Here sometimes business takes too long and people try to escape and be sneaky.

On the other hand one British manager in a parent company remarked about the blunt speaking of the Germans:

> Germans are quite insensitive. They can be kind and generous, but insensitive towards other people's feelings. They ask highly personal questions. They like involving themselves with the personal details of other people. They can be blunt and insensitive.

Such examples represent the more extreme end of both perceptions. Most of the comments by the managers on the differences were couched in less forceful terms. The following two examples are more typical. A German manager in a German subsidiary in Britain said:

> Germans are far more specific. They have a direct approach. The British talk around things. They wrap everything up. I prefer someone

telling me: You are an idiot, rather than wrapping it up, but thinking that I am an idiot anyway.

A British manager, in a company operating as a joint venture with alternating British and German top management, noted:

When it is the German term, you always know where you stand, they always state everything very clearly down to the smallest detail.

Comments were also made about the British referring to their colleagues by first names, whereas the Germans refer to their colleagues by title and surname. The tendency to address colleagues by title and surname is a general feature of the German culture, and a manager in a parent company in Britain commented:

Two German people I met [in the subsidiary established through a British takeover] retired two and a half years ago. Both worked all their lives together, but neither knew the Christian name of the other.

Another British manager described the way in which German managers tend to refer to one another as 'stuffy'.

But the German CE in a British subsidiary in Germany commented:

We have several group meetings every year with the managers in our [British] parent company. It is an occasion when we air all of our concerns. Normally all issues get cleared. It is of great advantage that people refer to one another by Christian names – that makes things much easier.

These examples suggest that the differences in linguistic styles can sometimes have strong negative meanings attributed to them by different nationals; as, for example, when the British are described as 'sneaky', and the Germans as 'insensitive'. Similarly, the form of addressing people seems to attract interpretations of a positive or negative character in interpersonal relationships. However, this is not an appropriate response since it applies the values of one culture to judging behaviour in another. A difference in forms of expression does not indicate the quality of relationships between people in the two countries. These have to be interpreted in each culture's own terms.

Thus some Anglo–German companies simply use both forms of address. The British CE in a subsidiary in Germany explained how the same people in the company refer to one another by Christian names when speaking English, but immediately change to title and surname when speaking German. For this company, the differences in address are simply associated with the difference in the languages.

But if a negative interpretation becomes attached to these characteristics, even though this may be through misinterpretation, the misinterpreted perceptions are subsequently likely to become relevant, and may influence the outcome of interactions between people from different cultures. For instance, as the examples show, the German managers addressed their British colleagues by surname, which was interpreted as a sign of 'stuffiness' on the part of the Germans, and to which the British themselves may well have responded in a less open manner. But for German managers this style of address is normal, and carries no negative connotations.

A positive cultural misinterpretation may also influence behavioural outcomes. When British managers address their German colleagues by their first names and this is interpreted by the Germans as a sign of social openness, it can result in more open, and even more efficient, relationships. As the manager in the example said: 'Normally all issues get cleared'. Our data have not recorded a case of a negative perception among German managers about being addressed by the British by their first name. But it is not difficult to imagine that there could have been cases when German managers would have felt offended by such 'overfamiliarity' and a perceived lack of a respect for status on being addressed by their first names.

A major difference regularly remarked on by both British and German managers is the British sense of humour in managerial interactions, compared to the German's absence of such a sense. One German CE in a subsidiary in Britain commented:

I enjoy working with the British. I prefer their sense of humour.

Another German CE in a financial subsidiary in Germany said:

I like the British understatement and sense of humour. My British colleagues are not pompous. They are pragmatic. They do not draw so much attention to themselves as managers in Germany tend to do.

In regard to the German lack of a sense of humour when dealing with management tasks, the German Chief Executive of a British pharmaceutical subsidiary in Germany said:

We are for precise planning. It is the Prussian bureaucracy, there it started. We are more hierarchical than in the UK. We are governed.

The UK has a relaxed atmosphere where you can show humour in any situation. Here even a pub is more formal. Business is a serious matter and joking about it is inappropriate.

The same view was endorsed by a German manager in a British car manufacturing subsidiary in Germany who said: 'We can perform better and achieve more here in Germany, because our people are very serious about business, and are goal orientated.'

The statements illustrate that a more serious approach to work, in which joking around is found inappropriate, is an integral part of the German work culture. It separates work from enjoyment. There is a time and place for showing a sense of humour, and that is outside work since it interferes with work efficiency. In contrast the weaker emphasis on work discipline in Britain allows more scope for sense of humour. It helps relaxed interpersonal relationships at work, and encourages self-expression and creativity.

Social atmosphere
This aspect of interpersonal relationships covers social openness and social distance. Social openness is demonstrated by a democratic attitude, an easy-going approach to work including socializing at work, and general social openness. In contrast, social distance refers to an autocratic attitude, confrontational behaviour, a lack of socializing at work, class consciousness and generally keeping social distance. Table 6.8 shows that the managers in this study perceive the social atmosphere in British and German firms as very different.

Comments about managers in German firms emphasize the social distance involved in organizational interactions, whereas comments about British organizational behaviour emphasise social openness. The distribution of comments shows that the descriptions attributed to the British and German social atmospheres are not divided according to the nationality of the interviewee. Thus, it is not just the British who believe that they have a more open atmosphere compared to the Germans. Far from this, most of the comments that the British atmosphere is more open came from German managers. Out of a total of 26 mentions, 17 came from Germans, 7 from British, and 2 from other nationalities.

Additionally, it is not just the British managers who believe that the German firms have a more 'alienating' atmosphere compared to the British. The Germans also endorse this view. Out of a total of 87 mentions indicating social distance in Germany, 70 came from British and 17 from German managers.

Table 6.8   *Social atmosphere**

	British	German	Other	Total
British social atmosphere				
Social distance				
Class consciousness	1	4	0	5
Social openness				
Democratic attitude	3	1	0	4
Easy-going	3	7	1	11
Socializing as part of work	0	4	0	4
Socially open	1	5	1	7
Total social openness	7	17	2	26
German social atmosphere				
Social distance				
Autocratic attitude	23	5	0	28
Confrontational behaviour	15	4	0	19
Jealousy and overambition	13	2	0	15
Lack of socializing	13	2	0	15
Keeping social distance	6	4	0	10
Total social distance	70	17	0	87
Social openness				
Openness present	0	0	0	0

*Mentions by managers.

Social atmosphere in British organizations

The British organizations' social openness has a number of aspects. Reference was made to the democratic attitudes of British managers compared to German ones. The British CE in a German subsidiary said:

> I am one of the workers here. I am not untouchable as the top German bosses are. My managers sometimes talk me out of things which I thought were right. They were not used to being treated like that before [under the previous, German Chief Executive].

The German Managing Director in a subsidiary in Britain felt that, compared to Germany, British business is more easy-going, by including more social occasions. He commented on the strengths of his British colleagues:

The British are best in situations where they can use personality and sense of humour; where you meet people and give speeches.

Another noted feature of the 'easy-going' approach is the ability to cope with unexpected events. Both German and British managers believe that German managers tend to struggle more, or may be even 'thrown off course' as soon as they face unexpected situations, whilst the British executives can cope with a fair degree of ease. To the question as to whether the subsidiary would welcome any changes on part of its parent company, one German manager in a British subsidiary in Germany replied:

> Of course the British managers behave quite differently compared to the Germans. The Germans are very serious about work, and so are the British, but in a different way. You are unlikely to see a British manager lose his composure. But you are likely to see this with the German managers. That way many potential conflicts can be avoided.

Socializing as part of work is regarded as characteristic of British management. When asked what was the first thing he had to get used to when arriving in Britain, one German manager in a financial subsidiary replied:

> All the social activities I have to get involved with. In Germany it was technical. I have to show my flag here. I say, they should pay my wife for all the socializing she has to do with me.

A German corporate Director in a parent company commented on his experience with the managers in the British subsidiary as being more socially open:

> The British and German management together make quite a good team. Between them they combine organizational skills with improvization. Our British colleagues tend to have a higher capability in social skills. They are more able to accept each other as a person. Their status may be clearly written down, but their cross status communications are more free.

One topic was raised which pointed to the social distance component in the British social atmosphere. It was that concerned with 'class consciousness'.

The German Chief Executive of a large German concern who has lived for many years in Britain aptly pointed to the difference in the major qualifying factors of social hierarchy in Britain and Germany by saying:

In Britain, class is important, whilst in Germany it is the rank that matters.

Unlike class, rank is a more meritocratic aspect of a society, and implies greater social mobility with more opportunities for ambition. This is commented on in the next section on German social atmosphere.

Social atmosphere in German organizations

The more alienating effects of the German work atmosphere were generally commented upon. The autocratic attitudes and confrontationary behaviour of German managers were regularly mentioned. The British MD in a German electronics subsidiary in Britain commented on the traditional autocratic attitude of the German management:

> The big thing that always struck me about my German colleagues is the fact that regardless the circumstances they will maintain that 'We are right'. It is impossible. The middle and upwards generation would never admit a mistake. Younger people in the company are far more genuine and helpful. They hate the German bureaucracy anyway. It is nice to see changes. Seeing XY [the company founder] was like seeing God.

And a British manager in a British company taken over by a German parent commented on the autocratic transition from British to German management:

> They [the German parent company] were originally very tight in strategies, wanted to keep a strong hand.

But he added, referring to the fact that the headquarters then became more aware of the differences between their subsidiaries in different countries:

> Later they became international, but in the meantime they were left with only 'yes-men'.

The confrontational behaviour of German managers can be problem in their collaboration with the British. The British manager in a German car manufacturing company felt:

> Our German colleagues seem to be much more direct, and can be rude. They are more ambitious. In the long run that gives tunnel vision, and we have noticed them in the last two years more arrogant than ever before. We [British managers in the subsidiary] react very badly to

arrogance, tend to oppose it, and the result is that the gap between us becomes wider.

A British manager in a German engineering subsidiary in Britain said:

I am always taken by the fact of how my German colleagues argue between themselves as soon as an unexpected problem arises. And their arguments soon become very personal.

This confrontational behaviour as perceived by others tends to be associated with the intense career ambitions of the German managers. A German Corporate Director in a large German chemical subsidiary in Britain commented about his colleagues in the parent company in Germany:

There are some very ambitious people. They would be very keen to cross their own lines of authority to personally involve themselves into our internal affairs in Britain. But we keep them at bay by being successful.

And a British manager in a large pharmaceutical subsidiary in Britain remarked:

Amongst the British managers there is a better trust in middle management. If a need to communicate with the parent company arises, it is easier for our managers [in the British subsidiary] to speak to top people in Germany, than to their opposite counterparts. Mistrust and jealousy in middle management [in the German parent company] make any communications difficult.

There is believed to be a less relaxed atmosphere in German firms, and, compared with British firms, there is a lack of socializing whilst working. This attitude is associated with the German tendency to strictly separate work and enjoyment. One British manager said:

My German colleagues put a lot of effort into enjoying themselves. Theirs is planned, talked about and organised enjoyment.

Another British respondent elaborated on the negative consequences of such planning:

They put so much effort into organizing enjoyment to start at 5.31 p.m. precisely after finishing work at 5.30 p.m. precisely, that when it eventually comes to it, I get tired of all the organizing and can't enjoy it.

And a German manager in a British subsidiary in Germany remarked:

> There is not a great deal of a social life in German companies. People are very status-conscious. Many of the jobs are created only to earn someone money.

A final aspect of the social atmosphere of German firms concerns maintaining formality and keeping social distance. A British manager in a financial subsidiary in Germany commented:

> Life here [in Germany] is a lot more formal. There is a lot more emphasis on status. There is no communication between colleagues in the office. In the UK people basically work as a team. Here you do not speak about your project. People are afraid of having to share their rewards. They are also afraid of getting on the wrong side of bosses. They abide by the rules. They do not query commands.

A British Corporate Director referring to the subsidiary in Germany said:

> I would love to make them [the Germans] a little bit less status-conscious. I have to go through the hierarchy, but I could be tempted to speak directly to German staff.

The status consciousness in the German companies also results in a greater transparency of the rewards associated with each step of the hierarchy, compared to the British companies. Rank in Germany is associated with defined and visible signs of status. For instance, one German manager explained how the exact design of the chair to which he was entitled (without hand rests, with hand rests, with hand rests and head rest, swivel, reclining or not) was upgraded each time he was promoted to a higher position within the organization. A British manager in a British parent company commented on how important their office is to the senior managers in their German subsidiary: the size of the room, whether it is south facing or west facing, the size of the windows and so forth. Such symbols of status in the larger German companies in particular tend to be accurately defined, and constitute closely monitored steps in the hierarchy.

Differences in social atmosphere

The characteristics of social atmosphere attributed to managements in a country are interrelated. In Britain class consciousness plays a part in social distance. But the overall lower status consciousness at work compared to Germany leaves more scope for relaxed interpersonal relationships between colleagues. The predominantly rank related status consciousness in Germany encorages greater competitiveness. The emphasis on achievements can contribute to higher efficiency of work, but not necessarily to a greater personal enjoyment from it.

DISCUSSION OF RESULTS

The results presented in this chapter illustrate the considerable degree of agreement between British and German managers about the aspects of organizational behaviour which they have raised as important in the interviews. The three issues given in Table 6.3 generated 57 topics. As Tables 6.4 to 6.8 show, the majority of the topics are mentioned by both British and German managers. The differences in comments discussed in this chapter underline that the managers were basing their viewpoints on their personal experiences of Anglo–German business collaboration, and one would expect to find personal variations. But there is also a great amount of agreement on the part of the managers about the nature of British and German organizational behaviour and the extent of differences.

We may now consider the propositions set up earlier in the light of the current data.

1. Management style
The management style in German firms is more highly institutionalized than in British companies.

Consideration of the data of Table 6.4 and the earlier discussion gives considerable support to this proposition. The higher institutionalization of management style is demonstrated by an emphasis on a disciplined approach to work, a lack of creativity in management, and the relative avoidance of taking initiatives. These are accepted as characterizing German management by those having experience of the operations of both nationalities. This may be contrasted with a lower institutionalization of management style. It is shown by a culture which emphasizes a creative approach, which seeks occasions for initiatives and takes them, and allows a lack of discipline, superficiality and overoptimism in work. The general view accepts this as a description of British management. These characterizations of national management cultures are made by managers of both nationalities.

2. Work attitudes
This institutionalization is associated with a greater degree of commitment in work attitudes on the part of managers and employees in German than in British firms.

The evidence from this study on this proposition is mixed. As far as management commitment to work content is concerned, as Table 6.5 shows, there are comments reflecting both high and low commitment among both British and German managers. The higher institutionalization of the German management style appears to allow for a lack of motivation on the part of individual managers, as expressed by a concern that hard work is not now so characteristic of German employees. The less institutionalized British management style encourages more initiative, which can generate greater individual commitment. Thus clear differences in work commitment stemming from differences in the degree of institutionalization of management style are not found.

But clear differences are shown in Table 6.6 regarding the second aspect of work attitudes raised in the interviews – identification with the current employer. The contrast between the British managers' lack of identification with their current employer and the German managers' strong identification is clearly noted by both British and German interviewees. So British lack of personal identification with the company, lack of continuity and 'entrepreneurial' attitude to work are associated with a lower institutionalization of management style. Whereas the German pride in work achievements, personal identification with the current employer, and a 'non-entrepreneurial' attitude to work, appear to flow from the higher institutionalization of management style. It may be different when this institutionalization is not so strong because the employer, as a foreign parent company, is not so well integrated into the German economic and cultural environment. Then this identification may not appear, as the two examples of financial subsidiaries illustrate.

This research therefore leads to a two-part reformulation of the second proposition:

2(i) This institutionalization is *not* associated with work attitudes on the part of managers and employees which show a greater degree of commitment and motivation to work in German than in British firms.

2(ii) This institutionalization *is* associated with work attitudes on the part of managers and employees which show a greater degree of commitment to, and identification with, the current employer in German than in British firms.

3. Interpersonal relationships
This institutionalization and commitment entails a lower degree of conflict, and is accompanied by greater harmony in interpersonal relationships at work.

The data on social atmosphere in Table 6.8 show considerable differences between the two work cultures. They appear to firmly reject the third proposition that the greater institutionalization of management and the greater commitment through identification with the current employer lead to a lower degree of conflict or greater harmony in interpersonal relationships at work. There is agreement that the German social atmosphere at work is characterized by an emphasis on social distance – autocratic attitude, confrontational behaviour, lack of socializing, etc. No manager, British or German, volunteered any example of German social opennness compared to British management. In contrast, in regard to social atmosphere, the British management culture was generally characterized as one of social openness – democratic attitude, easy-going, socializing as part of work.

There was one exception: class consciousness was noted as contributing to the social distance involved in the British management culture. This difference is striking to German managers as German society is more meritocratic. But this very fact may well invite more competitive behaviour, including the exhibition of jealousy, overambition and confrontational behaviour by which the social atmosphere in German firms tended to be characterized.

CONCLUSION

The results of this study have underlined the interrelatedness of all aspects of organizational behaviour. This creates a congruent system for each country's managers, since the management style, the work attitudes and the interpersonal relationships have considerable interactive impact on each other. They are also facilitated by the institutional framework as discussed in Chapter 3. Thus the characteristic aspects of German organizational behaviour are closely interrelated and facilitated through the institutional framework relating to employment in Germany, which is, in turn, linked to the structured characteristics of the German environment and culture. The liberal British environment has its own distinctive impact on organizational behaviour in Britain.

7 Problems in Cross-Cultural Parent–Subsidiary Relationships: The Views of the Subsidiaries

'I wonder what they [the British parent company] are doing with all the information. I am asking myself, if I do not need that infomation what are they doing with it?' German CE of a British subsidiary in Germany, describing the corporate reporting system

'My fundamental belief is that very, very few in the parent company make any decisions at all. There is a huge chain of command.' British CE of a German engineering subsidiary in Britain, describing his parent company's management

All complex organizations inevitably generate internal conflicts. An organization needs to employ many categories of specialists to get the benefits of their distinctive contributions. These include managers and workers; production, marketing and accounting experts, and many more. But the activities of the many specialists require integration towards a common goal. This generates conflict, because for specialists the more immediate specific goals of their department or function have much more salience than the farther removed and hazy common goals of the enterprise. The effective co-ordination of contributors with different values and goals is a key task, and problem, for the management of organizations (Pugh, 1979).

In organizations which have subsidiaries, conflicts between the central head office and the peripheral operating units are endemic. They are based on the inevitably differing views of the needs of the organization and their respective contributions to it. Their beliefs regarding what is the appropriate level of decision autonomy to allow to the subsidiary will almost certainly be different. Senior managers in subsidiaries usually regard the head office as exercising an over-centralized management structure of decision-making. Board members at the head office, however, often maintain that a great amount of operational autonomy is allowed to the operating subsidiaries. Brooke (1984) has insightfully

161

analysed one main cause of this tension. While corporate policies prescribe considerable delegation and board members encourage it, functional managers at the level below the board are likely to be communicating a steady stream of policy guidelines, recommended procedures and demands for control information. The managers in the subsidiaries inevitably interpret these as instructions, and feel that their autonomy is thereby reduced. They also resent the considerable amount of paperwork involved.

When the subsidiary is located in a foreign country, then additional factors exacerbate the situation. Language is always a considerable obstacle. Different insitutional and cultural environments have to be acknowledged, understood and adjusted to. Management processes are likely to be different in the two countries, even if similar formal structures are established (Hickson and Pugh, 1995).

THE PRESENT STUDY

The organizations in our study have felt the tension embedded in the parent–subsidiary relationship. This includes the usual range of centre–periphery problems of subsidiary autonomy, slow parent company response in decision-making, and so on. Further issues and problems stem from the cross-cultural nature of the relationship, including, for example, language problems, disparity in working arrangements and lack of corporate identity. These issues were explored in the interviews with the managers, and are analysed here.

As described in Chapter 2, the present sample includes managers of 91 subsidiaries in Britain and Germany. These respondents were asked about parent–subsidiary relationships in order to establish what are the major factors which are likely to disturb a managerially efficient and interpersonally smooth collaboration between the partners. The structured questions asked about the functional and organizational aspects of the relationship, such as subsidiary fit into the corporate structure, performance targets, and existing control mechanisms (questions 10, 13, 14). But relevant issues of managerial decision making, overall perceived satisfaction from the collaboration, and so on, were volunteered by the respondents in answer to questions in the semi-structured part of the interview (questions 20–27). Indeed, this subject is, together with that of organizational behaviour, the most frequent one. A total of 556 mentions (34 per cent of the total) were raised in the interviews, as Table 2.20 shows. The analysis in the present chapter is based upon the data they provide, and it therefore views these issues primarily from the point of view of the subsidiary.

THE RESULTS

Parent–subsidiary problems may be grouped into the following categories:

1. *Generic parent–subsidiary problems* – the problems built in to the parent–subsidiary relationship in all corporations for the reasons described above
2. *Cross-cultural parent–subsidiary problems* – the additional problems resulting from the fact that the subsidiary operates in a different country from the parent.
3 *Particular problems* – problems which are specific to one cross-cultural relationship. In this study these are of two types:
- *Problems of British subsidiaries and German parents.*
- *Problems of German subsidiaries and British parents.*

The problems will be discussed in order with examples.

GENERIC PARENT–SUBSIDIARY PROBLEMS

These problems are found in all parent–subsidiary relationships, even where the subsidiary is located in the same country as the parent company. Both British and German subsidiaries perceive them. They occur within the structural framework for the control of the activities of the subsidiary, which is set by three factors: (i) the degree of functional autonomy allowed to the subsidiary; (ii) the application of reporting control mechanisms in relation to its operations; and (iii) its influence on the setting of its own targets. Data on the sample relevant to these structural issues are first discussed and then the range of problems illustrated.

The structural framework of parent–subsidiary relationships

The replies in regard to the degree of functional autonomy allowed to the subsidiary are given in Table 7.1. It shows that, although there are a few subsidiaries with very little strategic autonomy (8 per cent), being concerned only with operational issues, most do have a strategic input. They are responsible to the parent company for strategy and report on it. Some, in addition, report on operational issues (35 per cent), but others have full operational autonomy (35 per cent). The distribution shows some differences between British and German subsidiaries. Five German

Table 7.1   *Degree of functional autonomy*

	Subsidiaries				
	British in Germany		German in UK		Total
	n	%	n	%	%
Subsidiary reporting to parent company on operational issues	2	4	5	11	8
Subsidiary reporting to parent company on both strategic and operational issues	13	29	19	41	35
Subsidiary reporting to parent company only on strategic issues: operational autonomy	15	33	17	37	35
Missing data	15	33	5	11	22
Total	45	100	46	100	100

subsidiaries in Britain have no strategic input, compared with only two British subsidiaries in Germany.

The concomitant reporting control mechanisms are given in Table 7.2. The most popular period of reporting for both British and German subsidiaries is monthly. But there is a considerable range. Some parent companies control through the annual budget only; others require daily updates. Again it would appear that the range is the same. But nine German subsidiaries reported that they were controlled primarily through the annual budget, compared with only two British subsidiaries in Germany, while seven subsidiaries in Britain were required to report daily or weekly, compared with only three in this position in Germany.

Target setting for the subsidiary is an important activity in parent–subsidiary relationships. The amount of influence that the Chief Executive of the subsidiary feels he has on the targets is given in Table 7.3. Some feel that they have low influence; only being able to comment on, or to attempt to negotiate changes in, targets set by the parent company. Most CEs feel that they have more influence, since the targets are discussed jointly before they are set. The distribution appears to be comparable for British and German subsidiaries, although more German subsidiaries in Britain are restricted to giving comments on targets already set (7 compared with 3).

The control framework demonstrated by the answers to the above questions appears to be generally similar, although there are somewhat

Table 7.2 *Control mechanisms relating to parent–subsidiary co-operation*

	Subsidiaries	
	British in Germany	German in UK
Control through the annual budget	2	9
Reporting three times a year	0	1
Quarterly reporting	5	1
Monthly reporting	30 (67%)	19 (41%)
Weekly reporting	2	3
Daily update	1	4
Other	2	2
Missing data	3	7
Total (= 100%)	45	46

Table 7.3 *Subsidiary CEs' influence in target setting*

	Subsidiaries			
	British in Germany		German in UK	
	n	%	n	%
Give comments	3	7	7	15
Negotiate the targets	10	22	8	17
The targets are discussed jointly	24	53	23	50
Subsidiary sets them: only important targets set by parent company	2	4	3	7
Other	0	0	2	4
Missing answers	6	13	3	7
Total	45	100	46	100

more German subsidiaries in Britain having a lesser degree of autonomy. Within this structural framework, a number of generic parent company–subsidiary problems are regularly raised. As listed in Table 7.4, they concern excessive bureaucracy, the parent company 'knowing better', and slow intra-company response.

Table 7.4   Generic parent company–subsidiary problems

	Subsidiaries		
	British in Germany	*German in UK*	*Total*
Excessive bureaucracy in communications	8	9	17
Parent company knowing better	6	16	22
Slow intra-company response	5	11	16
Total	19	36	55

Excessive bureaucracy in parent–subsidiary communications

The perception of excessive bureaucracy in communications is a common generic parent–subsidiary issue. A German MD in a British engineering subsidiary in Germany, when asked what he would like to change in the subsidiary's relationship with the parent company, replied:

> The reporting system. Reporting is worthwhile, but every week is stupid. Monthly is enough. If we have five bad months, we have to report every day.

As the German CE of another British subsidiary in Germany put it:

> I wonder what they [the parent company] are doing with all the information. I am asking myself, if I do not need that information what are they doing with it? It is annoying when different reports have to be written from those that are used here. For instance, about the number of accidents, we thought we could send them the report which we prepare for the trade unions, but that was not what they wanted.

As would be expected, there are many similar comments from the Chief Executives of German subsidiaries in Britain. Their views were neatly summed up by the British MD of a German engineering subsidiary who described the corporate reporting system simply as:

> It is three thousand ways of giving the same figures. Awful.

This problem is likely to be strongest following the takeover of an established company. As an example, the German Managing Director of a recently taken over German financial subsidiary in Britain, when asked what he believed the subsidiary managers would like to change in their relationship with the parent company, replied:

> I believe they think that the Head Office should leave them more space. They have now a lot of additional work because of reporting on day-by-day business. This often does not make sense to the English. But that is understandable.'

The increase in communication load after a takeover has good reasons. First, with a new takeover, the parent company needs to familiarize itself with the situation of the subsidiary. It will require more intensive reporting until the takeover becomes established. Secondly, the subsidiary is now part of a larger corporation with the inevitable increase in formalization that this brings (Pugh and Hickson, 1976).

Parent company knowing better than the subsidiary

The parent company's belief that it knows how to do things better than the subsidiary is a sensitive issue in all parent–subsidiary relationships. Typically the parent company considers that it has more expertise and experience and is therefore in a position to offer advice and guidance. But even though it is well meant in the interests of greater effectiveness, such managerial support by a parent may be seen by the subsidiary as a reduction in autonomy, or even a lack of trust. It is a generic problem that is built in to the relationship.

A nice example was offered by a manager in a British parent company with a subsidiary in Germany established for only one year. He noted:

> Initially we sent a man to help them, but they called him 'the secret service policeman', whilst he was only there to help.

A further example of 'knowing better' in relation to a British parent company was given by a German CE of a large British subsidiary in Germany. He used the German term *'Besser-Wisser'* for those who 'know better' when commenting:

> The attitude 'I know how to do it' does not go down well in other countries. I often get managers who complain and swear at the British *'Besser-Wissers'*. But I tell them: 'You should work with him, but

need not go to bed with him'. There is this attitude 'We are British and you work for us'. It does not go down well. But I believe it is just the same with subsidiaries of German companies in Britain.

Indeed, the same attitudes are found. In a British subsidiary of a German company in purpose clothing, the British CE explained his experience with his German superiors as follows:

They [the German parent company] would not give more autonomy to local markets. If something does not work, the Germans do not start thinking of something different, but believe that 'we did not have enough of what there is'. You cannot use the despotic German style to run UK, US, or French markets from Germany. The Germans would have to abolish themselves which they would not do. Our 'Xs' [a particular product] are harder wearing and more functional, but the customers want products that are comfortable and look good. But the Germans do not understand. They say 'No. We know what is good for you!'

The problem for the parent company of how far to intervene in the activities of the subsidiary is a classic example of the centralization dilemma. The problem appears to be a stronger one for German parent companies. Child and Kieser (1979) found a higher degree of centralization in German companies; and, as Table 7.4 shows, it is the British subsidiaries who report more problems of the German parent company 'knowing better'. This is also congruent with the finding (in Table 6.8 p. 152) that the social atmosphere in German organizations is characterized by more autocratic attitudes and confrontational behaviour than those of British organizations. In contrast, some British parent companies would appear not to show as high a degree of concern as the managers in their German subsidiaries would appreciate (see Table 7.8 below).

The task of maintaining the correct balance between centralization and delegation is a difficult one which has to be constantly reviewed by managements in both countries in the knowledge of the differences in managerial attitudes in the two cultures.

Slow intra-company response

Slow intra-company response, as another typical generic parent–subsidiary problem, was mentioned in both countries.

The British MD of the subsidiary in Britain of a German engineering company, when asked what changes he would like in the subsidiary's relationship with the parent company, replied briefly:

Reaction time.

The same problem of slow response was raised by the Chief Executive of a German subsidiary of a British machine tool company. He said:

We are unable to keep delivery dates, and we are losing customers. Today we send a fax [to the parent company] requesting an offer tomorrow, and you have to wait for two weeks.

The problem of slow intra-company response stems from the fact that staff in parent companies with no input to the host market are unlikely to be in a position to understand the issues and priorities involved there. Thus a problem or an opportunity which is urgent for the subsidiary and its customers may only be regarded as of marginal importance by the managers in the parent company. The problems may ease when staff in the parent company begin to understand the nature and problems of the host market. The examples given in Chapter 3 of 'support of the subsidiary' (see, for example, 'Company CA' and 'Company DA' on pp. 44–6) illustrate that in cases where specialist staff in the parent company provide regular support to the subsidiary's operations in the host market, the response time is not regarded a problem.

The generic problems illustrated above are classic examples of the centre–periphery issue which faces all multi-site organizations. They are commented on by managers in both the British and German subsidiaries, as Table 7.4 shows. It is difficult to achieve an appropriate balance of authority between the head office of the corporation and the outlying operating subsidiary. Often from the subsidiary's point of view the centre's involvement is demotivating.

CROSS-CULTURAL PARENT–SUBSIDIARY PROBLEMS

Cross-cultural parent–subsidiary problems are likely to be found in the relationships of all subsidiaries to their parent companies when the relationship involves different countries. They concern parent–subsidiary communiation channels, awareness of national identity, language differences, differences in accounting systems and barriers to corporate integration.

Table 7.5 *Channels of communications between the subsidiary and the parent company*

	Subsidiaries			
	British in Germany		German in Britain	
	n	%	n	%
Only the Chief Executive communicates	2	4	2	4
Only senior management communicates	9	20	10	22
All levels of management interact as needed	14	31	21	46
All staff interact with their counterparts as necessary	10	22	8	17
All levels of management interact with staff senior to their counterparts if needed	6	13	0	0
Missing data	4	9	5	11
Total	45	100	46	100

Parent company–subsidiary communication channels

The standard section of the interview included a question (question 16) on the channels of communication between the parent company and the subsidiary.

Table 7.5 lists a range of possible channels of communication that may be used for interactions between the subsidiary and the parent company. It shows a range from the most restricted – only the CE communicates – through use of continually wider channels to all staff interact as necessary. The widest channel use is when all levels of management can interact even with staff senior to their counterparts as necessary. The table shows considerable similarity between British and German subsidiaries in regard to the channels used. In both cases the most frequent practice is that all levels of management interact as needed (31 per cent for British subsidiaries in Germany and 46 per cent for German subsidiaries in Britain). But there is one striking difference. Amongst the British subsidiaries in Germany, six cases (13 per cent) were found where management interact with staff senior to their counterparts if needed, showing the widest channel usage. But no such case was found amongst the German subsidiaries in the UK. This may well be a reflection of the greater status consciousness of the German managers, and their greater tendency to follow defined procedures, as discussed in Chapter 6.

Table 7.6 *Cross-cultural parent company–subsidiary problems*

	Subsidiaries		
	British in Germany	*German in UK*	*Total*
Awareness of national identity			
'Us and them' attitude	7	24	31
'Superior nation' attitude	10	6	16
Language differences	13	18	31
Different accounting systems	1	3	4
Barriers to corporate integration			
Disparity in working arrangements	3	7	10
Insufficient information about other subsidiaries	1	5	6
Lack of corporate identity	1	5	6
Reluctance to integrate	3	1	4
Total	39	69	108

But in spite of the fact that the channels of communication are said to be reasonably free, a number of cross-cultural problems do occur. These are listed in Table 7.6.

Awareness of national identity

An important issue in cross-cultural parent–subsidiary relationships is the managers' awareness of the nationality of their colleagues, and how this affects the attitudes towards them. Managers in subsidiaries usually have negative perceptions of their counterparts in parent companies. These attitudes are likely to be exacerbated when the parent managers are of a different nationality. Several managers in our study believe that their collaborating partners show different approaches towards colleagues of their own nationality compared to the colleagues of the other nationality. They prefer their own nationals' way of doing things.

Table 7.6 shows the number of times this issue was mentioned in the interviews. There are two levels in the force of 'awareness of national identity'. At a weaker level it is manifested as an 'us and them' attitude. Those with this attitude refer to their counterparts in the company as 'the Germans' or 'the British', with an implicit danger of stereotyping. There are 31 mentions of this attitude. They come from both nationalities

(British 18, German 12, other nationality 1) and refer to both British and German managers (British managers 14 references, German managers 17 references).

For example, the German CE of a German subsidiary in Britain in the finance industry commented of his German predecessors:

> If you want to be in business here you have to be more flexible and give up the idea that the German way is the only way you can do it. Other Germans were here, and you could see the culture clash. Germans think that the English do not work hard enough.

A reciprocal view about the English was expressed by a German manager in a German parent company who, when asked what he believes the British subsidiary would like to change in their relationships with the parent company, replied:

> That we are not too German. They see us as organizationally too precise. Too concerned about details. But I say: I agree the results, but I do want to know how you intend to achieve it, and that is what they do not like – *Der Teufel ist im Detail*. The devil is in the detail.

A much stronger variation of the 'us and them' view is the 'superior nation' attitude. In this case, the characteristics associated with 'us' are generalized to the whole nation, whilst implying their superiority over the characteristics perceived in relation to the other nation. Table 7.6 shows that 16 mentions of this attitude were made.

It is more likely to be perceived by partners of different nationalities about one another, and less likely to be perceived by partners of the same nationality about each other. Thus all nine references regarding British managers as taking a 'superior nation' attitude came from German nationals. Although five such mentions out of a total of 7 regarding German managers came from British nationals, 2 came from German nationals themselves.

The British MD in a German subsidiary in Britain, when asked what was the first thing he had to learn when he first became involved in Anglo–German co-operation, replied:

> I expected a high degree of punctuality, but they are more serious than I expected them to be. I had to learn that they are quite a racist nation. Anti non-Germans. There is also some arrogance: 'Not German, not good.' However, when meeting them, they have good manners, are warmly welcoming, and are kinder and gentler than I expected.

And the German MD in a British financial subsidiary in Germany, when asked in what areas do the British and the German managers in the company have most difficulty in working together, replied:

> Simply in having to adapt to the ethical customs of the country. We [the Germans] have a vast feeling of superiority. But it is not the knowledge and the skill which are superior. We only have a very good system. The social and economic infrastructure are the real German trademark.

Similarly a German CE in a British pharmaceutical subsidiary in Germany said:

> Many Brits' experience with the former colonial style leads to the perception that on each end of the Channel there starts a completely different world. And that difference [i.e. of those overseas] is seen rather indifferently. It amounts to the perception that the Kenyan is not fundamentally different compared to the German. That leads to tensions.

Showing an awareness about national identity in cross-cultural situations through recognizing one's own nationals as 'us' and different nationals as 'them' is a natural initial human reaction. It may not become a problem in collaboration between people of different nationalities. It is likely to decrease in line with growing experience and the success of the collaborative venture. But when the 'us and them' attitude results in managerial intolerance towards 'them', then the 'superior nation' attitude becomes a problem.

Language differences

As shown in Table 7.6, a frequently mentioned cross-cultural problem relates to language. Of the 31 mentions made, 18 were in the German subsidiaries in Britain and 13 in the British subsidiaries in Germany. There are obvious difficulties when people do not speak the appropriate foreign language, but, in addition, the difference in the nature of the English and German languages can cause problems.

Problems of not speaking the language occur in German subsidiaries in Britain. In one subsidiary with 330 employees, of whom the German planning manager is the only German speaker, the British CE noted:

> They [the German parent company] send us German letters. These need to be translated before we can reply to them.

In a British company recently taken over by a German parent, the British manager complained:

> They use hundreds of abbreviations and different terminology. All correspondence, 99.9 per cent, is in German, but few people here speak the language. In our field we need competent technical staff; not many of these are linguists at the same time. This slows down the managerial process tremendously.

Despite problems in some cases, because English is established as the international business language, there are good practical reasons why the Germans use the English language much more frequently than the British use German. But, even so, some German managers describe the British as 'linguistically arrogant' (four mentions). A counter-argument is maintained by some British managers that the Germans are too keen to speak English; so much so that they do not give the British a chance to 'have a go' at German. In one large British corporation both interpretations were given: the former by the German CE of the subsidiary, and the latter by the senior British member of the parent company's board responsible for Germany.

The second problem concerns the structure of the English language and its idiomatic usage. For many German managers communicating in English, while individual words in the language are correctly interpreted and lack of vocabulary is not a problem, the overall message can still be misunderstood. This is because of the greater idiomatic content of spoken and written English. Since British managers do not adjust their idiom, the perception arises (as discussed in Chapter 6) that they are talking in 'nuances and hidden meanings'.

Commenting on the German problem of speaking the language but misunderstanding the message, a German CE of a British subsidiary in Germany said:

> Germans are formal and very accurate. When we first started communicating with the British, there was a hell of a lot of misunderstandings and misinterpretations. You did not realize what they wanted. We have a direct approach, the classic British do not have a direct approach. Sometimes we get a letter which starts as if it was saying "yes", but two pages later you find out that really, the answer is "no". My managers say: "Why the hell is he [the British boss] talking so much, he should just say 'No, it is not possible'." Then it would be simple and clear.

A further communication problem is the misunderstanding of the typical English tendency towards understatement. As discussed below, this may be wrongly interpreted by some German managers as a lack of interest in the work itself. Similarly, the 'warning signals' used in English about a likely dissatisfaction appear to Germans to be understated. So, for example, one German manager pointed out that it took him a long time to learn that if a sentence starts with 'Are you saying that...', then the matter is likely to be a serious one. The British manager is likely to be questioning an action or an attitude on the part of the recipient. But the German manager, merely translating the words into German, would consider the phrase to be a low key colloquial expression.

Conversely, the explicit German style of language can also entail friction and misunderstanding because it is likely to be perceived as 'too formal' in mode of address, and 'too blunt' in verbal expression, as discussed in Chapter 6 above.

Such language difficulties, and the possible misinterpretations of the motivations behind them, may be alleviated through more frequent, and more informal, personal contacts between the British and German managers. This could be made possible by company staff exchange schemes, or staff rotations between the parent and the subsidiary. Fifty out of the 91 companies in the sample said that they practise such schemes. Their duration ranges from two weeks to two years or more of experience in the host country. In one of them the British managing director of a German subsidiary in Britain commented:

> We export a lot of people here. It is successful to move people to Germany. Some permanently, some for a minimum of two years, some just for a few days. The main thing is to expose them to the contact with their German counterparts. Just to make contacts makes a great difference.

Of the companies who run the schemes only six mentioned language difficulties as a problem. The remaining 25 mentions of language difficulties came from the 41 companies who did not state that they run such schemes.

Differences in the British and German accounting systems

The British and the German accounting systems differ in important ways (Blake and Amat, 1993). Therefore, British and German companies need to convert their accounts from their home country format to that required in the host environment. The disparity in accounting systems in Britain and Germany was mentioned as a problem by four managers. One manager in a British subsidiary in Germany described the conversion of British accounts into the German format by saying: 'It is a nightmare.'

The Chief Executive of a large division of a German Corporation, the Divisional Headquarters of which is in Britain, commented:

> The German system cannot cope with the international accounting system. We have computers which translate our accounts into a, for us, inferior system.

But it also appears from one of the comments that the understanding of the rationale behind the different systems helps in reducing the problem. The German Managing Director in a British subsidiary in Germany stated:

> There was the problem that the British use a completely different accounting system. But once we learned to understand it, we found that it is a very good one.

This problem appears to be typical of the initial stages of a collaboration. Once either a set routine becomes established, or, at least, an understanding of the rationale behind the other system is grasped, the problems reduce. Indeed, several British subsidiaries in Germany indicated that they keep two sets of accounts, British and German, simultaneously, thus avoiding the need for conversion.

Barriers to corporate integration

Integrating an organization is a difficult managerial task, as explained above. If it has to be accomplished in a cross-cultural setting then additional barriers arise. Those indicated by the managers are listed in Table 7.6. They include disparity in working arrangements, insufficient information about other subsidiaries, lack of corporate identity and reluctance to integrate into the parent corporation. The table shows that managers in both British and German subsidiaries perceive some of these problems in regard to their parent companies. There are, though, differences in the intensity of the individual issues and the degree to which they are perceived negatively by managers in the subsidiaries.

Disparity in working arrangements

There are situations in which the managers in the subsidiaries feel that they are not given the work facilities that are available to the parent company. They consider that they are treated as 'poor relations'. The British manager in a subsidiary in engineering in Britain said:

> There is an element [in the parent company's approach] that 'the English are not us'. ... There is a disparity between the working conditions which they gave to themselves but did not ensure that their subsidiaries have. ... There is no corporate identity for subsidiaries as organizations. They have not made us a part of their computer system, for instance. I believe it comes down to time, attention and money. But what they are doing is spending my time and money for developing our own computers. I am sure that they now understand the cost of it. I get a kick out of doing it, installing our own system myself.

The Chief Executive of a British subsidiary remarked:

> We only have about a quarter of what they [the German parent company] have, for instance, in production facilities. There is no positive investment programme. They never invest in us, it would be nice if they would.

The Managing Director of a British subsidiary which manufactures parts for car engines said:

> We did get a large order to run continually for seven years, but our site here is too small. The land opposite [in immediate view of the MD's window] is offered for development. The latest situation is that we would even get a Government grant to develop that land. But the probability is that we [the parent corporation] will not make a positive decision. We will have to double production, and it is already crowded [in the current factory]. Not completing the order by ourselves is another alternative.

In the event the German parent company declined to invest in Britain, and the company is an example of a 'handicap of the subsidiary' as discussed in Chapter 3. Similar problems are reported in some subsidiaries of British parent companies, as shown in Table 7.6, although further details are not available in those cases.

Insufficient information about other subsidiaries

Insufficient information about other subsidiaries is sometimes perceived as a problem. The British manager in a German subsidiary in Britain, when asked what the subsidiary would like to change in their relationship with the parent company, replied:

> One of the concerns here is to get an understanding of other subsidiaries. We do not know about the other subsidiaries. We do not have meetings together.

The importance of sufficient information about other subsidiaries in contributing to increases in the efficiency of operations across the corporation was highlighted in the comments of a British manager in a British parent company in pharmaceuticals. He described the investment which the parent company put in to combat this problem:

> We [the parent company and the subsidiaries] have a European get-together every other month. Heads of companies; ten people meet. It is formal and informal at the same time. It brings good returns. The cost of this is peanuts, a few thousand pounds. But it builds mutual trust, confidence, etc. There is a need to communicate.

And the importance of subsidiaries having good information about each other as a contribution to the establishment of a corporate identity was underlined by the British MD of a German engineering subsidiary in Britain:

> We [the British subsidiary] get very good support from the Germans. Without them we could not do it. We do not write notes. Internal communications are not written. Now we are installing a new computer system. Everything is the same in the company. The different subsidiaries [in different countries] show each other opportunities. In our company we spend a lot on training. ... We were accepted into the family.

Lack of corporate identity

Feelings in the management group of a subsidiary of being identified with the parent corporation are not always present. A subsidiary's management can feel that it is being neglected by the parent, or that it is continually involved in intra-corporation conflicts. The British MD of a subsidiary of a major German engineering concern which was established through a takeover of a British company commented:

> When they bought us we were not making a lot of money. The parent company do not invest in us. They loaned us money in times of hardship. Their own investment takes priority. We are independent. I wish they were pushing us, but they are not. If they did, I could ask things from them and push them more.

This company is not fully utilizing its potential and is an example of 'handicap of the subsidiary' as described in Chapter 3. But even when the subsidiary's contribution to the parent company's output is substantial, as is that of 'Company JA', there may still be problems. The British CE of this highly successful British subsidiary of a German pharmaceutical company said:

> Our [the subsidiary's] line of business involves a lot of politics. There is always some pressure that investment should remain in Germany. The jealousy amongst the managers is shown at the middle management, rather than at the top. There is a lot of mistrust, and it is often easier to speak to top people in Germany than to our opposite numbers.

Although such problems may diminish over time they do not necessarily disappear. One British pharmaceutical subsidiary was sold, in the 1970s, by its then British parent company to a German corporation. Its Chief Executive, commenting on the ensuing change in managerial approach, said:

> Even after 20 years of experience, a management difference can still be noted. In our company it was due partly to education and partly to the culture of 'XZ' [the original company]. Managers had romantic ideas about business. It was more of an institution rather than a business. Its main characteristics were that it was highly ethical and very stable.

Subsidiary reluctance to integrate

Whilst several examples of a lack of corporate identity on part of the British subsidiaries in Germany are found, few attracted expressions of dissatisfaction about the situation by the managers concerned. The German subsidiaries in which the issue was raised were established as takeovers. They continue to perceive their original corporate identity long after the takeover, as also shown in the British example above. Indeed, in these German cases there is typically a reluctance to accept the corporate identity of the new foreign parent. Comments made by the managers of these British subsidiaries in Germany include:

> Our employees notice that we are a British company when we hoist the English flag outside the Head Quarters during an official visit from the parent company.

and

> The parent company attempts to integrate us, they are sending us company literature. For instance, the latest newsletter gave an article about the company's football team. But we [the subsidiary management] believe that the workers should concentrate on what is really important for the company, and that is to work.

The German CE of a large British manufacturing subsidiary in Germany commented:

> Up until the British parent company acquired 95 per cent of our shares we were still able to say that we are a German company. But now the linkage with the parent has become stronger. They [the British parent] even rejected a proposal of our *Aufsichtsrat* [Supervisory Board]. We see ourselves here naturally as 'XX' [name of the original German company]. But we all know that we are part of an English group now. We use, purely verbally, in business reports the British name of the Group. We do not use yet, as for instance the other European subsidiaries of the group do, the original English letterhead. It was once brought up that we should change, but that has now calmed down. Some subsidiaries display their Queen's honours' certificates and other symbols of English identity, but we are in that respect very held back. And we will not be forced. At the moment the parent company has other problems, anyway. There is no ill-will, and we are not being pressurised by them. It is possible that with the development of European operations completely new ideas will come forward, anyway.

The resistance to corporate integration by the managers in these subsidiaries is usually linked to a takeover of an established home company, considerable managerial autonomy, and a high degree of vertical integration entailing own manufacture of products sold in Germany.

The same situation can also exist in the British subsidiaries of German parent companies. The German Managing Director of a German holding subsidiary in Britain whose responsibilities include a large non-manufacturing subsidiary which was established as a takeover of a well-known British company commented:

> Our takeover was a friendly one, and integration is our strategy. But I think I know their [the British managers'] feelings. They think that the [German] head office should not interfere so much. They have a lot of additional work because of reporting, which is expensive. But this is a human kind of reaction and applies to all head office situations. For the parent company the acquisition was, so far, loss-making. They [the German parent] would also like to see that English management view themselves as part of 'XY' [name of the German parent]. Instead we are 'AB' [name of original British company], and things are different here. The English would be liked more if they did not want to keep the Germans out. The Germans do all kinds of integration, but the British do not respond.

These examples describe situations in relation to the managers in the subsidiaries which are similar in both countries. When it comes to takeovers of established companies, an initial rejection of the new foreign owner is common. Three factors contribute to this reaction. First, the perceptions of corporate identity and pride involved even in a national takeover, are likely to be complicated by nationalist feeling if the new parent is a foreign company. Secondly, a feeling of insecurity may well develop within the management of the subsidiary as a consequence of the newly introduced accountability to others. And thirdly, there is the burden of additional reporting to the new parent which may be particularly extensive in the initial stages following a takeover.

The existence of barriers to integration tends to be a reciprocal problem, typically with both the subsidiary and the parent company complaining, as illustrated in the examples above. In the British subsidiaries in Germany, the perception of a lack of corporate identity tends to relate to a lack of support by the parent companies. The parent companies' view, however, is likely to focus on the reluctance of the subsidiary to adopt the corporate identity. The issue may become a more serious problem when there is a lack of clarity, or a disagreement, about the role of the subsidiary in relation to the parent company's output. It is also exacerbated when interpersonal relationships between the managers in the parent company and the subsidiary are difficult. Examples of some takeovers suggest that the degree of reluctance is likely to diminish if the business situation of the subsidiary improves.

The range of cross-cultural parent–subsidiary problems, listed in Table 7.6 and discussed above, appear to face all multinational corporations which have to cope with the different cultures of their subsidiaries. The problems appear in both British and German subsidiaries, although the aspects emphasized may differ.

PARTICULAR PARENT–SUBSIDIARY PROBLEMS

These are problems which are specific to one of the cross-cultural relationships but not the other. They refer to the same areas of friction in both, namely: (i) the degree of autonomy allowed to the subsidiary; (ii) the parent company's decision-making approach; and (iii) its strategic and operational management skills. But on these three issues the impact of German parent companies on their British subsidiaries, and British parents on their German subsidiaries, are distinctive.

PARTICULAR PROBLEMS OF BRITISH SUBSIDIARIES AND GERMAN PARENTS

Three problems have been raised by managers in British subsidiaries of German firms. They concern: (i) the lack of autonomy given to the subsidiary; (ii) the rigidity of the parent company's decision-making approach, which is characterized by an emphasis on planning, an over-cumbersome structure, and a lack of flexibility; and (iii) the inadequate strategic skills of parent company managers. The data are shown in Table 7.7.

Subsidiary's degree of autonomy

Three of the formal aspects of subsidiary autonomy have been considered earlier in this chapter in Tables 7.1, 7.2 and 7.3. These showed that the control framework in British and German subsidiaries appears to be generally similar, although there are somewhat more German subsidiaries in Britain having a lesser degree of autonomy. It is within this structural framework that the issues of Table 7.7 are raised.

The issue of inadequate autonomy for decision-making in the subsidiary is raised in subsidiaries of German firms in Britain. In one subsidiary in the

Table 7.7 *Particular problems of British subsidiaries and German parent companies*

Subsidiary's degree of autonomy	
Pushing products onto the subsidiary	8
Parent company decision-making approach	
Excessive emphasis on planning	4
Inward looking	7
Over-complicated management structure	18
Rigidity in following rules and procedures	10
Job demarcation	4
Poor strategic management in parent company	6
Total	57

engineering industry, the British manager, when asked what he would like to change in the subsidiary's relationship with the parent company, made a plea for more autonomy. He said that he would like to change:

> Them [the parent company] being able to make strategic decisions, and allowing us to duly participate, or even do our own.

And the British Corporate Director in a large German chemical subsidiary in Britain said:

> They [the parent company] would like to have direct control of the business units in the UK. This has an influence on the motivation of staff here. The Germans would like to get rid of the corporate body here. They use cutting costs as an excuse.

Pushing products onto the subsidiary

A practice which is regarded by managers of subsidiaries as an extreme instance of reducing their autonomy is that of the parent company forcing them to take quantities of products for reasons quite unrelated to host country market demand. This issue of pushing products was raised by eight subsidiaries in Britain. The comments of a British MD of a trading subsidiary are typical:

In certain products we have the leading market share. But we are also trading in products which are by-products of manufacture for those companies which our parent company owns. Their strategy is to buy up trading companies to sell their manufactured by-products. They [the parent company] have products they want to get rid of, and they push them on us.

A more extreme example is given by the British MD of a subsidiary in Britain of a large German engineering company. When asked what was the subsidiary's main purpose, he replied:

To sell the products of the parent company at a profit which should [just] sustain the operation here. They [the parent company] can control our costs more if we do not make a profit. The evidence suggests that the situation is fairly similar in other subsidiaries of 'XY' [the parent company].

The manager explained his view of the situation:

At the end of the year they need to get rid of their stocks, and they [the parent company] dump them on us. The first three months of a year are locked in, and they are not interested whether it is realistic. Their whole management and accounting system for sales is wrong. When they ship a machine to us, that counts as a sale on their management accounts. But they do not admit the consolidated accounts. Management in 'XY' [company name] is a fiddle, because they [the senior managers in the parent company] have a personal interest in the business. I had enormous rows with them. At the end of the year they used to take all the machines left over and dump them on our order. Our stock in May was worth a sum which was ten times the sum of our annual turnover! Liabilities moved from a country with low interest rates to one with the highest. We then had to raise a loan half the amount of our annual turnover, so that a small company in the UK can be used as a sales dump. Their excuse is that it keeps the factory going. It is a production led-company.

The problem of pushing unwanted products onto a subsidiary was mentioned only by British subsidiaries of German parent companies. The examples given suggest that a strict planning system, as described below, is likely to entail disadvantages as well as advantages for the subsidiary. While it offers measurable yardsticks to oversee production performance, it may also encourage an emphasis on manipulating book figures divorced from real performance in the market. In a classic centre–

periphery conflict, it is difficult for a subsidiary to accept that, from the parent company's point of view, such a manipulation may be to the overall longer-term benefit of the corporation.

German parent company decision-making approach

Decision making in German firms has been characterized in Chapter 6 as highly institutionalised. It is based on detailed forward planning, emphasizing the use of appropriate structures and procedures, and valuing transparency and consensus to gain commitment. It is clear that these characteristics may cause problems for managers in foreign subsidiaries.

Excessive emphasis on planning
A comprehensive planning approach to work aids the formalization of procedures and output, and so facilitates their easier control. This is typical of the German approach to management (Hickson and Pugh, 1995). In general, planning can help to maintain good operating efficiency. But whilst German planning was seen as a strength (cf. Chapter 5), the usefulness of applying such a comprehensive approach to all areas of work is sometimes questioned. Four managers in the German subsidiaries in the UK felt that the amount of time and effort spent on planning in the German parent companies is excessive and unjustified. The British MD in a subsidiary of a large German engineering corporation commented:

> The amount of time spent on planning is totally unacceptable. We have a three year plan which is revised ongoingly and updated every June. The system is very difficult. It is very bureaucratic and the information required is excessive with so much detail. The amount of money and effort put into planning is unjustifiable. It leads to slow response coupled with the inability to see the urgency of certain things.

The British MD of a subsidiary in Britain of a large German engineering corporation, when asked what he believes the parent company would like to change in its relationship with the subsidiary, replied:

> They would probably like to see us producing more strategic type marketing planning information. Me, to write more analyses. I call this approach 'Talking more about selling the "As" [products] than selling the As'. We had a three-day strategy workshop. Very interesting. Informative and hard work, but I am not sure what will come out of it.

But not all managers of subsidiaries complain of excessive planning. The benefits of planning were firmly pointed out by the German Chief Executive of a British subsidiary of a major German engineering concern, the management board of which consists of German expatriates. When interviewed in July, the CE said:

> We are currently planning for next year. We have over 20 years of planning experience. It is a routine. We get a formula from Germany. Our attitude is always to do to 150 per cent; British attitude is to muddle through. They do not think in long term, only next quarter.

German parent inward-looking
Both British and German subsidiaries may regard their parent companies as 'inward looking' in regards to their concerns but the grounds on which they do so are different. German parent companies are regarded as insufficiently aware of how business activities operate abroad. The British CE of a German insurance subsidiary in the UK commented:

> There is a big difference between Germany and the UK. We are a much freer market. Germany is bureaucratic. The German supervisory authority [in the insurance industry] still controls policy wordings. There is a strong discipline within the market. ... In our business, the UK is international, Germany is domestic.

And the British Marketing Director in a subsidiary in electrical consumer goods, established by a takeover, commented:

> They [the parent company] consult you [on market strategies] and then they do what they want. All marketing material is done centrally in Germany. For us [in the subsidiaries] they make translations. There is no understanding of anything else than German. All correspondence comes in German, although few people here speak the language.

As discussed in Chapter 4, the German approach to the market is inward looking, as corporate managers find it difficult to accept that other markets have different characteristics.

Overcomplicated management structure of German parent companies
There are many complaints by the managers of British subsidiaries that the management structures of the German parent companies are over-complicated, and therefore inefficient. The British CE of a large German

insurance subsidiary in Britain described his experience with the German parent company's management:

> Everything has to be structured just for the sake of it. Pigeon holes for everything. It is their [the Germans'] strength and weakness. Germans have tidy minds. We [the British] are far more flexible.

The British manager in a subsidiary of a German engineering company commented:

> My fundamental belief is that very, very few in the parent company make any decisions at all. There is a huge chain of command.

A British manager in the HQ of the German subsidiaries in Britain of a large German enginering corporation explained:

> Our Group restructured itself and created worldwide divisions. Instead of reporting to 'XY' [name of the parent company] we report to several divisions. There are separate divisions for individual products. It is a technocratic and fragmented structure. The parent company has a terribly technical management and rules the company as a machine.

A British manager in a subsidiary of a large German engineering organization stated:

> Our German company is not sales oriented. They are technocratic. They do not manage. The managers are highly trained in the engineering field with less practical experience across the board. There is very little contact between the upper and lower management levels. Upper management try to become modern by classifying things by catch words – which they do not take notice of. Everything revolves around the plan. People who are doing the work and are responsible, they never see the managers. When I started there was 'XY' [name of the company founder]. Then the current corporation bought the company. The owner visited the shop floor. The corporation people do not. ... The sales department slows things down, they have less experience and often do not understand our questions.

Rigidity in following rules and procedures by German parent companies
In addition to the overcomplicated structure, with many departments and procedures, British subsidiary managers also consider that their German

colleagues stick to the rules too closely. For example, there is a more bureaucratic emphasis on getting decisions in writing.

The British Managing Director of a German subsidiary in specialized clothing, when asked what was the first thing he had to learn when he first became involved in Anglo–German collaboration, replied:

> The German accent on controlling. Controlling is a very important factor for a German company.

And to the question of what would the manager like to change in the subsidiary's relationship with the parent company, he replied:

> We are slyer than the main board [of the German parent company]. I would like to change a lot of little things. Just day-to-day bits. I am not a fan of German management. They do not stimulate initiative; there are rules for everything. They are not real life managers. I take all the flexibility I need.

The British MD of a German engineering subsidiary commented:

> [In the parent company] there is a greater necessity to get things in writing. They are bureaucratic or highly professional or something between the two.

The British CE of a British engineering subsidiary in Germany, with much experience in that country, put this inclination of German management to get everything down in writing in a much broader cultural context:

> Just look at the administration here [in Germany]. Everything needs to be put on paper. In England we rely on "what is fair and reasonable", and thus emphasise the spirit of the law rather than the letter of it. If you transgress against the spirit of the law in England, you are for it. Here you have to contradict the letter of the law in order to be for it. And if you find a hole, you get off. And therefore the paper-war gets bigger and bigger, because people try to fill any holes with papers. I can give you an example. You might ask me to build you a plant for the production of sulphuric acid. I think it is easier to build it than define in over 40 pages exactly what is to be done. So what happens if I complete the plant and it does not work? If applying the British spirit of the law, I am for it. If applying the German letter of the law, I only need to refer you to page 38 where it says that the plant should really not be built, and I get off.

The rigidity of the decision-making process was mentioned as a weakness of German parent companies. One British manager in a large German chemical subsidiary in Britain, with many years of experience working in Germany for the parent company, when asked what are the subsidiary's main internal limitations replied:

> Rigid central control, both in a negative and a positive sense; delegating authority. The decision-making processes are arduous. But I know the machinery and I know how to oil the machinery.

The British MD in an electronics subsidiary commented on the parent company's approach:

> I find them [managers in the parent company] more serious. They would never admit a mistake. I struggle with them in relaxing. They are quite formal. Sometimes I feel in admin and control they are a bit harder and harsher. They tend to avoid risk, would not take a chance as I would. Younger people are far more genuine and helpful.

The tendency of the German management to stick to appropriate procedures was also acknowledged by some German managers interviewed in Germany. But they emphasized the strengths of a more formal approach. For example, the German Chief Controller of a British subsidiary in Germany in consumer goods said:

> The Germans are naturally much more bureaucratic, but they are also more accurate. The English tend to float on the surface. If we produce a number, we know how we got it, whereas the English are just happy to have some numbers.

Job demarcation

Associated with the practice of complicated management structures in the German companies is job demarcation. The manager's job is precisely defined and the limits of his competence strongly respected. The British Managing Director of a German engineering subsidiary in Britain, when asked what was the first thing he had to learn when he first became involved in Anglo–German co-operation, replied:

> There is a great difference [between German and British companies]. The general employee in Germany will work within much higher hierarchy with much more defined job descriptions. That creates problems. We will often say he is stubborn, as his answer will often be "no",

because it is not within his competence or he does not want to involve himself. In Germany they need to apportion the blame before they tackle the problem. Here [in Britain] we first resolve the problem, and later worry about what was done.

And a German manager in a German subsidiary in electronics in Britain commented:

Whilst specialists here are quite willing to cross the demarcation lines and use initiative, their counterparts in Germany will always follow the procedure. The Germans are very strongly structured and bureaucratic.

A British manager in a British subsidiary of a major German engineering corporation said:

People in Germany may work in a field for 20 years, but need to refer to someone specifically appointed for any particular aspect of work. For instance, a sales engineer with lifetime experience cannot address himself a fairly common aspect of product design, but needs to officially refer to the production engineer, who may be much younger and less experienced than the sales engineer is, just for the sake of following the procedure. It is a very rigid system. It makes the decision-making process slower than it should be. Less rigidity would make our life easier in relation to the customer. The reaction time of the Head Office is twice as long as it ought to be, because the 'system' has to be followed.

Poor strategic management in the German parent company

Some subsidiaries in Britain encounter problems which the managers regard as stemming from the poor strategic management skills exercised in their German parent companies. Table 7.7 shows six mentions of this issue (in only one case were managers in British parent companies regarded as having poor strategic skills). This view of German parent companies is usually combined with a characterization of their operational skills as excellent (9 mentions, compared with only two mentions of British parent companies).

The German parent company's characteristics of poor strategic management combined with good operational management were commented on by the British CE of an engineering subsidiary in Britain. He said:

There is a great tendency for a secure and safe route in Germany [in the parent company]. A German-middle ranked manager would always go for fixed interest rates. Englishmen like speculation. Production line efficiency is second to none. Efficiency in organizing the business is top-heavy. Operational management is OK, strategic is appalling. German managers are not so smart in understanding the market place. Sometimes you have to move quickly to protect yourself in the market place. But they need to spread the responsibility, to get full consensus.

And the British Managing Director of a subsidiary manufacturing car parts, when asked in what areas do they have most difficulty in working together, replied:

They [the German parent company management] should ask questions before coming to conclusions. Strategic decision making, general management, there we do not work well together. There is a failure to understand the differences betwen the German and British economy. Understanding our environment is also still a problem from the commercial point of view. In UK it is different than in another German company. There are big legal differences.

The mentions of poor strategic management in German parent companies tends to be associated with the consensus method of decision making favoured in Germany. The managers describe it as longer-term oriented but slow, inflexible, and allowing personal initiative and responsibility to be avoided. The German chief executive of a German subsidiary in Britain, when asked what he would like to change in the subsidiary's relationship with the parent company, replied:

Time they need to make some decisions. They always mount a very deep insight into future activities. It takes sometimes a bit too long. It is the group policy.

However, it was admitted by both British and German managers to have a number of advantages. These include reliability, and commitment to the decision as a result of the consensus. In addition managers regarded consensus methods as effective when used by the Germans, since they build on a methodical and planned approach in an accepted strategic framework.

This picture can be illustrated through the perceptions of the German CE of a British subsidiary of a German engineering company. In reply to the question what was the company's last major strategic decision and how did it come about, he maintained that:

> I do not make any grand decisions. Politicians think that they can do it. I have not made any strategic decisions whatsoever. I stuck my neck out for the 'XY' site [a recent acquisition in the UK], and lobbied people [in the parent company] to sign it [the deal]. That was it.

And in reply to the question of what does he believe the German partner would like to change in their relationship with the subsidiary, the CE replied:

> They would tell me: 'Sell more'.

This statement of a senior German manager, whose career was all spent with one company, implies that all the decisions he takes are concerned with one underlying stable strategy – long-term continuous company growth in the same product markets. Because of the implicit nature of such an integral strategy, there may well have never been the need to formulate it as such, since it is not likely to be challenged. Hence his concern was limited to manufacturing and sales operations.

This example is a good illustration of the difference in the emphasis between British and German managements. British management emphasizes strategy because it has to survive in a liberal environment where the ability to change direction is often a condition for success, and, not infrequently, a condition of survival. But in Germany the structured environment, stemming from the longer-term orientation of the economic and industrial infrastructure, allows for the emphasis to be shifted to operations.

The comment of a German manager in a British electronics subsidiary illustrates the difference. In reply to the question of what was the first thing he had to get used to when working for a British company, he replied:

> The fast response to business developments, in particular to any negative ones. That was something I had not experienced before.

In general, the nature of the particular problems that British subsidiaries have with their German parent companies are a reflection of the environmental and cultural differences of the the two countries. As discussed in previous chapters, the structured nature of the German environment leads to a concern with succesful operational management, a reliance on comprehensive forward planning, and an emphasis on precision in product quality and correct managerial practice. These strengths in the German environment often become problems for the subsidiary in the liberal British environment. They show there as a lack of strategic skill, rigidity in structure and decision making when flexibility is required, and unwarranted reductions in autonomy.

PARTICULAR PROBLEMS OF GERMAN SUBSIDIARIES AND BRITISH PARENTS

The particular problems of German subsidiaries with their British parent companies are different. They concern: (i) lack of interest in subsidiary affairs; (ii) parent company's decision-making approach, which is characterized as insufficiently defined and inward looking; and (iii) the inadequate operating skills of the parent company managers. The data are shown in Table 7.8.

Degree of autonomy

The issues of subsidiary autonomy raised by German subsidiaries are different from those of their British counterparts. They focus on the different parent company approach, which can be misinterpreted.

Lack of interest in subsidiary affairs
Even the perception that sufficient autonomy is given by the parent company to the subsidiary can have negative connotations. Managers in three German subsidiaries believed that the subsidiaries are given high autonomy due to the importance of the German market and the size of

Table 7.8 *Particular problems of German subsidiaries and British parent companies*

Subsidiary's degree of autonomy	
Lack of interest in subsidiary affairs	3
Parent company decision-making approach	
Insufficiently defined management structure and procedures	2
Inward looking	5
Poor operational management in parent company	5
Total	15

the subsidiaries' contributions to their British parent companies. A German Chief Executive of a British subsidiary in Germany suggested that, provided the subsidiary is performing successfully, the British parent company does not have a great interest in its affairs. He said:

> To the British, the employees in the German subsidiary are simply the 'spinners' [i.e. the lower level workers]. One has to give them a free run. Therefore the British do not object greatly if we take actions on our own behalf.

In contrast, the German CE of a British financial subsidiary noted:

> I find the British style of management very relaxed, but that does not mean that things get neglected. A problem that I noticed with some German employees is that, if they are not sufficiently familiar with the English language and style, they mistakenly presume that they can relax their approach to work in a British company. That, of course, is not the case, and the realization of the mistake always comes as a shock.

The reason for the apparent lower level of interest of British parent companies in the operations of their subsidiaries compared with German parent companies, was commented on by the German MD of a British engineering subsidiary in Germany. He explained:

> The difference between a German and an English firm is in its climate. The controls and all the rest of it depend in principle on the target achievement [in a British company]. We have our targets. One is profit; then it is cash-flow. And the climate changes in accordance with the degree of achievement of these. That means if we report good figures, no questions are asked. Then we can write commentaries which will be, as a rule, believed. But if you start producing bad figures, then the climate is of course, quite different.

But opportunities for a more participative style of management as offered by British senior managers may not always be taken up by the German staff. When asked whether he had introduced a British style of management into his subsidiary, the British Chief Executive of a subsidiary in Germany replied:

> Ah, that is difficult. You try to get anything out of the people, and you will see just how difficult that is. Brainstorming in Germany is really complicated. It all comes down to this attitude: 'I will not tell him

what he would not like to hear.' To undermine such barriers is really almost impossible.

British parent company decision-making approach

A most comprehensive critical view on the decision-making processes in British parent companies was given by the British corporate director in a large British chemical company. Comparing the British and the German styles of decision making, he said:

> In the British companies a decision can be reached on a minority of views. But one of the weaknesses here is that people always feel free to try to undo a decision. This is because everybody questions everything. Germans are much less questioning, but they are clearer in what they do. The individualistic culture slows down decisions. The decision-making process in Germany is more ponderous, but once taken, it is absolute. Here to reach a decision takes a shorter time, but it keeps on being modified afterwards. As a result it is slower. On balance, to reach a decision in Britain is a slower process.

This view has wider cultural implications. If retaining flexibility is important for management in the British environment, then this will compromise the degree of reliability of decision making. In contrast, the stable German environment supports the more lengthy consensus method of decision making, a main feature of which is the reliability of the decision once it has been made.

Insufficiently defined British management structure and procedures
The greater desire by the German managers to rely on clearly defined structures and procedures was endorsed by a German manager in a British subsidiary in Germany, who said:

> The British parent company is responsible for major organizational changes of which we are informed. But the reporting structure is never sufficiently clearly defined by them. For instance, it is never clear which levels of authority in the parent company correspond to which levels of authority in the subsidiary in Germany, and to whom in Britain are individual German departments accountable.

The lack of emphasis on procedure by some British parent companies was noted by the German MD of a British transport company subsidiary.

When he was asked what was the first thing he had to learn when he
started co-operating with the British, he replied:

> I had to get used to their rules of the game. For instance, when they
> [the British parent company] said 'we do this'. Then they went and did
> it; long before it would have been formulated in writing.

That manager did appreciate the British parent company approach.
Similarly, the German Chief Executive of a major British chemical subsidiary in Germany was enthusiastic about the parent company's decision structures:

> In our company all is a matrix. We all have several bosses. It depends on
> the subject. You cannot operate a company effectively if you do not have
> a matrix system. We in the company do not have an organizational chart.
> Each business has their own organization. In Germany everybody has
> their pigeon hole. Here we do not have that. Other German companies
> find it strange... We report business to business. Across departments.
> Depends what it is, and as and when appropriate. ... Last year we were
> the most successful non-German company in Germany.

British inward-looking in approach

The problem of British inwardness as seen by German management is
that British managers are believed not to consider themselves to be a part
of Europe. Therefore British firms are not receptive enough in understanding the continent, and not aggressive enough in European markets.

A German manager in a British engineering subsidiary in Germany said:

> One of the problems [in the collaboration] is that the Brits always
> think in terms of 'England and the Continent'. It was very difficult for
> them to come to terms with the fact that we have here the DIN regula-
> tions." (DIN regulations are the German equivalent of BSI standards.)

This view of British managers' inwardness held in German subsidiaries is shared by others. The German CE of the British subsidiary of
a large German engineering company said:

> UK is not Europe. I never expected that UK is so absolutely different
> than Europe. Attitudes, education, patterns of behaviour, perhaps
> climate. They did not wake up to the fact that the Empire is long gone.
> Brits do not realise anything else than British. Commonwealth market
> is still a reserve market, but they cannot retain it longer. Europe can

survive without the Brits, but the Brits cannot survive without Europe. Success in Britain is overexaggerated. They are kidding. British industries do not realise how far they are behind.

Poor operational management in the British parent company

In contrast to comments on the poor strategic management of German parent companies, German subsidiaries see problems in the poor operational management of their British parents. The British Chief Executive of a subsidiary in mineral extraction in Germany noted:

> The problem in Britain is that everyone always questions everything, and that is why work is seldom concluded in an efficient manner. The advantage here [in Germany] is that work gets done. But the quality of it depends on who gave the instructions. If the instructor is a poor one, then you get problems afterwards, because no one asked: 'Why?'

The German CE of a British subsidiary in Germany in engineering explained that the British parent company is renowned for the top quality of its products worldwide. But in relation to some management issues the manager said:

> The British tend to be sluggish, perhaps conservative. We should have finished building the stock hall that was finished recently, one year earlier. We would have saved the company around DM 150,000. The collaboration [with the British parent company] in all production related matters is cumbersome.

The German Chief Executive of a British subsidiary in Germany producing industrial regulators, when asked what he would like to change in the relationship with the parent company, and, conversely, what he believes that the parent company would like to change in its relationship with the subsidiary, replied:

> We would just like to see when they [the British parent company] start organizing themselves in a more efficient manner, and display a better quality of management ... In turn I should imagine that to the British we moan too much, in particular about the quality of the goods.

As the above quotation illustrates, associated with the inadequacies in operations, comments were made in the subsidiaries about the lower standards of quality of British goods. The German Managing Director of a British subsidiary in consumer goods said:

Quality used to be a problem and we had disagreements [with the parent company] about that. Then they allowed us to establish our own quality control department [for the goods manufactured in the UK], which made things a little easier for us.

From the point of view of the German subsidiaries, these inefficiencies are likely to be associated with the British employees' lower degree of work discipline and identification with their employers (as discussed in Chapter 6 above). In addition the lack of apprenticeships and middle level qualifications on the shop floor are relevant, as discussed in Chapter 5 above.

CONCLUSION ON PARTICULAR PARENT–SUBSIDIARY PROBLEMS

The particular parent–subsidiary problems shown in Tables 7.7 and 7.8 reflect the differing emphasis in the two cultures on the degree to which structures and procedures are defined and followed. Whilst the German parent companies are believed to be strictly structured and relying on defined procedures by their British subsidiaries, the British parent companies are more likely to be seen as insufficiently structured by their German subsidiaries. The German insistence on procedural definitions is perceived by their British subsidiaries as 'technocratic' management. The British preference for procedural flexibility is perceived by their German subsidiaries as a lack of procedural and organizational clarity.

The German approach reduces scope for initiative and improvization which the British managers in the subsidiaries tend to perceive as frustrating. The British approach increases the degree of uncertainty which the German subsidiary managers, as part of their structured approach to work, prefer to avoid. An understanding of the strengths and weaknesses of both approaches in relation to different areas of work is likely to reduce the scope for possible misunderstandings and enables a positive utilization of the strengths of each, as will be discussed in Chapter 8.

CONCLUSIONS

The formal structures of parent–subsidiary relationships, as shown in Tables 7.1, 7.2, 7.3 and 7.5, do not appear to show great differences between British and German multinational corporations. The ranges of differences in functional autonomy, control mechanisms, communication channels and target setting are similar in both groups in the sample. The generic problems of excessive corporate bureaucracy and slow intracompany response generated at the interface between parent companies and their subsidiaries of both nationalities are also similar and typical of centre-periphery issues, as shown in Table 7.4. Cross-cultural problems focus on a number of comparable topics such as language issues and barriers to corporate integration, but these show greater differences in management approach (Table 7.6). The particular problems discussed of British subsidiaries with German parent companies, such as rigidity in following rules and procedures (Table 7.7), and German subsidiaries with British parent companies such, as poor operational management (Table 7.8), diverge considerably.

Table 7.9 summarizes the characteristics of the British and German parent companies' approaches to the management of foreign subsidiaries. The less well-specified organizational procedures of the British approach puts a high value on flexibility. Speed of decision making is favoured, encouraging the granting of more autonomy to subsidiaries. This is viable because the parent company's concern focuses on strategic decisions, allowing more scope for the subsidiary to utilize oportunities at the operational level. The general approach may be viewed as congruent

Table 7.9   *British and German parent company approaches to the management of foreign subsidiaries*

British (liberal)	German (structured)
Organizational procedures	
Less well-specified	Highly specified
Flexibility valued	Reliability valued
Decision making	
Transparency neglected in favour of speed	Transparency emphasised at the expense of speed
Autonomy	
More autonomy with lower degree of centralization	More centralized planning with less autonomy
More scope for subsidiary to utilise opportunities	Easier control and co-ordination by the parent company
Content of decision making	
More concern with strategy	More concern with operations

with the liberal nature of the British economic and industrial environment as discussed above.

The more highly specified procedures of the German approach, based on more detailed centralized planning, puts a higher weight on accuracy and reliability. The emphasis on transparency and propriety in decision making, at the expense of speed, reduces subsidiary autonomy and facilitates easier control and co-ordination by the parent company. This is viable because the parent company's concerns focus on operational management. This general approach is congruent with the structured nature of the German environment as illustrated in earlier chapters.

Both approaches have strengths and limitations. As shown in this chapter, both throw up distinctive problems which form the pitfalls awaiting a firm from one country wishing to operate in the other. These are discussed in Chapter 8 below, together with the potential benefits that are available if effective collaboration across the cultures can be developed.

8 Pitfalls and Potentials in Anglo–German Business Collaboration

'The legal side of things here [in Germany] is very demanding, the tax situation and the operating principles of German companies are really complicated. A Brit is bound to find it difficult to understand how Mitbestimmung works. Although these things have their advantages, of course, the British are bound to be horrified by all of it. But I should imagine that a German coming to Britain must find it equally difficult. You move from a clearly defined formal environment into a world of uncertainty.' British Chief Executive of a subsidiary in mineral extraction in Germany

'The Germans are best at being efficient and organizing; the British are best at being creative and improvizing. Their combination gives the best of everything.' German Chief Executive of a subsidiary in light engineering in Britain

The nature of the British and German environments has been shown in this study to be contrasting, and British and German cultures seen as orientated towards different, and often divergent, values. The business conditions, practices and market expectations in each country reflect the different characters of their two environments. The 'structured' national environment of Germany presents barriers to British companies in entering and operating there. Similarly, the 'liberal' national environment of Britain offers obstacles to German companies.

When these barriers are unrecognized, or not overcome, they become pitfalls which hamper, and may destroy, cross-cultural business ventures. The success of company operations in the host country will depend on its managers' ability to deal with the differences effectively. Companies considering exploring the opportunities which the German and British markets present need to learn about them. They will then be in a position to realistically assess their own position in relation to entry and operation.

This recognition and assessment of the difficulties is the first stage in the management process of avoiding or overcoming the pitfalls. In the second stage, companies will have to provide the management knowledge and skill to capitalize on the different strengths and weaknesses in both environments. Successful cross-cultural management is based on balancing these to achieve an optimal combined output. A company needs the ability to adjust its strategy and operations to the different conditions in the host environment. If this is achieved, then the very existence of environmental and cultural differences provides a basis for the considerable potential for successful business activity.

Based on the experiences of 99 companies operating at the business interface between the two countries, this study has identified the key difficulties involved. In this chapter, we shall, first, summarize the barriers which could become pitfalls to the unwary. Second, we examine some of the practical ways in which the potential of Anglo–German business collaboration can be exploited.

VARIATIONS IN BARRIERS ACCORDING TO INDUSTRY

The difficulties of entry into an environmentally different host market do not apply equally to all industries and types of operations. As discussed in Chapter 3, different industries have different environmental requirements. Their degree of sensitivity to variations in environmetal conditions also differs: some are more dependent on the nature of the environment than others. These variations have to be taken into account in understanding the nature and impact of the barriers in each business situation.

Table 8.1 gives an overview of the degree of dependence on, and the congruence with, the British and German environments of the different industries found in the sample. As analyzed in Chapter 3, specific industries (such as finance and publishing) are the most highly dependent on the environment, indifferent industries (such as commodities), the least. Industries harmonious with the environment of a country have a considerable level of dependence. The table shows that industries harmonious with the British environment, such as biotechnology, are dichotomous with the German environment. Similarly, industries harmonious with the German environment, such as mechanical engineering, are dichotomous with the British one.

These industry differences must be taken in account when estimating the strength of the barriers. Three classes of barriers can be identified:

(i)   Those arising as the result of *environmental* differences between Britain and Germany (as discussed in Chapter 3).

Table 8.1   *Congruence of industries with the British and German environments (with their degree of environmental dependence)*

Specific	Harmonious with UK (dichotomous G)	Harmonious with G (dichotomous UK)	Indifferent
highly dependent	*dependent*	*dependent*	*less dependent*
banking	biotechnology	mechanical engineering	commodities
publishing	flexible electronic systems	chemical	consumer goods, e.g. food, clothing
	consumer electronics specialities	electrical materials for the building industry	transport services mineral extraction

(ii)   Those arising from *market* differences (Chapter 4).

(iii) Those caused by differences between the two countries in *organizational behaviour* (Chapters 5 and 6).

Based on the problems identified in those chapters, a listing of the business barriers between Britain and Germany, and their intensity across the range of industrial types has been constructed. These will be discussed in the following sections.

BARRIERS TO BRITISH OPERATIONS IN GERMANY

The barriers to British companies in Germany as shown in Table 8.2 are considerable. The number of asterisks shown indicates the intensity of the barriers. They vary though, according to whether environmental, market or organizational behaviour barriers are being considered. The variation is even greater across industry types. An inspection of the table suggests that environmentally specific industries have the greatest strength of barriers, followed by those industries in harmony with Germany. The environmentally indifferent industries have a lesser strength of problems, and those industries environmentally dichotomous with Germany have the weakest barriers. We shall now examine in more detail the barriers applicable to the various types of industries.

Table 8.2   *Barriers to British operations in Germany*

Barriers	Specificity	Harmony with Germany	Dichotomy with Germany	Indifference
A. Environmental (ch. 3)				
1. Substantial initial investment likely to be required	***	***	*	**
2. Long term presence required	***	***	*	**
3. Continual investment intensity required		***	*	*
4. Entry likely to require the takeover of an established indigenous company	***	**	*	*
5. Need for integration into the industrial infrastructure	***	**	*	*
6. Regulatory restrictions to operations	***	**	*	**
7. High degree of managerial flexibility required	*	*		*
B. Market (ch. 4)				
1. Domesticated market resenting foreign entry	***	***		**
2. Subject to extensive approval procedures	***	**	**	**
3. Different market infrastructure	***	***	*	**
4. Differences in technical specifications	***	***	*	*
5. Different market approach required	**	**	**	**
6. Differences in customer product preference	**	**	**	***
C. Organizational Behaviour (ch. 5, 6)				
1. Language differences	*	*	*	*
2. Differences in qualifications and skills of German employees	**	*	***	
3. Differences in decision making	***	**	*	*
4. Differences in management style	***	**	*	*
5. Differences in interpersonal relationships	**	*	*	*
6. Differences in the nature of employment	***	*		
7. Differences in motivation	**	**	*	*

ENVIRONMENTAL BARRIERS TO BRITISH OPERATIONS IN GERMANY

The German industrial environment is structured, and less easily accessible for foreign competitors. In general, compared to Britain, it takes longer in all industries to become established in Germany and requires more capital input. An important indicator of establishment is the degree to which a foreign company becomes accepted by the German industrial infrastructure (such as technical supervisory bodies, local trade associations). But within this general position, considerable variation according to type of industry exists.

Environmentally specific industries

The main problem for environmentally specific industries is the lack of demand in the host markets for their products. The characteristics of the German finance market, for example, are different in many respects from the British one: 'In Germany people strive for safety. There is a developed fixed rate finance market, and people pay on time.' Because of this fundamental difference, establishment in the market requires substantial initial capital investment (barrier A1). Four out of 5 UK financial subsidiaries in Germany in the study named 'establishment in the host market' as their main target – even though one of them has been operating there for 71 years! (barrier A2). Since the industry does not use capital equipment such as heavy machinery, the demand for continuous capital investment is absent (absence of barrier A3).

Typically a foothold in the market is gained through the acquisition of an established indigenous company (barrier A4). This is likely to entail some resentment within the company taken over, partly because of the specificity of the operations, as the examples of resistance to corporate identification in Chapter 7 illustrate. Compared to Britain, the German finance industry is characterised by such activities as: greater consideration given to the non-financial potential of a client company in relation to loans, the granting of unsecured bank loans to companies, a lesser willingness to call in receivers as soon as financial liabilities exceed current assets, and a more supportive export credit finance system. A British firm will have to conform to these requirements (barrier A5) and also with the greater regulatory restrictions, in particular in insurance services. 'The nature of our business has a very strict legal background, we have to have standardised products.' (barrier A6).

Because of the difference in the range of company activities between the home and host environments, and the need to adjust to the different conditions in the host environment, a certain amount of managerial flexibility is required (barrier A7).

Industries harmonious with the German environment

In industries in harmony with the German environment, British firms operate from a base of dichotomy in their home environment. They therefore enter from a position of environmental disadvantage. In order to counteract this, such companies have to undertake a considerable, and sometimes long-term, initial investment in Germany (barrier A1). Thus 'Company GC' in Chapter 4 (p. 92), a car manufacturer, had to carry the losses of its German subsidiary for 15 years before establishing a niche in the market. If that input proves to be successful, however, then the operation in the host environment can compensate the parent company for its handicap (see, for example, 'Company KA' in Chapter 3 (p. 58), manufacturing engine parts for the automobile industry). Companies in a situation of home country dichotomy, which may not be in the position to exercise a substantial degree of initial investment, have slim chances of a success in Germany (e.g. 'Company IA' in the machine tool industry in Chapter 3 (p. 55), in the situation of the handicap of the parent company).

In Germany the sound reputation of a firm is traditionally more important than offering special deals. 'German customers need to buy the company first before buying its products.' Customers carefully examine the past record of a company before entering into important deals with it (barrier A2). 'The problem is, that when we started the "Company IA" name was good, only later we have lost a good name, and you cannot change that now. ...With a German name it would be somewhat easier.' In addition, particular industrial operations are likely to be subject to more detailed regulation in Germany than in Britain; for example, in relation to environmental pollution in the chemical industry. This is likely to slow down any implementation of change. The establishment of new production facilities or the introduction of a change in technology by a British parent company may thus have to be delayed in its German operations compared to Britain (barrier A6).

In these industries, harmonious with the German environment, but dichotomous with the British environment, British companies with limited financial potential are likely to find that the barriers and difficulties develop into a pitfall.

Industries dichotomous with the German environment

It is always expensive to establish operations in Germany in all industries, but for those industries in environmental harmony with Britain, and therefore in a dichotomous situation in regard to Germany, entry should be easier. They have greater support from their home environment than their competitors in Germany. Returns may also be generated faster. Thus 'Company BA' in Chapter 3 (p. 42), in the sector of consumer electronics, grew from zero to DM 305 million turnover in three years. 'Company BC' in Chapter 3 (p. 43) became sufficiently established to focus on its English name, dropping the word *Deutsche* from its title. The barriers listed in Table 8.2 are therefore much weaker than for other industrial types.

But some of the typical German barriers may still apply, though to a much lesser degree than, for example, in heavy engineering. For example, operations in pharmaceuticals and biotechnology are highly regulated and restricted (barrier A6).

Environmentally indifferent industries

In this situation the managerial requirements of the industry are environmentally indifferent; that is, the differences between the environments do not have a decisive influence on the company's output. For example, in the food and clothing industries, fashion changes do not require substantial industrial adjustments. However, this does not mean that there are no barriers, particularly compared to those industries in dichotomy with Germany, as Table 8.2 shows. Indifferent industries are highly competitive with the presence of indigenous suppliers (who are not disadvantaged) or, indeed, other foreign competitors.

The general barriers to entry and presence typical for Germany still apply, that is, initial capital investment is required (barrier A1), long-term presence is necessary for acceptance in the market (barrier A2), and regulatory restrictions on the industry are likely to be greater (barrier A6).

MARKET BARRIERS TO BRITISH OPERATIONS IN GERMANY

In general, the German market is more domesticated. Both industrial and private customers prefer to buy German products rather than those of foreign manufacturers. A longer market presence is therefore necessary in order to acquire a reputation for offering appropriate high quality products. A product may be considered inappropriate for four reasons:

(i)   Its quality or range may be insufficient in relation to the higher expectations of the German market. This problem appears to be typical for companies in the situation of dichotomy in relation to the host market.

(ii) A specific portfolio may not have the same market appeal in Germany as in Britain. The differences in market appeal relate to the differences in values between the cultures which are reflected in different customer preferences (e.g. 'Company GC' in Chapter 4, p. 92, in car manufacture shows how the product had to be developed to appeal to the host market).

(iii) The product may be inappropriate for the different needs in the host market. This would be likely to apply to environmentally specific industries, such as the finance industry or publishing.

(iv) Product specification and licensing in particular industries (for example, the pharmaceutical industry) are likely to be subject to stricter and more lengthy approval procedures in Germany than in Britain.

These barriers will develop into a pitfall if companies fail to recognise the existing market differences, and endeavour to offer the identical home country range of products in both countries.

Environmentally specific industries

The highest potential for market related problems occurs in environmentally specific industries. Both their products and operations are designed to suit specific environments (barrier B4). Whilst in other industries merely an adjustment to the product may suffice in order to satisfy the culturally distinctive demands of the German market, in the environmentally specific industries the differences are so great that, typically, a different product range is required (barrier B6). The problems caused for British financial subsidiaries in Germany, for example, are underlined by the comment that all industrial clients of all non-German banks in Germany represent only about 3 per cent of the market (barrier B1).

Industries harmonious with the German environment

For industries harmonious with the German environment, British subsidiaries are disadvantaged in their market whilst their home competitors have the advantage of their environment. Thus, for example, British heavy engineering is handicapped in Germany from two points of view: First, it is in an extremely competitive market where home producers have the advantage of harmony, and the market in this industry is thus used to very high technical standards (barrier B4). Second, the market is used to German selling techniques (barrier B5).

A key barrier is the 'way in which the German market works'. Because of the structured nature of the market compared to the British, a correct understanding of the market infrastructure in Germany is vital. The learning process about its dynamics will take time, typically some years. Trade associations, agents, suppliers and distributors, need to be acknowledged in appropriate ways in order to be able to enter effectively into the appropriate business community, and to become accepted by it (barrier B3). This, too, requires time, since foreign companies are not easily accepted, but the worth of long-standing company and personal relationships in business in Germany cannot be overestimated (barrier B1). This is because conducting business is done on a more personal basis, and in corporate relations having a long-standing good reputation is a fundamental consideration for being accepted as a business partner (barrier B3).

Technical product performance specifications, product quality and reliability are important matters in the German market, which stresses the latest developments in technology, high performance and reliability. Products are subject to extensive approval procedures (barrier B2). In this sector, more than in any other, the German market prides itself on its high quality and high price. Traditionally, in this way of thinking, one could not 'overengineer' (barrier B6). But in recent years the pressures for competitive production worldwide have led to some indications of a growing price consciousness even here. This might, in time, lead to a weakening of these barriers.

Industries dichotomous with the German environment

In general, industries in dichotomy with Germany have easier access because the indigenous suppliers are disadvantaged. For example, in consumer electronics, (e.g. 'Company BD' and 'Company BA' in Chapter 4, p. 93) the problems experienced are minor. 'Company BA' is flourishing; its product is acceptable (barrier B4) and so is its overall market approach (barrier B5). In the six UK subsidiaries in this industry in the sample, only three mentions of any problems in the German market were reported. This suggests that for this industry, the British market approach can also be effective in Germany.

But in relation to other dichotomous industries, such as the pharmaceutical industry and biotechnology, product specifications and licensing are subject to stricter and more lengthy approval procedures in Germany than in Britain (barrier B2). Indeed this degree of regulation may be one of the reasons why these industries are in a dichotomy in Germany, being less progressive compared with Britain.

Environmentally indifferent industries

In environmentally indifferent industries, such as consumer goods, the national environment is of little importance for the industry's operations. But in the German market, differences relating to customer preferences become pronounced. The marketing approach must therefore close the gap between the products and the market expectations, by adjusting the products (barrier B4) or influencing the market's preferences through advertising (barrier B5), or both. In the German market the overall product quality needs to be emphasised more. As discussed in Chapter 4, 'value for money' is not as attractive a consideration in Germany as it tends to be in Britain, and 'cheap' is generally unattractive. As Table 4.2 shows, for the German market in general the most effective competitive advantages are the quality and reliability of the product, and its high performance specifications (barrier B6).

ORGANIZATIONAL BEHAVIOUR BARRIERS TO BRITISH OPERATIONS IN GERMANY

The organizational behaviour problems of British companies in relation to German staff primarily relate to management style and interpersonal relationships. Since German managers speak English much more frequently than British managers speak German, a language barrier can arise from their restricted degree of understanding of the idiomatic nature of spoken and written English. Although German staff appear to cope reasonably well with the more personal and relaxed style of management of their British managers, misunderstandings sometimes occur, as when the British style of understatement is misinterpreted as a relaxed attitude to work.

Two of the most frequent comments that the British parent companies make in relation to German staff concern: (i) the tendency on the part of the managers to rigidly follow procedures; and (ii) the clear separation made between work and socializing. From the British parent companies' a dissatisfaction is felt with German staff due to 'lack of creativity', 'bureaucratic attitude' and 'social distance'. Typical comments include: 'They are clerical people, not problem solving', 'Everything in Germany takes longer, because procedure needs to be followed'. Interpersonal relationships in Germany are found to be less smooth and more alienating than in Britain. 'They keep themselves to themselves, they are afraid of getting on the wrong side of their bosses.' The professional jealousy, associated with the more intense career ambitions of many German managers, is a more important motivating factor in Germany than it tends to be in Britain, where, for many managers, personal enjoyment at work is seen as important.

The decision-making processes in German corporations are regarded as more cumbersome and slow, as the result of the consensus method used. Its strength is in reducing the amount of risk involved in a decision, but owing to the time it takes to make a 'sound decision', fast-developing opportunities can be missed. An advantage of the method is its reliability by gaining the commitment of all involved.

Any of these differences, if not understood and managed appropriately, will become a barrier to effective operations. Compared to environmental and market barriers, much less variation occurs across the types of industry. Organizational behaviour is much more affected by culture than by the environment.

Environmentally specific industries

In the environmentally specific industries, the above organizational behaviour barriers apply, and some aspects will become more pronounced.

In the finance industry, for example, the position and motivation of managers can be very different from that of their British counterparts, since decision making in regard to lending in Germany is based on personal relationships and trust as opposed to the emphasis on securities in Britain (barrier C3). Thus, managers in Germany enjoy a higher degree of personal freedom in decision making. The lack of understanding of this difference can be a barrier and, if overlooked, can turn into a pitfall as the examples in Chapter 6 show (barrier C7).

Industries harmonious with the German environment

These are the traditional German industries with their characteristic emphasis on relevant technical qualifications and long-term continuity in employment. Their operations benefit from a disciplined approach to work with attention to technical detail. These are not identified as amongst the British strengths. At the interface, these differences, together with those in decision making and management style, become particularly relevant. Because these industries are likely to include major deals, such as plant purchase in heavy engineering, the substantial interaction required on both sides can generate problems. At contract negotiations, for example, German customers typically regard British salesmen as lacking sufficient technical knowledge and being inadequately prepared for the necessary detailed examination of the issues raised. They may thus spend 'most of the time on the telephone to the head office'.

Industries dichotomous with the German environment

The operations of industries dichotomous with the German environment, such as flexible information systems and biotechnology, are fast-changing and rely strongly on specialised skills which are not equally available in Germany. The lack of qualified personnel can be a barrier (barrier C2). The British employers may need to subsidise their German staff with the skills and expertise of British specialists in these areas. For example, in the German subsidiary of 'Company DA' in Chapter 3 (p. 45), supplying flexible electronic systems, approximately 50 per cent of software engineers are British.

Environmentally indifferent industries

In these industries only the general differences in organizational behaviour described above were found to apply.

BARRIERS TO GERMAN OPERATIONS IN BRITAIN

The barriers for German companies in the UK are shown in Table 8.3. In general, they appear to be less strong than those shown in Table 8.2 in relation to British operations in Germany, and they are of a different nature. As before, they vary according to whether environmental, market or organizational barriers are being considered, and across industry types. Again the environmentally specific industries appear to have the most formidable barriers, followed by those industries in harmony with Britain. The environmentally indifferent industries encounter weaker bar-

Table 8.3 *Barriers to German operations in Britain*

Barriers	Specificity	Harmony with Britain	Dichotomy with Britain	Indifference
A. *Environmental* (ch. 3)				
1. Substantial initial investment likely to be required	**	*		
2. Long term presence required	**			
3. Continual investment intensity required				
4. Entry likely to require the takeover of an established indigenous company	***	*		
5. Need for integration into the industrial infrastructure	**			
6. Regulatory restrictions to operations				
7. High degree of managerial flexibility required	***	***	**	***
B. *Market* (ch. 4)				
1. Domesticated market resenting foreign entry	**			
2. Subject to extensive approval procedures				
3. Different market infrastructure	**			
4. Differences in technical specifications	***	**		
5. ifferent market approach required	***	***		***
6. Differences in customer product preference	***	***	*	***
C. *Organizational Behaviour* (ch. 5, 6)				
1. Language differences	*	*	*	*
2. Differences in qualifications and skills of British employees		**	***	**
3. Differences in decision making	***	**	**	*
4. Differences in management style	**	*	*	*
5. Differences in interpersonal relationships	**	*	*	*
6. Differences in the nature of employment	*		**	*
7. Differences in motivation	**	**	*	*

riers than these, and those industries environmentally dichotomous with Britain have the weakest barriers. We shall now examine in more detail the barriers applicable to the various types of industries.

ENVIRONMENTAL BARRIERS TO GERMAN OPERATIONS IN BRITAIN

The British industrial environment is characterized as liberal, but that does not mean that it does not present barriers for entry to German companies. But the nature of the barriers differs from those encountered in Germany. They are less formalized in that they consist of fewer regulations and explicitly formulated operational restrictions. The barriers primarily comprise the need for a sound understanding of the strategic and operating characteristics applicable to conducting business in Britain. This means understanding the British environment, and the ways in which business can be efficiently conducted there.

A major feature of the industrial infrastructure in Britain compared to Germany is that it is less clearly defined, less centralized and less cohesive in character. This can present drawbacks as well as advantages for German companies in Britain. Because of the relative lack of legal and institutional backing, the transparency of the infrastructure is lower. Fewer rules may apply, but those that do may be more difficult to comply with if host companies are not familiar with the principles according to which they work. They are less likely to be spelled out legally or bureaucratically. The emphasis is on socializing with professional colleagues and competitors to establish and maintain 'good business practice'. A major overall difference in Britain compared to Germany is the much greater demand on managerial flexibility. A company's inability to cope with the faster dynamics of the British business environment may well present as formidable a barrier as those resulting from restrictive regulations. The problems of the home entertainment company 'Company FA' in Chapter 4 (p. 86) in adapting to the British market are a good example.

Environmentally specific industries

In the liberal UK environment, financial services are seen as an industry which has the right to operate on the same basis as any other industry. Thus it is expected to cater primarily for its own survival and profits. It is not subject to the same restrictions or limited to set procedures as in Germany. But because the market requires products which differ fundamentally from those offered in Germany (such as different insurance policies) substantial initial investment in the host environment may be required for gaining a market share (barrier A1) and a quick establishment even in a liberal environment is unlikely (barrier A2).

Entry through a takeover is common even in Britain, in particular for corporate customers (barrier A4). One German manager in a financial subsidiary in Britain commented: 'One of the problems [for the company] is that in Britain the "old-boys' network" in this industry is very strong' (barrier A5). Because of the major changes to German products which have to be developed in this industry, which is less regulated than the German financial industry, managerial flexibility is a major asset required for success (barrier A7).

Industries harmonious with the British environment

These industries, such as consumer electronics and pharmaceuticals, do not have major specific environmental barriers in addition to the general ones of entering and operating in the British environment as described above. Some investment may be required in order to accommodate the different demands and expectations in the British market (barrier A1), and gaining market share may be easier if an established company is taken over (barrier A4). But the largest barrier is the need for managerial flexibility, which is very high in these industries (barrier A7). As discussed in Chapter 3, this is because flexibility is required on many levels. First, the UK environment as a whole is less stable than Germany. Second, the industrial environment is faster, and product specifications change frequently. 'Company FA' in Chapter 3 (p. 49) in home entertainments illustrates these barriers.

Industries dichotomous with the British environment

These industries (e.g. mechanical engineering, chemicals) are strong in their supportive harmonious German home environment. They also have an advantage in Britain, where their indigenous competitors are in a dichotomous disadvantage. The liberal structure of the British environment also allows easier access. German companies in these industries have a good reputation and this 'opens doors' (such as 'Company CA' in Chapter 3 (p. 44) in precision engineering, which can sell a range of innovative high quality products backed up by good service, drawing on the support of its German company). Therefore, only very weak barriers are listed for this industry type in Table 8.3. The one exception is that of managerial flexibility (barrier A7), which is always a necessity in the British market.

Environmentally indifferent industries

For industries environmentally indifferent (such as commodities or consumer goods) the British market offers relatively few and weak barriers to operations, as shown in Table 8.3. As before, the British market has to be understood and changes made in the product to suit it. 'Company LB' in Chapter 4 (p. 88) in the food industry became successful when it made the relatively small changes needed to appeal to a speciality British market, while developing market volume through its own label supplies. This example again emphasizes the need for managerial flexibility (barrier A7), and, as frequently happens, this was obtained through replacing the German Managing Director with an Englishman.

MARKET BARRIERS TO GERMAN OPERATIONS IN BRITAIN

Because the British market is more liberal and less domesticated, on the whole it presents fewer restrictions for foreign competitors than the German market. As was discussed above, this lower institutionalization of the British infrastructure can have negative consequences if it is not understood and managed. The nature of the products offered in the market must be seen as appropriate. A product may be considered inappropriate for three reasons:

   (i)   Its quality or range may be insufficient in relation to the particular expectations in the British market. This problem appears to be typical for companies in the situation of dichotomy in relation to the host market. For example, in Chapter 4 (p. 86) the range of 'Company FA's' products did not have a feature that every other brand offered.
  (ii)   A particular range of products may not have the same market appeal in Britain. Differences between the cultures are reflected in different customer preferences as is shown by the example of 'Company LC' in Chapter 4 (p. 89) in kitchen furniture. This company had continually to fight for the retention in its portfolio of a product popular in Britain but not in Germany.

(iii)   The product may be inappropriate for the different needs in the host market. This would be likely to apply to environmentally specific industries (such as finance industry and publishing) which would have difficulty in offering identical products to compete with indigenous offerings.

These barriers develop into a pitfall if companies fail to recognize the existing market differences, and endeavour to offer the identical products in both countries.

Environmentally specific industries

The highest potential for market related problems occurs in environmentally specific industries, since their products and operations are designed to suit specific environments. Whilst in other industries an adjustment to the product may suffice in order to satisfy the culturally distinctive demands of the host market, in the environmentally specific industries the differences are so great that, typically, a different product range is required.

In the UK, financial services are more flexible and individual, with such products as credit cards and non-standard insurance (barrier B4). In competitive situations, British insurers are much more flexible in their willingness to take on risks compared to the German insurance industry. 'The British are very flexible, they have it in their stomachs' (barrier B5). German banks are far behind the UK banks technically, and in terms of know-how in these fields. For example, 'Company ME' in Chapter 4 (p. 82) in insurance needed to generate a completely new product portfolio for the British market because the parent company's German products were uncompetitive (barrier B5). But it is also the case that the one single mention in the whole study of a 'Buy British' attitude was made by a manager of a German subsidiary in the insurance industry.

Industries harmonious with the British environment

Subsidiaries in these industry types are handicapped by an extremely competitive British market, used to high standards promoted by British marketing techniques. There is a requirement for a different market approach from Germany with an emphasis on appropriate consumer marketing (barrier B5). For example, 'Company FA' in Chapter 4 in consumer electronics had to reorientate both its product portfolio and sales outlets in order to stay in business (barrier B6).

Industries dichotomous with the British environment

As explained in Chapter 3, German industries such as heavy engineering and chemicals have a clear advantage in Britain over indigenous competitors. This is illustrated by the minor nature of the few marketing problems occuring in these industries. As the example of 'Company AG' in Chapter 4 (p. 91) in heavy engineering suggests, there is a need to adapt to some extent to the demands of the British customers, and this may present some difficulties for German managers (weak barrier B6).

Environmentally indifferent industries

In these industries, the barriers to the British market lie in the requirement for a different market approach with an emphasis on appropriate marketing.

In consumer goods, for example, different customer product preferences, due to different tastes, different lifestyles, and different perceptions about competitive advantages, necessitate a different market approach (barrier B5). Difficulties can arise when there is a lack of willingness to recognize and respect these differences by German suppliers. Rather than adjusting the product and the market approach to suit the British customers, some German companies wish to 'educate' the market to suit their outputs. But the typical German emphasis on quality as the main, and often the only, competitive advantage of a product is generally not as effective in the British market as the German companies tend to expect (barrier B6). British customers are more likely to be persuaded by an appropriate product image encompassing a variety of competitive advantages (for example, price, functions, fashion trends), rather than by the information on the product's impressive technical parameters. Thus a problem for German companies in Britain is to learn how to market effectively in Britain by recognizing and respecting these differences (barrier B6). Typically, the product can be adjusted to suit British customer preferences, or it can be marketed in such a way that the British market is likely to respond. In most cases, a suitable combination of these changes is effective.

ORGANIZATIONAL BEHAVIOUR BARRIERS TO GERMAN OPERATIONS IN BRITAIN

Amongst the most frequent comments that the German parent companies raise in relation to the organizational behaviour of British staff is the shorter and less stable nature of employment, the lower degree of match of qualifications with currently held positions, and a less disciplined, though more creative, attitude to work. German employers tend to perceive a problem with British staff due to such issues as, in German terms, 'disloyalty to the current employer', 'lack of discipline' and 'lack of attention to detail'. Such comments are often related to the difficulties of finding technically qualified staff in Britain.

But the German approach to managing also tends to generate considerable resentment. In general the more structured management style of German managers does not go down very well with their British staff, who see it as 'technocratic' or 'autocratic'.

Comments were made on the uncalculated and risky decisions coming 'as a gut reaction' by British corporations. A problem may arise if German managers expect a well-calculated reliable decision in every case. British managers value flexibility and sometimes feel free to question a decision after it is made.

As before, these differences of organizational behaviour need to be understood and managed in order to avoid their becoming barriers to effectiveness.

Environmentally specific industries

The particular nature of the environmentally specific industries in Britain contrasts with their position in Germany. In the German insurance industry, for example, there are much stronger constraints on the products offered. These outputs are not appropriate for the British market, and firms therefore need to change their whole approach to the market and the customers. This necessitates the employment of indigenous British experts to direct the operations. Unless complete autonomy is given to the subsidiary management, then these different approaches need to be co-ordinated at the parent company–subsidiary interface. This puts considerable demands on the decision-making and management styles of the managers involved and can present considerable barriers (barriers C3 and C4).

Industries harmonious with the British environment

These industries, such as pharmaceuticals and consumer electronics, being dichotomous with the German environment, operate under a handicap. This can have effects on the parent–subsidiary interface. The German decision-making and management styles are not congruent with the management required in these industries in Britain. This can pose a problem if these differences are not understood and accommodated by the parent company (barriers C3 and C4). As the example of 'Company FA' in Chapter 3 (p. 49) in home entertainments illustrates, having an indigenous Chief Executive is conducive to understanding the industry, the market and the staff in the host country (barrier C2).

Industries dichotomous with the British environment

In industries dichotomous with the British environment, such as engineering, the staff problems in the subsidiary can become a major problem. As discussed in Chapter 5, German employers tend to perceive a lack of qualifications and skills in Britain in traditional manufacturing and engineering in particular (barrier C2). Training is important, but 'as soon as we train them, they go elsewhere'. The German managers see their British staff as lacking discipline, being insufficiently technically qualified and lacking company loyalty (barriers C6 and C7).

Environmentally indifferent industr.ies

In these industries, in particular consumer goods, the general differences in organizational behaviour described above were found to apply. In addition, since these industries involve marketing to the general public, it is particularly beneficial to have indigenous managers with the knowledge and skills of marketing in Britain (possible barrier C2). 'Company LB' in Chapter 4 (p. 88), for example, had to replace its German MD with a British manager, in order to be successful in the British market.

CONCLUSION ON BARRIERS AND PITFALLS

There is clearly a wide range of possible barriers in Anglo–German business collaboration, and to the unwary they may well become pitfalls. They flow from the differences in the environments and cultures of the two countries. But the existence of these two sets of strengths and weaknesses suggests that these differences could form the basis for fruitful collaboration among those who are knowledgeable about the pitfalls and skillful in avoiding them. In the next section we examine some of the effective collaborations which have been achieved.

EXISTING EFFECTIVE ANGLO–GERMAN BUSINESS COLLABORATIONS

With the increase in understanding of the other culture through co-operation, the differences causing the problems become less important and companies can learn to build on their different potentials and strengths through utilizing options in the environment. We now explore the outcomes which were generated as the result of effective Anglo–German collaboration which overcomes the barriers and avoids the pitfalls. The potential of three categories of combination will be considered: *specialization, collaboration* and *synergy*.

- In the *specialization* situation, each country concentrates on a different type of output, for the execution of which it is better suited. These outputs are then exchanged between the countries.
- In the *collaboration* situation, each country is attributed tasks for the execution of which it is better suited compared. These tasks are then contributed as part of their joint output.
- In a situation of *synergy*, the joint output generated by the collaboration of the two countries (or their nationals) in a common process produces a more effective result than would be the sum of their individual contributions.

The companies in the study have identified these potentials, and brought about combinations of contributions which have become effective. In Chapter 3, British and German industrial potentials were discussed. Chapter 4 explained how German subsidiaries or agents can assist British companies to approach the German market effectively, and how British subsidiaries and agents can assist German companies to do the same for the British market. We may now analyze what are the different British and German contributions to effective collaboration.

Successful combinations of British subsidiaries and German parent companies

Table 8.4 lists successful combinations of British subsidiary contributions to German parent company operations. They are classified according to the three types of combination.

An example of effective *specialization* in publishing is 'Company NA' (p. 62). The industry is an environmentally specific one, requiring the operations in each country to be different and distinctive. The corporation is managed as a joint venture. Thus the two components of the company, British and German, each look after their own specific markets with distinctly different enviromental needs. Because the management of this organization is an efficient one which is aware of, and capitalizes on, the combination of the different strengths, the end-result for the corporation as a whole, is very effective. The German input supplies stability, and the British shrewd financial management. The corporation, which operates across continents, also uses its British and German market understanding to advance in other culturally related markets.

Amongst the most frequent forms of *collaboration* is the supply of products by the parent company which is complemented by the subsidiary's contribution of specialized knowlege of, and access to, the host market. The family-owned 'Company CA' (p. 44) in precision engineering is an example. The parent company's strengths are drawn from the structured conditions of its German environment. These spill over to its British subsidiary, which capitalizes on these circumstances and in turn provides its German parent with access to the British market. The collaboration generates high returns.

The German 'Company LB' (p. 88) in the food industry is a further example of successful *collaboration*. It initially offered the identical product portfolio as offered in Germany. But this did not have the same appeal to the British market. The collaborative potential of this company was utilized when the British MD of the subsidiary, with the backing of the German parent company, developed products specifically designed to suit the British market. Of its three current best-selling products, two were developed for the UK market and do not sell in Germany. In this case the potential was realised through the collaboration of German parent company's manufacture complemented by the subsidiary's contribution of the market knowledge and marketing skills required in the British consumer industry.

The large corporation 'Company FB' (p. 50) dealing in, amongst other product lines, building materials, is an example of *synergy*. It combines the efficient management of standard industrial operations on the part of

Table 8.4 *Successful combinations of British subsidiary contributions to German operations*

German contribution (German parents)	British contribution (UK subsidiaries)
Specialization	
Engineering R&D and manufacture ('Company EA')	Engineering R&D and manufacture marketing and sales of own product
Engineering ('Company EB')	Low-cost, high-volume manufacture, and tendering
Commodities ('Company LA'), looking after defined territories	Commodities, looking after defined territories, different territories than German office
Publishing ('Company NA') catering for the specific needs of the German market, full vertical integration	Publishing catering for the specific needs of the British market, full vertical integration and operational autonomy (joint venture company)
Collaboration	
Heavy engineering R&D and manufacture ('Company AA')	Market knowledge and access to it, sales and servicing
Precision engineering R&D and manufacture ('Company CA')	Market knowledge and access to it, sales and servicing
Chemical industry R&D and manufacture ('Company AC')	Market knowledge and access to it, manufacture and some R&D
Electrical and industrial electronics R&D and manufacture ('Company AD')	Market knowledge and access to it, manufacture and R&D in electronics
Consumer electronics R&D and manufacture ('Company FA')	Market knowledge and access to it, incl. responsible for own marketing as different from parent, sales
Food manufacturer 'Company LB'	Sales, marketing, product development for UK market. Market knowledge and access to it.
Synergy	
Trading in building materials ('Company FB')	Divisional HQ for the corporation for product, i.e. management ability and skills needed in a fast moving industry

Table 8.4   *Continued*

German contribution (German parents)	British contribution (UK subsidiaries)
Information technology, hardware manufacture, standard systems ('Company HA')	Flexible electronic systems custom-made designs, marketing, sales, servicing the UK market and looking after other related to UK markets on behalf of the parent company
Pharmaceuticals R&D and manufacture ('Company JA')	Corporation-wide responsibility for hi-tech 'speciality' R&D and manufacture, British market knowledge and access to it for parent company's products.

the German parent company and the management of fast-moving businesses by the British subsidiary. Because the nature of the business involves buying, processing, and selling a wide range of associated products worldwide, speed of response to the market, and speed of decision making are important for success. Recognizing its own weakness in this regard and the subsidiary's strength, the German parent corporation delegated the responsibility for the fast-moving businesses to its subsidiary in Britain.

'Company HA' (p. 53) in information technology also operates in a *synergistic* situation. Because of the differences in the requirements in the British and German markets in this industry, the subsidiary offers flexible custom-made designs in Britain, whilst the German parent company supplies reliable hardware. Only standard packages are sold in Germany, but the subsidiary in Britain offers a 'Total System Solution' to the customer. The subsidiary is given autonomy, and invests mainly in people, expertise and specialisms to develop its distinctive product approach. In addition, it was made responsible on behalf of the parent company for other European markets. It covers Italy, France and Spain because the demands on the industry in these countries come closer to the product options offered by the British subsidiary, rather than those of the German parent company.

The British subsidiary of 'Company JA' (p. 57), which is a large German pharmaceutical company, also demonstrates a *synergistic* combination. It was given the exclusive corporation-wide responsibility for a major hi-tech 'speciality' product line. The British CE, a member of the parent company's main board, explained that the quality of research in Britain and its efficiency were responsible for this decision. The subsidiary's main strength is drawn from the availability in this field of British scientists with exceptional qualifications. This strength complements the German parent company's manufacture and R&D in the more traditional pharmaceutical areas.

Successful combinations of German subsidiaries and British parent companies

Table 8.5 lists successful combinations of German subsidiary contributions to British parent company operations. As discussed above, they are classified into *collaboration* and *synergy*.

'Company DA' (p. 45) in electronics is an example of an effective *collaboration* between the supply of products by the British parent company complemented by the supply of specialized market knowlege and access

Table 8.5   *Successful combinations of German subsidiary contributions to British operations*

British contribution (UK parents)	German contribution (German subsidiaries)
Collaboration	
Consumer electronics design and manufacture ('Company BA')	Market knowledge and access to it incl. responsibility for own marketing as different from parent, sales
Flexible electronics systems ('Company DA')	Market knowledge and access to it, marketing, sales, project work, hardware installation, maintenance
Pharmaceutical R&D and manufacture ('Company BC')	Market knowledge and access to it, marketing, sales
Chemical R&D and manufacture ('Company GA')	Market knowledge and access to it R&D and manufacture
Articles used in the building industry ('Company FB') R&D and manufacture	Market knowledge and access to it, some R&D and manufacture
Synergy	
Engineering R&D and manufacture ('Company KA')	Engineering manufacture and some R&D, German market knowledge and access to it, access to other markets related to Germany on behalf of the parent company

to the host market by the subsidiary in Germany. The parent company's strengths lie in inputs for which the liberal British environment is favourable. Its main strength in both the British and the German markets is the specialism of the parent company's British staff in computer systems knowledge. The German subsidiary mediates between the parent company and the customers. It assists in arranging their direct interaction on more specialist aspects of business, and provides technical systems support within the market, such as project work, software implementation, and hardware installation and maintenance. The parent company provides the product, and the subsidiary an efficient technical sales support service.

An example of *collaboration* through providing market knowledge and marketing in the German market is given by the British 'Company BA' (p. 42) in consumer electronics. Its subsidiary helped to develop the company's image in the German market, to one of quality and good value for money.

The large German subsidiary of 'Company KA' (p. 58), which manufactures engine parts for the automobile industry, is in a *synergistic* combination. As a profit centre, it has total operational autonomy. It uses all the advantages of its environment to build up its own identity, and it has a good market share. The subsidiary is responsible on behalf of the UK corporation for certain lines of business, and looks after other territories culturally related to Germany. The parent company is in a handicap, but the synergistic effects, generated through the collaboration between the British and the German parts of the company, support the parent company in its less favourable home environment.

BRITISH AND GERMAN STRENGTHS AS POTENTIAL CONTRIBUTIONS TO EFFECTIVE COLLABORATION

Based on the examples in the previous section, Tables 8.6 and 8.7 summarize the strengths of each country's potential contribution to effective collaboration. They are heterogeneous, deriving from the environmental, marketing and organizational behaviour strengths of the two countries as they have been described in previous chapters.

It is unrealistic to expect that only the strengths of each partner would be utilized in a collaboration. But any sensible collaboration would at least not ignore the strengths of each of the partners, whilst trying to build on their weaknesses! Getting it correct is not straightforward, because the usual initial inclination for each cross-culturally collaborating management is to attempt to shape its partner in its own image. This,

Table 8.6   *British strengths – potential contribution*

---

as part of:

Specialization

R&D in the pharmaceutical industry
R&D for the hi-tech industry and less traditional areas
Low cost manufacture in some traditional industries
Catering for the British market of environmentally specific industry on behalf
  of foreign owners

Collaboration

Management of fast moving businesses, strategic management in particular
Marketing in the UK and other related markets
Access to other markets culturally related to the UK
Sizeable domestic market for suitable German products

Synergy

Flexible information systems
Improvization and creativity

---

in fact, negates the potential, since the strengths are complementary. Collaborative potential comes from the recognition and exploitation of the differences.

An effective *specialization* can be built on German efficient manufacture in traditional areas, such as the electrical engineering industry, in collaboration with its British counterpart in the associated area of electronics. The German strengths in this situation are good vocational competence, technological innovation, emphasis on operational efficiency, and developed traditional skills. In terms of workforce skills, attention to detail and good discipline are assets. The British strengths are based on the availability of qualified and skilled personnel in speciality areas, where a substantial degree of innovation and managerial initiative are beneficial.

The commonest form of *collaboration* is built on R&D and manufacture in one country and sales in the other with a sizeable domestic market. The British and the German strengths in this respect are equal. They are based on an indigenous understanding of the different host culture. They provide direct access to the industrial and market infrastructure, including access to other culturally related markets. The important condition in this situation is that the subsidiary's expertise is taken seriously by the parent company. It may suggest product adjust-

Table 8.7   *German strengths – potential contribution*

---

as part of:

Specialization

Efficient manufacture in traditional industries
R&D in traditional manufacturing areas
Catering for the German market of environmentally specific industry on behalf
of foreign owners

Collaboration

Efficient management of standard industrial operations
Providing German market knowledge and access to it
Access to other markets culturally related to Germany
Sizeable domestic market for suitable UK products

Synergy

Traditional manufacture
Organizational and planning skills

---

ments and changes in market approach which may have to be implemented in order for success to be achieved.

In a *synergistic* situation each of the partners can contribute in a way which enhances the overall output. Thus the British strength in developing flexible information systems coupled with its managerial improvization and creativity may lead a German firm in a traditional industry to exploit new opportunities through product modifications and adjustments to suit different markets. Such a situation can stimulate the introduction of new products and aid the development of modern industries from the more traditional ones.

CONCLUSION

These examples and analyses suggest that the strengths of the two partners are deeply rooted in their particular cultures and are facilitated and perpetuated through environmental and institutional differences in Britain and Germany. Thus the industrial and market related strengths of the two countries are congruent with their strengths in education and organizational behaviour. The combination of the different strengths of the British and German management can also be seen as potentially synergistic. The organizational and planning skills of the German managers can combine with the improvization and creativity of the British managers to bring effective results.

Where companies have entrusted specialized functions involving these strengths to the appropriate nationals, the results are very good. So employing a German planning manager in Britain is likely to bring synergistic results, if the planning is made part of the more creative and flexible British approach to management. Similarly, employing a system designer or a marketing specialist in a traditional German manufacturing company can be effective.

The British approach benefits from German accuracy and the German approach benefits from British flexibiliy. Managers of both nationalities with very long-term experience (25 years and more) of Anglo–German business collaboration entirely overlooked the negative aspects of differences between the British and German approaches. They concentrated on the positive work contributions to be derived from a combination of both.

Bibliography

Bennett, Robert J., Günter Krebs and Horst Zimmermann (1993) *Chambers of Commerce in Britain and Germany* (London: Anglo–German Foundation for the Study of Industrial Society).

Blake, John and Oriol Amat (1993) *European Accounting* (London: Pitman).

Brooke, Michael Z. (1984) *Centralization and Autonomy: A Study in Organizational Behaviour* (London: Holt, Rinehart and Winston).

Budde, Andreas, John Child, Arthur Francis and Alfred Kieser (1982) 'Corporate goals, managerial objectives, and organizational structures in British and West German companies', *Organization Studies*, 3, 1–32.

Campbell, Adrian and Malcolm Warner (1993) 'German management', in David J. Hickson (ed.) *Management in Western Europe* (Berlin and New York: de Gruyter).

Chandler, Alfred D. (1962) *Strategy and Structure* (Boston: MIT Press).

Child, John and Alfred Kieser (1979) 'Organization and managerial roles in British and West German companies: an examination of the culture free thesis', in C.J. Lammers and D.J. Hickson (eds), *Organizations Alike and Unlike* (London: Routledge).

Feddersen, Knut (1991) *German Subsidiary Companies in the United Kingdom* (London: German Chamber of Industry and Commerce in the UK).

Hickson, David J. and Derek S. Pugh (1995) *Management Worldwide: the impact of societal culture on organizations around the globe* (London: Penguin Books).

Hofstede, Geert (1980) *Culture's Consequences: international differences in work-related values* (California: Sage).

Lane, Christel (1989) *Management and Labour in Europe* (London: Edward Elgar).

Lane, Christel (1992) 'Britain and Germany compared', in Richard Whitley, (ed.), *European Business Systems: firms and markets in their national contexts* (London: Sage).

Lane, Christel (1994) 'Britain: a stalled social system of production?', paper prepared for the American Conference of Europeanists, Chicago, March 31–April 2.

Lawrence, Peter (1980) *Managers and Management in West Germany* (London: Croom Helm).

Lorenz, Andrew and David Smith (1993) 'Secret report reveals shocking state of industry', *The Sunday Times*, 14 March, 1.

Maurice, Marc, Arndt Sorge and Malcolm Warner (1980) 'Societal diferences in organizing manufacturing units: a comparison of France, West Germany, and Great Britain', *Organization Studies*, 1, 59–86.

Millar, Jean (1979) *British Management versus German Management* (Aldershot: Saxon House).

Noelle-Neumann, Alisabeth and Strümpel, Burkhard (1984) 'Macht Arbeit krank? Macht Arbeit glücklich? Eine aktuelle Kontroverse'(Munchen: Paper).

Porter, Michael E. (1990) *The Competitive Advantage of Nations* (London: Macmillan).

Prais, S.J. (1981) 'Vocational qualifications of the labour force in Britain and Germany', *National Institute Economic Review*, 98, 47–59.

Pugh, Derek S. (1979) 'Effective co-ordination in organizations', *SAM Advanced Management Journal*, Winter, 28–35.

Pugh, Derek S. (1990) 'Introduction to the third edition', in D.S. Pugh (ed.), *Organization Theory: selected readings*, 3rd edn (London: Penguin Books).

Pugh, Derek S. and David J. Hickson (1976) *Organizational Structure in its Context: the Aston Programme I* (Aldershot: Gower).

Randlesome, Collin, 1993, 'The Business culture in Germany' in Randlesome, Collin, William Brierley, Kevin Bruton, Colin Gordon and Peter King (1993) *Business Cultures in Europe*, 2nd edn (London: Butterworth-Heinemann).

Scholz, Christian (1993) *Deutsch–Britische Zusammenarbeit: Organisation und Erfolg von Auslandsniederlassungen* (Munchen und Mering: Rainer Hampp Verlag).

Schröter, Marco (1994) *Effektivität deutsch–britischer Zusammenarbeit in Unternehmen* (Göttingen: Cuvillier Verlag).

Stewart, Rosemary, Jean-Louis Barsoux, Alfred Kieser, Hans-Dieter Ganter and Peter Walgenbach (1994) *Managing in Britain and Germany* (London: Macmillan/St. Martin's Press).

Trompenaars, Fons (1993) *Riding the Waves of Culture: understanding cultural diversity in business* (London: Economist Books).

Whitley, Richard (ed.) (1992) *European Business Systems: firms and markets in their national contexts* (London: Sage).

Index